THE Q FACTOR

THE Q FACTOR

The Elusive Search for the Next
Great NFL Quarterback

BRIAN BILLICK
and JAMES DALE

TWELVE
NEW YORK   BOSTON

Twelve
Hachette Book Group
1290 Avenue of the Americas, New York, NY 10104
twelvebooks.com
twitter.com/twelvebooks

First Edition: September 2020

Twelve is an imprint of Grand Central Publishing. The Twelve name and logo are
trademarks of Hachette Book Group, Inc.

The publisher is not responsible for websites (or their content) that are not owned
by the publisher.

The Hachette Speakers Bureau provides a wide range of authors for speaking events.
To find out more, go to www.hachettespeakersbureau.com or call (866) 376-6591.

Library of Congress Control Number: 2020938824

ISBNs: 978-1-5387-4992-0 (hardcover), 978-1-5387-4991-3 (ebook)

Printed in the United States of America

LSC-C

10   9   8   7   6   5   4   3   2   1

To football: the most complex, fascinating, strategic, frustrating, challenging, hope-inspiring, and heartbreaking game there is. And to quarterbacks, the element of the game that begs for analysis and then always surprises us. We tried to untangle it; perhaps we came close.

Contents

Foreword by Michael MacCambridge   ix

I.   The Draft: Hype, Hope, and Hoopla   3

II. What Is It About Quarterbacks?   49

III. Billick's Extrapolations: Observable, Projectable
         Trends...Not Wishful Thinking   69

IV. Rookie Year Report Card: Premature but Predictive   107

V.   Year Two: The Real World   143

VI. Is the Game Changing?   179

VII. Can We Do Better?   211

         Acknowledgments   249

         About the Authors   251

Foreword

By Michael MacCambridge

There was a great quarterback once.

Big, strong, smart. He could spin it, he possessed all the tools, and he'd forged his game in the high-level pressure and competition of the SEC.

Pro scouts were raving about him early. They admired his poise and brains; they liked his field vision. He was a leader of men, a true can't-miss prospect.

Then he was drafted, and though he was all the things that scouts said he was, he labored in relative obscurity for more than a decade in the NFL.

Injuries. Setbacks. Interceptions.

He played for three different teams, and never made the playoffs. Never even played on a team with a winning record.

So the great quarterback was *perceived* as a journeyman.

Those are the breaks. He soldiered through it and (this is another part of being a great quarterback) he never complained.

Also: He was a family man. Had some good kids, a couple of whom were named Peyton and Eli.

And here, in the example of Archie Manning's professional

career, we have the vexing conundrum that Brian Billick and James Dale are attempting to unravel in *The Q Factor*.

I suppose some would consider the elder Manning a disappointment in the pros, though I think of his case as more of a cautionary tale.

Football is so different than baseball or basketball. Mike Trout gets to the majors and it doesn't matter how hopeless his teammates are; he's going to hit his 40 homers, steal his 30 bases, and win multiple MVP awards. LeBron James is drafted by the hapless Cavaliers, and he'll still win Rookie of the Year, go to the All-Star Game, and within a few years win the MVP and carry a nondescript group of teammates to the NBA Finals.

But football is a harsher, much more interdependent environment. You can have all the skills in the world, but if you get drafted by the wrong team, you will never reach your true potential as a pro quarterback.

It was Archie Manning's misfortune to be drafted by the New Orleans Saints at a time when they were about the wrongest team in all of professional sports.

How much of a shambles were those Saints teams of the early seventies? The year before Manning was drafted, the Oakland Raiders picked a player in the first round of the NFL Draft who was nowhere to be found on the Saints *entire* draft board (the gifted tight end Raymond Chester of Morgan State). A year after Manning was drafted, the Saints hired a general manager named Richard F. Gordon, who possessed precisely zero football experience. Gordon had just retired as an astronaut at NASA, and had orbited the Moon forty-five times as the command module pilot on Apollo

12, but the skills required for that mission proved not particularly relevant to pro football.

So Manning took his lumps behind a woeful offensive line. He broke his arm and came back too early. His best offensive weapon was a slow, steady wide receiver named Danny Abramowicz, who looked (and ran) like Buck Owens in shoulder pads.

Alternative histories could be written about what might have been. For instance: Suppose Terry Bradshaw (drafted a year earlier) had gone to New Orleans instead of Pittsburgh, and Manning had wound up with Chuck Noll's Steelers instead of the Saints, and had spent his career handing off to Franco Harris and throwing to the likes of Lynn Swann and John Stallworth. If that happened, which do you think is more likely: That Bradshaw would still be in the Hall of Fame? Or that the Manning family would now have eight Super Bowl rings? (At least.)

These circumstantial hypotheticals aren't just ancient history, either. They are the sort of things that football people discuss deep into the night. What if Andrew Luck hadn't had the joy of football pounded out of him by a woeful offensive line in Indianapolis? What if Pete Carroll had stubbornly stuck with his big-money free agent signing Matt Flynn as a starter, rather than the rookie Russell Wilson, whom a vast majority of scouts felt was "too short" to succeed in the NFL? What if the Chicago Bears had selected a more mobile quarterback—Patrick Mahomes or Deshaun Watson—in the 2017 draft?

Football is circumstantial. We realize this in the main, but we often forget about it in the rush of pre-draft hysteria. H. L. Mencken once wrote, "The public wants certainties; there are no certainties." Mencken wasn't writing about the tortuous, high-risk, high-reward process of evaluating college quarterbacks. But he could have been.

We are, however, becoming incrementally wiser. And what Billick and Dale accomplish here is nothing less than a treatise on the eternal challenge of projecting what twenty-one- and twenty-two-year-olds are going to do in the crucible of professional football.

We do know this: Great quarterbacks do great things. And among those great things is they make great throws.

I have watched a lot of football games in my life. There are some things I've seen that remain imprinted on the brain. There's a pass Joe Namath made in 1968 that I still daydream about every once in a while. You can see it in the opening minutes of the NFL Films Super Bowl III highlight video. It came in the 1968 season opener, on the road against Kansas City. Namath took his normal deep drop, then threw with an easy motion down the left hashmark. But the ball emerged from his hand as if from a rocket launcher. It is the most effortless pass you've ever seen that travels more than fifty yards in the air. Don Maynard caught it in stride for the Jets' first touchdown of the season.

Billick and Dale understand the intoxication of those kinds of passes. But they also understand the hard work, preparation, and study that goes into the process, well before the play is ever called and the pass is ever made. They recognize that great quarterbacks *also* do simple, prosaic things. Like getting to the facility early in the morning. Like mainlining film study. Like spending hours on their mechanics, so that during the game, they don't have to think about their footwork, or their throwing motion, or varying their snap count.

Foreword

The mystery of thinking outside the box to find the perfect quarterback is nearly as old as the game itself. In 1946, Paul Brown sought out Otto Graham, because he was impressed by Graham's basketball-playing skills at Northwestern, and thought that the very same traits of court vision and quick, adept hands would be crucial in running the T-formation offense he wanted to install on the Cleveland Browns.

By the end of the sixties, as the twin examples of Johnny Unitas's stoic purposefulness and Joe Namath's slangy self-assuredness were on display, people began to recognize that the traits of a great quarterback called not for one specific thing but for a blend of skills. There was a monthly magazine called *Pro Quarterback* in that era, with a recurring comic feature by the artist Jack Davis, titled "Superfan," about Y. A. Schmickle, a "mild-mannered, boring accountant" who was miraculously transformed into a star quarterback when an old coach injected him with the secret-formula PSCWPLB ("**P**assing of Unitas, **S**crambling of Tarkenton, **C**onfidence of Namath, **W**isdom of Starr, **P**oise of Lamonica, **L**eadership of Dawson, **B**elly of Jurgensen"). Scouts have been seeking the magic elixir ever since.

They have also, since that time, become much savvier about data. One of the things I most enjoyed about this book is the enlightened view it provides of the role analytics plays in the modern scouting process. I respect analytics. I spend quality time with analytics. But even I have come to realize that, though we are now armed with terabytes of next-gen data, the challenge of speculative discernment about the quarterback position remains nearly as much of an art as it is a science. The Browns' Paul DePodesta says it best elsewhere in this book: "Analytics don't work by themselves."

There's something else as well, beyond the data, and beyond whatever does or doesn't happen at the combine. With the best quarterbacks there is a sense of poise that is hard to quantify but easy to recognize. I've heard some scouts call it "grace under pressure" (the phrase is attributed to Hemingway, but it translates well to the position of quarterback). At its best, there is an almost mystical aspect to it. Think of the best quarterbacks you've ever seen, and how they behaved in the crucial moments of big games.

This composure—everything is done in the nick of time, but never in a rush—is a rare and timeless quality, long valued in our most accomplished athletes. "Speed is not part of the true Way of strategy," noted the Japanese swordsman Miyamoto Musashi in his seventeenth-century text *The Book of Five Rings*. "Speed implies that things seem fast or slow, according to whether or not they are in rhythm. Whatever the Way, the master of strategy does not appear fast... Of course, slowness is bad. Really skillful people never get out of time, and are always deliberate, and never appear busy."

Yes. That. The best quarterbacks share that ability to keep their heads when surrounded by chaos and mayhem. Think of Joe Montana in the Super Bowl. Or Ben Roethlisberger, bodies falling left and right around him, instinctively moving away from the carnage, to carve out enough room to fire another accurate pass on the run. They never appear busy.

The special blend of qualities that make a quarterback remains elusive.

But after fifty years of watching football, you can witness glimpses at times, and you know it when you see it.

Foreword

On New Year's Eve 2017, Kansas City Chiefs rookie quarterback Patrick Mahomes started his first game. The Chiefs had already qualified for the playoffs, and were locked into the number 4 seed, so the season-long starter Alex Smith, who'd mentored Mahomes throughout the year, took to the bench.

Mahomes played well, and came out of the game in the fourth quarter with a comfortable 14-point lead, replaced by third-stringer Tyler Bray. But then Bray made a couple mistakes, and the Broncos rallied to tie this essentially meaningless regular season finale.

Then, because it's football, and coaches are competitive even when there's absolutely nothing at stake, Andy Reid put Mahomes *back in the game*, for the final two minutes.

Soon enough, there came a play I'll never forget: The Message.

Score tied at 24, 1:44 on the clock, Chiefs ball, first and ten at their own 32, trying to move the sticks to get into field goal range. Trips right, Mahomes takes the snap from the pistol, fullback Anthony Sherman to his left; soon the pocket collapses and Mahomes scrambles back and to his right. The Broncos rushers, DeMarcus Walker and Von Miller, are closing in on him, and Mahomes keeps scampering back and away, drifting toward the right sideline. He is all the way back to his own 16-yard line when he backpedals one more step and jumps back to throw, just as Walker is diving into his chest. If you've seen plays like this a hundred times, you know that often the quarterback doesn't even get the ball to the line of scrimmage, and gets flagged for intentional grounding. But this is Mahomes, so what transpires is another pass—half a century after Namath's throw—that expresses open contempt for the laws of physics and the time-space continuum.

Off balance, fading back, under pressure, Mahomes fires an absolute dart, thirty yards on a rope, right to DeMarcus Robinson, who catches it surrounded by three Broncos defenders before going out of bounds.

In the press box that day in Denver, two writers from the *Kansas City Star*, the columnist Sam Mellinger and the beat writer Terez Paylor, literally came out of their chairs in dazzled astonishment. There was a brief, involuntary fandango of adulatory commotion, and then Paylor —who loves football as much as anyone I've ever known—exclaimed, "*I am but a man.*"

Some throws make you shake your head; some throws open the doors of perception and leave colleagues agape with stupefaction, on the floor of the press box.

"It was plainly unprofessional," admitted Mellinger of his comportment in the moment. "And I have no regrets."

That's the sort of response that the best quarterbacking can inspire.

In the end, the story of football, the story of great quarterbacking, and the story of great quarterback evaluation are all about fine margins.

I can remember visiting Billick once. He and his wife Kim are wonderful hosts, and on this day Brian and I were walking in the woods behind his home, and talking football. We were discussing the process of breaking down game film, and he told me something I've never forgotten. When you go back and look at a game, and are reviewing how a quarterback handled his progressions, you will inevitably see numerous instances where both the primary and secondary receivers are covered. "But the best quarterbacks," explained Billick, "are able to throw it into that coverage and complete the pass anyway."

This seeming contradiction was echoed by Peyton Manning, in telling the story about his NFL learning curve. It was his rookie season in Indianapolis, and his quarterback coach was Bruce Arians. It was a Monday morning after a typically difficult game (the Colts went 3-13 in Manning's rookie season, and he threw 28 interceptions). As they were watching film, they came upon a play where Manning, under pressure, held on to the ball until the last instant, then just threw it away.

"Why didn't you throw it to someone?" asked Arians.

"Nobody's open," protested Manning, holding his thumb and index finger about an inch apart. "The window was like that."

"Peyton," said Arians evenly. "That *is* open in the NFL. That's what getting open looks like here."

Those are the hard truths that the great quarterbacks internalize.

There are other hard truths and cautionary tales in this book. Especially of the very human trait of people (even really smart people making seven figures a year to acquire and evaluate football players) allowing themselves to fall into the trap of seeing only what they want to see, discounting crucial factors, and making decisions based on hope. That's how Jake Locker, Blaine Gabbert, and Christan Ponder all go in the top 12.

It's an illustration of how difficult the process can be, and provides a message of humility to armchair quarterbacks (and volunteer general managers) everywhere: For every rule that's ever been written about what it takes to succeed at the most difficult position in sports, there's probably a quarterback in Canton who was an exception to that rule.

So the search continues. But when you see what the great quarterbacks can accomplish, from Otto Graham and Bobby Layne to Patrick Mahomes and Lamar Jackson, you understand why the searching and studying and the agonizing are all worth it.

This book underscores why evaluating quarterbacks remains one of the most fascinating exercises in all of sports, and helps us to be smarter about that process. The next NFL owner with a prime pick would be well-advised to read this book, and view the prospects with a rigorous, clear eye for the most salient factors.

Also, probably don't hire an astronaut to be your next GM.

THE Q FACTOR

Challenge:

There is no position in sports more important or challenging to fill than quarterback. You can win games without a great one, even the Super Bowl, but it's hard, very hard. I know; I did it—but not for lack of searching. Winning a championship without that elite QB took the best defense in the modern history of the NFL (almost as hard to find as a quarterback). Ever since then, after leaving the coaching ranks and gaining the clarity of distance, perspective, and analysis, I've been determined to see if there's a better way to evaluate quarterback talent and potential. I set out in search of the Q Factor.

Hypothesis:

Study a small, select group of highly rated, high-draft-pick quarterback prospects—their skills, stats, and character traits—and track their performance and circumstances, and you may uncover patterns of what separates great from merely very good...and maybe reveal methods for spotting and developing future talent— that is, the Q Factor.

Laboratory:

We're putting the 2018 draft class, the most touted quarterback draft class in a decade, under the microscope—who they are, how they got here, who they're playing for, how well they do and why, and what each is made of: talent, character, metrics, and magic. Studying the '18 class may reveal the path to better measurement and better prediction, to finding a formula for prognosticating slightly better. And slightly better, just fractionally better, may be enough to make the difference between good and great, between salary-cap dollars spent well instead of burned, to finding a few more leaders and a few fewer busts. For the next class. And the one after. Maybe even a formula that translates into identifying "quarterback-types" in fields beyond the football field.

I

The Draft: Hype, Hope, and Hoopla

April 26, 2018, 8:00 p.m.—Arlington, Texas, AT&T Stadium

NFL commissioner Roger Goodell, flanked by Dallas Cowboy legends Troy Aikman, Jason Witten, and Roger Staubach, strides into his realm—blinding klieg lights, pulsing highlight screens, earsplitting music, choreographed frenzy and fanfare. The fans jeer Goodell, the big-time wrestling bad guy a crowd loves to hate, while stomping and cheering for their hometown heroes and the Game of Football. The 2018 NFL Draft is about to begin. A hundred thousand stalwarts are packed into and around AT&T Stadium. Ultimately over 45 million people will watch this year's draft, live on network and cable television, and streaming on sports apps.

The first draft was held in a hotel room in Philadelphia in 1936, with ninety names written on a chalkboard and owners taking turns making their selections, a bigger version of a backyard pickup game. This was before scouts, and agents, and the Combine, well before 1980 when brand-new cable channel ESPN approached Commissioner Pete Rozelle for rights to broadcast the event. He agreed, even though he thought no one would watch.

This was before the NFL discovered what Cirque du Soleil, Wall Street, and even NASA learned long ago—spectacle is good entertainment and good business. Put all the elements together and the show is even better. Sight, sound, and lighting wizardry now treat stock market IPOs, space shots, and the NFL Draft like Las Vegas extravaganzas. At the draft, borrowing from NASA, the players/astronauts are in one place, the draft brain trusts/Houston are in another, and the ceremony/liftoff is in still another. It's all about the show. Of the 250 players in the draft, the twenty-two top players are at AT&T Stadium. But there's live video of the other players, at home around the country, surrounded by anxious mothers, fathers, and grandparents, college teammates, agents, and hangers-on. And there are live feeds from each of the thirty-two teams' nerve-center draft rooms back in Phoenix or New York or Detroit or Green Bay. At the draft itself, there are largely ceremonial reps from each team to accompany their picks onto the stage. But if you're a fan, it all happens in one place, on *your* screen—TV, laptop, tablet, mobile phone, sports bar, or man cave—wherever you are. The team picks, the kid pumps his fist, his mother weeps, and he walks onstage draped in his new jersey…all brought to you by the NFL to fuel the hype for next season months before it starts.

Who gets picked? When? And why?

Who was the standout quarterback at the Combine? Who ran the fastest 40? How good is that running back from the Pac-12? How about that blitzing linebacker from the ACC? The blazing wide receiver from the Big Ten? Is that kid from the SEC going to play football or baseball? Who's the top player in the draft, and who will be the overall number one pick? They may or may not be the same.

There's always lots of talk—endless debate, analysis, emotion, arguments, predictions on future stars and future busts—every year, and this year is no different. Except this year, almost all of the talk is about one position: quarterback, quarterback, quarterback. This year, the experts say, there is a batch of potential first-round quarterbacks to rival the historic drafts of 1983—Dan Marino, John Elway, Jim Kelly, Ken O'Brien, and Tony Eason—or 2004— Ben Roethlisberger, Philip Rivers, and Eli Manning.

> "NFL teams needing help at quarterback will have no excuses this year with a crop of talent worthy of comparison to even the renowned Class of 1983."
>
> NFLDraftScout.com

> "Quarterbacks are going to dominate the conversation surrounding the 2018 NFL draft. It's possible five signal-callers could get selected inside the top 10."
>
> Bleacher Report

> "The numbers this year will show that this is a quarterback-rich draft class."
>
> *Sports Illustrated*

The prevailing wisdom is that, yes, as many as five could go in the first round of 2018. Up to nine could be picked in total. The combination of talent, need, and hyperbole is the making of a true feeding frenzy.

Quarterback is unlike any other position on a football team. The quarterback is the only player who is at the center of every offensive play. The quarterback may get a play called into his headset, but he decides whether to carry it out or call an audible, depending on what he sees at the line; he may execute his audible or go to a checkdown play; throw deep or dump the ball off short; he may hand off or he may fake the give and roll out, or keep the ball himself and run; or scramble to find a receiver late, or throw the ball away on purpose to save a sack or loss. He makes more decisions than anyone else on the football field with the possible exception of the head coach. And his decisions can mean the fate of a down, a series, the quarter, the score at halftime, an entire game, or a season. Yeah, a quarterback is important. In fact, the position is arguably more important than any other single position in any team sport. A quarterback can literally make or break a football team. You can win without a great one (I know; I did it), but it isn't easy, and you can't *keep* winning without one. Finding a great one, a franchise quarterback, may be the hardest challenge in football, or in all sports. So this year, with its promising, tantalizing collection of talent, is getting more attention than any draft in almost forty years.

Roger Goodell waits for the applause (and jeers) to die down, welcomes everyone to the 2018 draft, takes a dramatic pause—drumroll—and announces: *"The Cleveland Browns are on the clock…"*

Thanks to a losing record, the worst in football for yet another season, the Browns have the number one pick. In fact, they also have the number four pick. They're on the clock, so they have ten minutes to submit their first selection. There's been a lot of talk around the league, in Cleveland, in the media, online, anywhere football is spoken, about who they'll take. One thing is for sure: They need a quarterback. The Browns have an almost remarkable (laughable if you live anywhere but Cleveland) record of drafting badly, especially quarterbacks. In 1999, with the number one overall pick, they took Tim Couch out of Kentucky. He played only five seasons, made the postseason once, was plagued by injuries, and was replaced by his backup. The Browns then went through a laundry list of NFL journeymen—Jeff Garcia, Luke McCown, Trent Dilfer, Charlie Frye, and Derek Anderson—before finally taking Brady Quinn from Notre Dame with the twenty-second pick in 2007. But Quinn could never quite nail down the starter's job, battling with Anderson until he was traded to the Broncos for the 2010 season. From there, it was back to the backup department with a succession of stalwart placeholders from Colt McCoy to Jake Delhomme to Seneca Wallace. In 2012, the team used its first-round pick to take Brandon Weeden, who, after struggling in his early college career, had a record-setting senior year at Oklahoma State, enough to earn him the number twenty-two pick in the draft. But a combination of interceptions and injuries ended in only two seasons with the Browns.

In 2014, midway through the first round, the Browns took controversial Texas A&M quarterback Johnny Manziel. Nicknamed "Johnny Football" by his Aggie fans, he beat seemingly unbeatable Alabama and set Heisman passing records. He opted to enter the NFL Draft after his junior year and was deemed to be either the next great superstar or, in the words of Barry Switzer, "an arrogant little prick," too full of himself to be coached. Unfortunately, the Browns' twenty-second pick (maybe it was the number 22, like Quinn and Weeden) made more headlines off the field than on (fines for hand gestures, party videos, visits to Las Vegas, and domestic violence charges) and was cut loose before the 2016 season. He hasn't been able to sign on with another NFL team since.

After three more seasons of back-to-the-backups—Brian Hoyer, Josh McCown, Cody Kessler, Robert Griffin III, and then trading for DeShone Kizer—it was finally time for Cleveland to get another shot at the number one overall pick in 2018. Would they break their quarterback jinx…or were they really cursed? The cynics were betting on the curse. Nine minutes and counting…

The Browns are facing a classic draft dilemma (in some ways a good problem to have). They have both the first and fourth picks in the first round. Do they take a quarterback with the number one pick or play it more strategically? Picking a franchise quarterback is hardly a science, and Cleveland has the record to prove it. The draft tends to sift out the best players and push them to the top—it does not predict greatness, only pretty goodness. The Browns' coach, Hue Jackson, has a 1-31 record and is under a lot of pressure. Maybe the wise move would be to pass on a quarterback with the first pick, take the consensus draft superstar, Saquon Barkley, running back out of Penn State, and set out to notch some wins under veteran QB Tyrod Taylor, signed in the off-season. Then, with their number four pick, they could draft the best available quarterback. The Giants were picking number two, and with their commitment to Eli Manning, they were unlikely to take a quarterback. The Jets at number three were going to take a quarterback, but that would leave four of the top five prospects on the board for Cleveland's number four pick. Plenty of draft rooms had Baker Mayfield (Oklahoma) at the top, but plenty had Sam Darnold (USC) number one, followed by Josh Allen (Wyoming) and Josh Rosen (UCLA). Since there is no obvious winner, Cleveland might well get their favorite anyway. Sound strategy…but not what the Browns are known for.

The Cleveland Browns take Baker Mayfield… Cleveland's pick was something of a surprise. Not only did they take a quarterback with their number one pick, they took Baker Mayfield, a guy with a lot of promise and a lot of questions. The Browns' draft room was split, with Hue Jackson and offensive coordinator Todd Haley not in the Mayfield camp, but GM John Dorsey and owner Jimmy Haslam wanting Mayfield. Is that just scuttlebutt? Hardly. Multiple sources reported the room was divided and Todd Haley texted a close associate that Baker Mayfield "was not my guy."

Here's a pre-draft snapshot of Mayfield, Oklahoma:

NFL COMBINE: Physical: 6 ft. 1 in., 215 lbs. • 40 yd. dash: 4.84 secs. • Vertical jump: 29.0 in. • Broad jump: 111 in. • 3 cone drill: 7.0 secs. • 20 yd. shuttle: 4.28 secs. • NFL evaluation: 6.09, NFL instant starter

Baker Mayfield has guts…or confidence…or a chip on his shoulder. Despite an impressive high school career, he didn't have big-name colleges beating down the doors at Lake Travis High in Austin to sign him. So instead of playing for a second-tier school, he walked on at Texas Tech and won the starter's job and a full ride. Then, in spite of a 5-0 record before an injury, the coach opened up the competition. So Mayfield became a walk-on again, this time at Oklahoma, and once eligible, won the starter's job and a full ride once again. He led the Sooners to the Rose Bowl. And he won the Heisman Trophy. He's a little arrogant. But maybe he's earned it.

Mayfield has a very different evaluation than Sam Darnold or Josh Rosen; he's more of today's spread quarterback. The good and bad is that he creates beyond the strict scope of the play but doesn't go through the 1-2-3 progression-read from under center within a protected pocket. This is not to say he can't do the progression from under center, but it wasn't the game style within the Oklahoma offense.

Mayfield completed 70 percent of his passes in his last season in college, with 43 touchdowns to just 6 picks. He led the country in passing efficiency, breaking his own record from the season before. So while you aren't going to look at his 70 percent completion percentage and question his accuracy, that doesn't mean the questions aren't there. Mayfield, more so than Rosen, Darnold, or Allen, was often throwing to wide-open players rather than "throwing them open"—that is, throwing into a tighter window. Mayfield could afford to miss a window and still complete the pass because the offensive scheme was to throw to wide-open reads, so a slight miss was still a good stat on his sheet.

His completion percentage also benefited from horizontal throws and quick screens (the typical kind of spread college passing you can compare to Cam Newton when he was a prospect). The throws are good and effective, but as one executive scouting him said, he could only find about 20 percent of his throws from Mayfield's full season that would extrapolate into NFL play.

Mayfield is light on his feet and quick to elude rushers and use his running game. He uses his eyes well and knows exactly where his guys will be on the field. He shows total command of the offense—an offense built for him—throws well on the run, and is a playmaker when the initial plan breaks down. He can do what is asked of him but can also play outside the framework of the play. He was a 67 percent passer when on the move. His smart reads save his arm talent a lot of times. Admittedly, because of his playmaking ability, he will take some unnecessary risks and incur some unnecessary sacks when trying to make a play or wait for a receiver to break open down the field.

The knock or potential knock on Mayfield has been attitude: taunts, brashness, defiance—they've given it all kinds of labels. He did a "crotch grab" as silent trash talk to Kansas. He made a neck-slash gesture to an opposing team after a TD. He carried a sign into the Rose Bowl that read "Pretenders" because a sportswriter had said the Sooners didn't belong there against Georgia. But he also admitted a member of the Georgia team had the right to mock him because they won the game. He's emotional, yes. He's brash, yes. He has a chip on his shoulder. But I see it differently. His emotion is generally aimed at the other team, not his own teammates. He's tenacious. He's a competitor. His teams seem to rally around him. That's worth a lot. I wasn't alone in my initial take. One of my insiders—one who didn't have a high pick or a seeming QB vacancy—said Mayfield was "the guy we liked the most…He made very few mistakes…Now, he had balls deflected, but in terms of making timing and accuracy, yeah, he had it all." He tempered his assessment, "You were a little bit worried about coachability, personality, and the… immaturity, things like that," but his team still had Baker at the top.

Comps: The typical comparisons for Mayfield range from Doug Flutie to Russell Wilson (small for a quarterback) to Johnny Manziel (questionable attitude) to Dak Prescott (though a later draft pick). Like Flutie and Wilson, he may be small for a quarterback (6 ft. 1 in.), with a worry about lower release meaning batted balls, but he compensates with his other skills. Like Manziel, there are concerns about attitude, but I see his brashness as leadership on the field, not the egotism of Manziel. And I see him most like Marcus Mariota in his playmaking ability and the type of offense they ran in college. Like Mariota, Mayfield was an absolute stud in the red zone and rarely turned the ball over. He will have to develop the traditional

NFL QB skills to consistently win from the pocket, but he is smart and has a major work ethic that also feels a lot like Mariota.

Bottom line: If he can adapt to NFL-style football, if he can make the transition to playing under center, if he can "walk on" again, Baker Mayfield could turn a franchise around from day one. Big ifs, big upside.

So . . . the biggest questions on Mayfield are whether his accuracy, his 68.6 completion percentage, his ratio of 129 TDs to 29 INTs, and his ability to run—404 carries for 1,083 yards—will translate to the NFL. In my opinion, his high completion percentage is a little misleading. Mayfield, unlike some of the other top-rated quarterbacks, was surrounded by perhaps the best offensive talent in college football. When you look at the film or tape (the football catchalls for any kind of video—what used to be film, and then videotape, and is now digital files), yes, he completed the passes, but often they were not the spot-on throws that he'll need against NFL defenders. As my first NFL mentor, legendary coach Bill Walsh taught me, judge accuracy less by down-the-field throws and more by where the QB places the ball for short and intermediate targets, the throws that allow a receiver to gain yards after the catch without having to break stride to catch the ball. Many of Mayfield's easy flare routes and slant routes were placed all over the field, sending a warning to me that he may struggle to attain this same level of accuracy in the NFL. Another plus that may translate as a minus is that Mayfield was very productive in college with runs in critical situations, leading people to call him a good running QB. Here's the but: His size and physical makeup will not allow him to have the same productivity running in the NFL . . . and will likely get him killed (we've seen that movie before). Maturity issues have also plagued Mayfield, but his post-draft news conferences suggest he is learning to present himself in a more professional, poised manner.

Will he play? The Browns acquired former Bills starter Tyrod Taylor. This could be an interesting competition . . . if it is a competition. When a club commits the first overall pick in a draft, I'd say the competition is over. The question isn't if, it's when the top pick takes the field. Taylor is a seven-year vet who spent his first four seasons backing up Joe Flacco in Baltimore. He went to Buffalo as a free agent and was a respectable 62 percent passer with 51 TDs to 18 INTs, diligently following the game plan they gave him: sub 450 throws per season, nurture a running game, don't turn the ball over. Even though he did what he was asked, or maybe because of it, Buffalo decided he wasn't good enough to win, so off to Cleveland he went. I can't imagine what fiction Hue Jackson spun to sign Taylor, knowing the team was mandated to get a top QB in this year's draft. Unlike Josh McCown in New York, who was signed specifically to mentor whomever the Jets would choose, Taylor likely had to be sold on the promise he would be the starter, be able to keep the job as long as he was winning, and even with a first overall pick in the wings, be assured he'd at least get the chance to show his skills for the next team to sign him. Jackson has even reiterated that Taylor will be the starter. It is interesting that Taylor, like Mayfield, is an alpha male who has had to fight for everything he has ever gotten. Although he was polite after the Browns' pick, I can't imagine Taylor is genuinely interested in mentoring Mayfield.

How will all of this play out? Hue Jackson, a head coach with an abysmal win-loss record, is now saddled with a QB not of his own choosing, nor of his offensive coordinator's. Plenty of sites and experts did have Mayfield ranked number one with stats to back them up.

But others disagreed. And relying on pure analytical data is danger-ous. Ask even the most ardent analytics devotees and they'll tell you that the best athlete assessments are comprised of a *combination* of elements: numbers, experience, and observation, the last being the tie-breaker. If you don't see it with your own eyes, it's not there. They'll also tell you that baseball players can be sized up analytically on individual performance—pitcher, batter, fielder—much more accurately than football players who interact with ten others on every play. The way to pick a quarterback is by consensus of knowledge, not by a set of num-bers or a power struggle in the draft room. But despite that wisdom, according to my sources, it seems that consensus was lacking when the Browns' pick was made. And that means trouble. How are the GM and coach supposed to work together when they're not in sync? Why is the owner again "helping" make draft picks? How will all that work in the meeting room and on the field? Yes, Jackson ultimately endorsed the Mayfield pick, but it seems he was just parroting the party line, to appear to be in line with his bosses. Of course, if things go south, Haley can invoke an "I told you so" in looking for his next job.

So with Mayfield, when and how does the quarterback transi-tion take place? If Taylor starts to turn the Browns around, when/how do you pull him for Mayfield? If he isn't winning but they don't play Mayfield, how long can Hue Jackson last? Just ask John Fox. When the Bears took Mitchell Trubisky with the second overall pick in 2017, Fox's plan was to start Mike Glennon, bringing along Trubisky, letting him adjust to the NFL, learn from Glennon, and between the two, chalk up enough wins to enable Fox to keep his job for another year. Then, once Trubisky had his legs, and the team was improved, Fox and the Bears could play at their best the follow-ing season. The best-laid plans…When Glennon started out 1-3,

Fox had to turn to Trubisky early, who wasn't ready, and proved it with a 4-8 record—59 percent completion, 7 TDs and 7 INTs. Fox was fired. So much for "bringing along" the quarterback.

In Cleveland, one thing that does match up in Taylor and Mayfield is that they're both ball protectors. Taylor, like Alex Smith in Kansas City, may carry it to extremes, avoiding turning the ball over but, as a result, not taking chances down the field, even when bolder decisions are what's needed. On the other hand, Mayfield is gutsier, more of a gunslinger—which can be effective in college but usually not so much in the NFL, which requires that elusive, perfect balance of bold and wise. The good news is that with their similarities, the offense won't have to change a lot in the transition from Taylor to Mayfield. And it will happen. Probably sooner rather than later. Just ask the owner.

"The New York Giants are on the clock..." With the draft favorite— "once in a generation" running back Saquon Barkley—still on the board, the Giants grab him with the number two pick. As predicted by insiders, but defying fan and jock sports-radio demands, they doubled down on betting their near future on Eli Manning at quarterback. The Giants' brain trust—GM Dave Gettleman, assistant GM Kevin Abrams, head coach Pat Shurmur—collectively said they "do not see a franchise QB in the draft worthy of passing up Barkley for." To back that up, they let it be known they wouldn't have taken a quarterback even if the Browns had scooped up Barkley. But in the fourth round, they did opt for quarterback Kyle Lauletta out of Richmond.

"The Jets are on the clock..." Back to the quarterback feeding frenzy, it's the Jets' turn. They're almost as desperate for a franchise QB as the Browns. Back in 1965, the Jets used their number

one overall pick in the then-independent AFL to take Alabama's Joe Namath (outbidding the NFL's St. Louis Cardinals), and brash, flashy, fun, pantyhose-modeling Namath led the team to a Super Bowl upset, complete with a pregame win guarantee, over the Baltimore Colts...followed by a multi-decade franchise quarterback drought. In 1983, the Jets took Ken O'Brien out of UC Davis with the twenty-fourth pick (surprisingly over Dan Marino), and while he attained over 25,000 yards passing in his pro career and achieved a rare perfect passer rating (158.3), he was only able to get to the postseason once and managed a single winning season.

The team then ran through a variety of stand-ins and/or big names in their waning days—Browning Nagle, Boomer Esiason, Vinny Testaverde, Chad Pennington, and an aging Brett Favre. It wasn't until they used the number five pick in 2009 to take Mark Sanchez out of USC that there was a spark of QB hope. Coach Rex Ryan bet on the rookie and he led the team to the postseason in 2009, albeit thanks to the Bengals resting their starters in the final regular-season game, and the Jets made it all the way to the AFC Championship for only the third time in the team's history (though they lost). The following year, thanks in part to another gift—a late-season loss by the Jaguars—the Jets were in the postseason again, and again made it to the AFC Championship (and again lost). Unfortunately, the bubble burst shortly after, Sanchez was released, and his career devolved to a tour of backup duty for the Eagles, Broncos, Cowboys, Bears, and Redskins. Soon after Sanchez's departure, Rex Ryan, who had guaranteed a Jets Super Bowl not once but three times, was shown the door. (He landed in Buffalo, where he made the Super Bowl guarantee again. And again it didn't happen. I might suggest a different PR tactic.) For the Jets, after Sanchez came another succession of QB placeholders—Geno Smith, Ryan Fitzpatrick, and veteran/mentor (not always one and the same) Josh McCown.

The Jets needed a quarterback, a real honest-to-god franchise quarterback, to bring the team and the fans a shred of hope that the glory days of Broadway Joe might return. And—due to some complex pick-swapping, basically giving up a lot of later-round opportunities—they had the number three pick to get one. I won't say the Jets tanked in 2017 in order to get in position for a high pick in 2018, but management gave Todd Bowles (in year four of his contract, going 5-11 the last two seasons) an extension to underline that they understood what taking a rookie QB usually means—hope and promise, not immediate results. Or to give Bowles one last chance. Not sure if the Giants would or would not take a quarterback, the Jets had to believe at least three other QBs were worthy of being taken that high (my strategy for the Browns, which wasn't followed).

The Jets, like a lot of teams, had Sam Darnold at the top of their draft board. Whether a team has an early pick or not, or a position need, they evaluate all the top players. One of my sources at the Ravens, who were lukewarm on Darnold, said, "We liked him, thought he would be good for somebody, but it wasn't like we're were thinking, 'Oh man, this guy…'" But at the Eagles, who were banking on a healthy Carson Wentz, their VP of player personnel, Joe Douglas, told me, "Sam Darnold was the number one QB on our board in Philly. We did not interview him but did a more clinical evaluation." A "clinical evaluation" from Joe Douglas means a lot. Joe worked his way up the personnel ranks, scouting for me at the Ravens, then at the Bears as director of college scouting, then the Eagles. He did his homework on Darnold and liked him. And Joe was hardly alone. (Joe's early opinion of Sam would turn out to have consequences later on.)

*   *   *

"With the number three pick..." The word is, the Jets liked Darnold best, but thought highly of all the top QB prospects *except* one: Baker Mayfield. So when the Browns took Mayfield, the Jets breathed a sigh of relief. Supposedly, VP of player personnel Brian Heimerdinger leaned over to GM Mike Maccagnan and said, "You have a horseshoe up your ass." And then, when the Giants opted for Barkley and not a quarterback, the Jets were thrilled to have their top choice, Sam Darnold. When they'd made the trades earlier in the year, it's unlikely they thought Sam Darnold would still be available, but Cleveland gave them a gift. Well inside the draft clock's ten minutes, Maccagnan was ready to put Darnold's name on the board but, due to the script for televised drama, the team had to wait...and wait. Having followed Darnold for almost four years—the combined work of Heimerdinger, head coach Bowles, offensive coordinator Jeremy Bates, and the whole scouting team, what was another few minutes? A lifetime, it seemed. Finally they put Darnold's name in and they hoped the future was now.

Pre-draft snapshot—Sam Darnold, USC:

> NFL COMBINE: Physical: 6 ft. 3 in., 221 lbs. • 40 yd. dash: 4.85 secs. • 26.5 Vertical jump: 26.5 in. • Broad jump: 105 in. • 3 cone drill: 6.96 secs. • 20 yd. shuttle: 4.4 secs. • NFL evaluation: 7.00, Pro Bowl caliber

As a coach evaluating players, you try not to have biases based on your own past experience, good or bad, particularly when it comes to the school the player comes from. But sometimes you have biases anyway. Mine was UCLA. I just never had much luck with prospects from there, with one big exception—offensive tackle Jonathan Ogden, one of the greatest players I've ever coached. When it comes to quarterbacks, USC has kind of earned its own stigma. It's been discredited, fairly or not, because of draft picks who didn't live up to their promise: Matt Cassel, Matt Leinart, and Matt Barkley (hey, maybe it's just guys named Matt). To some extent, Mark Sanchez and Carson Palmer would be the exceptions. Still, Sam Darnold is fighting the unfair USC stigma already.

Physically, Darnold is impressive. He has good size and frame and is a thick, solid six foot three, but he doesn't sacrifice any athleticism with his size. He ran a 4.85 dash in the Combine, and the game tapes show he's a more than competent runner with the ball in his hands when needed.

But primarily, Darnold is a pocket-first passer in the tradition of USC offenses. He can read the field and keep his eyes on the secondary while sensing the rush. He trusts his reads and gets the ball out quickly. He does have an elongated release that is hard to ignore, but once he makes a decision, he can execute any throw on the field. He trusts his arm (critical) and has a good feel for the open spaces on the field.

What I like on tape is that Sam doesn't make it harder than it is. If his primary read is open, he'll take it. He doesn't overcomplicate his reads. He's already mentally moving on to the next play. He has a strong tendency to throw a catchable ball, and he's accurate. That's more than just his completion percentage; he hits his pass catchers in stride, and that allows them to run after the catch. That's something we focus on for the receivers but it's an underappreciated trait for a quarterback.

More about his elongated throwing motion: It's very circular and drops all the way down to his hip, almost like Tim Tebow in his long baseball throwing motion. The problem is it can allow the defense to jump his passes. And that's what the stat sheets show: 20 picks in his last 20 games; 22 turnovers in 2017—13 picks and 9 fumbles. And he had 24 turnovers the year before. You have to worry that it's not a fluke; it's a style of throwing that can lead to a pattern. That's a red flag.

Some of his misses come from trying to use all upper body on his throws and not bringing in his lower body. His touch and accuracy were probably best in 2016, not as good in 2017. And he took sacks when he could have/should have gotten the ball out and, at worst, thrown an incompletion. An incompletion is way better than a sack and lost yardage. While he can run, he doesn't always protect his body as well as you'd like in the open field, and that's dangerous.

Comps: Sam reminds me of Carson Palmer on a number of levels. Not only did both quarterbacks play at USC, Palmer was the overall first pick in the 2003 NFL Draft, and whether Darnold went to the Jets or not, he was going early. Palmer played eight seasons for the Bengals, led the team to their first playoff appearance in fifteen years, and was a two-time Pro Bowler. After that, his performance declined; he blew out his knee, had a conflict with ownership, was traded to the Oakland Raiders and then to Arizona. With the Cardinals, Palmer continued his run of dependable performances when in the game, but was injury plagued and out a lot. His most successful post-Bengals year was 2015, helping the Cardinals advance to the NFC Championship game and being named to his third Pro Bowl. After spending much of the 2017 season on the injured reserve list, Palmer retired. All in all, Palmer was a solid player in the NFL for a number of years but lacked a certain leadership quality, with a demeanor not unlike Darnold's. In fairness, it was certainly not all on Palmer that he had only four playoff games to his credit: One of the hardest things to do is to mentally separate a quarterback from what goes on around him—the weapons he's given (or not given), injuries, team management and ownership. Nonetheless, we all look for the elusive quality of leadership.

Sam has a similar body and mechanics to Andrew Luck when Luck was a prospect. But Darnold's motion is hardly as refined. Luck had a lot of preseason hype but lived up to it. Sam played well but has the turnover problem. All in all, he may be the least risky QB in this class (not meant as a backhanded compliment), but I don't think he is going to transform a team from day one like a healthy Andrew Luck did the Colts.

Bottom line: Sam Darnold is a solid player with the size, tools, and mental ability to play the position for a long time. Leadership is an unknown...and almost always is at this point. His throwing motion is a tough pill to swallow—and turnovers are a worry—but he definitely has more positives than negatives. Which team he ended up with could make all the difference. If the Browns had grabbed him with the overall first pick, the question would have been: Would he play a while behind Tyrod Taylor, or would the win-now pressure be too much to keep the new savior out of the game? If the Giants had taken Darnold, it's likely he would've spent time learning from Eli Manning, working on his mechanics and maybe getting some leadership lessons. But neither of those scenarios played out; Darnold is with the Jets. His success will ride not only on himself but on the Jets' supporting cast too—his teammates and coaches. Unlike the Browns, the Jets didn't make many moves to add to the offensive side of the ball in free agency, so all of their chips are on Darnold to be the difference-maker in an offense that ranked 28th (out of 32) in total offense and 24th in both scoring and passing. Isaiah Crowell at running back and Terrelle Pryor at wide receiver aren't big enough weapons on their own. So when Darnold finally does go in, like Jimmy Garoppolo in San Francisco, he is going to have the onus to turn it around with his play.

The key phrase there is "when Darnold finally does go in." The Jets starter is longtime veteran Josh McCown. McCown played college ball at SMU and Sam Houston State, was drafted by the Cardinals in the third round in 2002, and also played for the Lions, Raiders, Dolphins, Panthers, Hartford Colonials, 49ers, Bears, Buccaneers, and Browns (it may have been easier to list where he didn't play). He comes from a quarterback family, as he's the older brother of former NFL QB Luke McCown and younger brother of former Texas A&M QB Randy McCown. The Jets specifically signed the thirty-eight-year-old to mentor whomever they selected, which may well work, since Josh wants to go into coaching when he's done playing. This is about as ideal a situation as a rookie can have. Darnold knows he will not be put in, barring injury, until he's ready to function successfully. Of course, there is a wild card: Teddy Bridgewater is also here and he isn't going to roll over and abandon his comeback just to make way for Darnold. But Bridgewater has a history of being realistic and mature. He had an excellent working relationship with Case Keenum in Minnesota. He's a competitor but he's not a disrupter.

As to when Darnold will actually go in, coach Todd Bowles put it this way: "We're not going to throw him in there, but at the same time, we're not going to hold him back either." Now there's a statement to cover all possibilities, including GM pressure, owner pressure, fan pressure, and wanting to hold on to your job.

Sam Darnold has all the tools to be a successful NFL quarterback, but yes, he has turned the ball over a good deal. Does he have the "command presence" you like to associate with your face-of-the-franchise pick? I'm not sure. (If there were analytics for leadership, picking a franchise quarterback would be a piece of cake.) But it does look like Darnold can handle the spotlight. Off the field, he can deal with the attention and hype of being a starting QB in New York. Darnold was the favorite of the USC Trojans, and they may as well be an NFL franchise in terms of celebrity, glitz, and pressure. It's not the Big Apple but it is the LA Coliseum.

For me, after the supporting cast, after the spotlight, after the rookie adjustments, here's the key for Darnold: Jeremy Bates, Jets offensive coordinator. Jeremy told another coach, who in turn told me, that Sam Darnold is the *kind* of player he wants—that is, not just a good quarterback, but the type, style, and demeanor of player he believes can win in his system. Bates is a Mike Shanahan/Jon Gruden kind of coach who sets up a system—a structured scheme—for the offense, and then finds the quarterback that fits it, not the other way around. He does not put a priority on a QB that makes plays "outside the design of the offense" (à la Baker Mayfield or Lamar Jackson) but rather on one who makes plays within it. Darnold is the definition of the player who plays within the system. The Jets and Bates don't see what other people call a lack of "command presence." They see a system player—therefore an asset, not a liability. If Bates is right, he's got a winner. *If* Bates is the OC for a while...

With the fourth pick... The Browns were next on the clock and now obviously didn't need a quarterback. There were several good choices on the board, but they passed on some tempting ones: Bradley Chubb, a pass-rushing end from NC State, and Quenton Nelson, an outside linebacker from Notre Dame, both considered the highest-rated non-QBs after Saquon Barkley. Instead, the Browns took Denzel Ward, a highly touted corner from Ohio State. To bear out the prevailing wisdom, Chubb and Nelson went at number five and six respectively, to Denver and Indianapolis. Again, the Browns surprised everyone. In a good way? Or in the old way? Time will tell very soon. (Spoiler alert: All three picks—Chubb, Nelson, and Ward—had outstanding NFL rookie years, with Nelson and Ward named to the Pro Bowl.)

"The Buffalo Bills are on the clock…" Ten minutes to change their fate. Like the Jets, the Bills are a long way from their glory days. Jack Kemp out of Occidental College, seventeenth-round pick of the Lions in 1957, came to the then-AFL Bills to lead them to five Championship games and two wins, before he went on to serve in Congress, as secretary of housing and urban development, and later flirted with a run for president. After Kemp, it was twenty-one years until Buffalo had another star quarterback: Jim Kelly, one of five first-round QBs in the famed class of 1983. Kelly was picked by Buffalo but initially went to the USFL Houston Gamblers before coming to the Bills. He led the Bills to a then-record four consecutive Super Bowls—unfortunately no wins—and Kelly was a first-ballot Hall of Famer. That was the end of the good times in the Nickel City and the beginning of a parade of not-quites: Todd Collins—round two from Michigan; Doug Flutie; and Drew Bledsoe, all on the downside of their careers; J. P. Losman—round one from Tulane; Trent Edwards from Stanford, Ryan Fitzpatrick

for four valiant years, E. J. Manuel out of Florida State—their last first-rounder; then Kyle Orton, Matt Cassel, and Tyrod Taylor. And as the QBs came and went, head coaches did likewise.

Interesting stat: Throughout Jim Kelly's career he had one head coach, Marv Levy. Levy was head coach of the Bills for eleven years. After Kelly, there were twelve starting quarterbacks and ten head coaches and exactly two postseason appearances, both losses. Coincidence? No. It's hard to find and develop a franchise quarterback. And it's almost impossible for a head coach to do that in a single season...but not uncommon for owners and fans to expect the coach to do it. Sean McDermott is in his first year as head coach as the team makes its 2018 QB draft pick. Buckle your seat belt. The Bills traded with Tampa to move up to number seven, which, at this point in the draft, gave them a chance to get one of the "Joshes"—Allen out of Wyoming or Rosen from UCLA. They were leaning toward Josh Allen and were surely looking over their shoulders thinking Arizona might have their eyes on him too. McDermott had been the defensive coordinator for the Panthers when they took Cam Newton, and Allen had been compared to Newton more than once—similar size, similar arm strength, both solid runners.

In a last-minute wrinkle, on the morning of the draft a story surfaced about racist tweets, complete with the N-word, posted by Allen when he was in high school. Some questioned whether this would affect how teams looked at Allen. My sense is the Bills were confident in their reading of a more mature Allen who, to this point, had received nothing but ringing endorsements about his character. Cynics might conjecture that somebody found and planted the story at draft time in hopes of getting teams to come off of Allen. Or even that the Bills had done it to keep others from taking Allen earlier. Can you imagine anyone doing something manipulative like that in big-time sports or business?...he asked cynically. Who knows? But it makes for good conspiracy theories. To Allen's credit, the moment the tweets surfaced, he was forthright, saying that when it occurred he was "young and dumb," a statement of the obvious but one that had to be made.

Growing up in rural Firebaugh, California, Allen declined the opportunity to play high school ball in the more cosmopolitan Fresno, opting to remain in his hometown farming community, mostly white and Hispanic, with limited exposure to African Americans. That's hardly an excuse for those tweets, but it does seem that going off to play big-time college football at the very least changed his perspective. One of the guys who was most vocal in favor of Buffalo drafting him was his former Wyoming teammate Eddie Yarbrough, now a linebacker for the Bills, who is Black.

Here's a pre-draft snapshot of Allen, Wyoming:

NFL COMBINE: Physical: 6 ft. 5 in, 233 lbs. • 40 yd. dash: 4.75 secs. • Vertical jump: 33.5 in. • Broad jump: 119 in. • 3 cone drill: 6.93 secs. • 20 yd. shuttle: 4.4 secs. • NFL evaluation: 5.9, become NFL starter

Déjà vu Kyle Boller. Evaluating/rationalizing Josh Allen is like reliving the Ravens selling ourselves on Boller in 2003. We had accuracy and completion concerns but tried to justify his weaker stats with excuses: lack of talent around him, second-rate receivers, not enough time in the pocket due to his offensive line, etc. We fell in love with his strengths and had blind spots for his glaring weakness: consistently far below 60 percent completion stats. In fact, his college best was only 53.3 percent. (By way of comparison, Peyton Manning had four college seasons at 60 percent plus, Dak Prescott had three out of four seasons above 60 percent, Tony Romo had two, Mark Sanchez two.)

And I'm not alone in my concerns. One of the guys who was very much part of picking Kyle Boller, and who is now in the position of evaluating and rating players on the draft board, said this about Josh Allen: "We liked a lot about him. He [did] have all this stuff off the field. But what goes into completions, yeah, that's what scared us...I hate to say this, but it was just like Kyle...was the same thing...I just see this guy at times, he's just not a naturally gifted, accurate passer."

Granted, Josh Allen has the elite frame at six foot five you look for. He's strong and has the ability to shake off some arm tackles in the pocket and extend the play, à la Big Ben Roethlisberger. But "à la Big Ben" comparisons are usually wishful thinking. Lots of guys are big, but not Ben. Shaking off a tackle doesn't make you a Super Bowl quarterback. Better stats and better decisions do. And the problem is, Allen's accuracy breaks down when he's forced off of his spot. He does show the ability to make some throws no one else in this draft class can match—long and deep without much effort. There will be some QB coaches who think they can build on that potential and fix the accuracy issues (another common delusion we coaches fall for).

On the plus side, Josh Allen has taken a fair amount of snaps from under center, so you can extrapolate a good number of throws and project him as an NFL-style passer. That's clearer than trying to evaluate a lot of college spread QBs that are single read and then they take off and run. Allen scans the entire field and goes through a progression, again NFL-style. There's some good tape of him as a play-action passer as well, turning his back to the defense and making a quick read and decision. He hits intermediate-level throws pretty well, particularly with a clean pocket (though there's no guarantee of that in the NFL). Allen can run when he has to, but he's a pass-first quarterback who makes plays with his legs, not the opposite, a run quarterback who can make some throws; and given the choice, you want the former.

But—and it's a big but—from my perspective, Allen is a rerun of the Boller show, even down to the circus they're having over his arm strength. He can heave the ball ninety yards. Wow. But how many times do you need that in a game—or a career? Once maybe. And it's usually when you're in pretty deep trouble, late in a game, hoping for a miracle. Much more telling is his completion percentage. After no initial NCAA Division I interest and a year at Reedley College, in both of Allen's two full seasons as a starter at Wyoming his rate was 56 percent. Regardless of the second-tier talent around him, that's hard to overlook. And keep in mind, in the Mountain West Conference he was always throwing *against* subpar defensive talent. In his two games versus Power Five teams, he was a virtual no-show: 23 of 40 for just 174 yards and 2 picks against Iowa, and then 9 of 24 for only 64 yards and a pick against Oregon. So he had a weak completion percentage against weak defenses and was far worse against better teams. Boller-esque.

Allen, typical of big-arm quarterbacks, tries to make up too much with arm stretch, convincing himself he can beat a safety or an outside-breaking cornerback with his pass velocity. It leads to too many poor decisions and breakups—or worse, interceptions. His throws are similar to Cam Newton's, with his deep ball coming out flat. When he tries to compensate with a touch throw, it's often short-armed and soft, floating away. Josh needs to find a way to harness both weapons, where he can unleash a cannon but, when needed, also throw with touch. And he needs to improve his timing with better footwork. Right now, when he moves around the pocket, he doesn't keep his feet under him and stay in delivery mode. He has to reset in order to throw, and that makes him late. Similarly, his anticipation throws leave a lot to be desired.

Not to get too negative here, but there's one other factor we have to put in the mix: signature games. That's when you see potential star quality, leadership moments, indelible performances. You want to look at the tapes and see games where the quarterback was clearly the best player on the field. I looked hard and I can't find those games. Even when he was playing small-ball college. He had just one game over 300 yards. One. That's hard to imagine. Where was his moment? That has to make you second-guess him as a top ten pick or even a first-rounder.

So…Josh Allen is your classic boom-or-bust player. For sure, some GMs, coaches, and scouts are going to talk themselves into believing that this kid can be great. That's a fantasy I've lived. In the end, Allen is a cross between Kyle Boller and Jake Locker—Boller for the arm strength but poor completion numbers, and Locker for athleticism but also abysmal completions. Boller and Locker have another distinction—first-round picks with losing records in college—which fortunately Allen doesn't share. I don't want to bury Allen with these comparisons, and he does have some high ceilings—moments, if not games, when he's been brilliant—but he's hit some low floors often too.

There's one other comp that's likely to be raised by some people: Like Allen, Carson Wentz came out of a second-tier program, in

29

his case North Dakota State in the NCAA Football Championship Subdivision. But that's where the parallels diverge. With knock-out completion percentages (high 60s), school scoring records, two FCS National Championships, graduating with a 4.0 average, and a memorable Pro Day, Wentz rose to the number two pick in his draft class. He was taken by the Eagles and went on to set rookie records and have a dazzling second year that positioned Philadelphia for the Super Bowl (prior to his late-season injury). Josh Allen is not Carson Wentz, no matter how hard we wish it.

If I'm a coach and I find myself rationalizing the negatives—accuracy, completions, yards—or hoping for a fairy-tale ending, I tell myself to wake up. I don't want to hitch my wagon to this kid if my job depends on it...*and it always does.*

But despite the concerns, mine included, there were plenty of pluses, and the Bills took Allen. Now the question was: When will he play? Even though the team says they're committed to not putting Allen in too early, they don't have many options but to start him soon. They picked up A. J. McCarron from Cincinnati in March to replace Tyrod Taylor, but he was obviously a placeholder for their first-round pick. On paper, you'd think it looks positive that Allen is going to a team that was the seventh-ranked rushing attack in 2017. The problem is, a lot of that was due to (1) Tyrod Taylor, an agile running QB, (2) the protection of offensive guard Cordy Glenn, and (3) offensive tackle Seantrel Henderson. But (4) thanks to trades and free agency, they're all gone.

So...the pressure will be on the big arm of Allen and the big target of wide receiver Kelvin Benjamin. To coach Sean McDermott, that combo looks and feels a lot like Cam Newton—strong arm, so-so throwing touch, but huge target(s). Will Allen be able to deliver in Buffalo like he did at Wyoming? He has determination. He has self-confidence. He had meager college offers but made the most of what he got. He played in the second tier of NCAA football but like Carson Wentz was taken in the first round. You have to like his grit and character, assuming it's the mature version. Now let's see if he has the NFL tools...

Pick number 10... The Bears and 49ers picked at number eight and nine, a linebacker and an offensive tackle. And then it was back to the quarterback show. Arizona has been through a lot of transition. Head coach Bruce Arians, a one-of-a-kind, colorful, demanding/nurturing, no bs, f-bombing guy, retired at age sixty-five after five years and the most wins in Cardinals history: fifty. Lasting five years—and leaving on your own terms—turns out to be well beyond the average head-coaching tenure (and the average is raised by Bill Belichick's nineteen years at the Patriots, almost double anyone else). Arians said it was time to take a break from the game. (As it turned out, his break lasted one season, after which he signed on as head coach of the Bucs). Since Arians had surrounded himself with famously silver-haired assistants, lovingly called his "geezer staff," GM Steve Keim was not inclined to promote from within. He hired Steve Wilks, defensive hotshot from the Panthers, who had impressed several teams the previous year. Getting him was considered a coup. And for Wilks, it was a chance to sit on a very hot seat, trying to succeed the almost legendary Arians, revitalize an aging team, and quickly turn a rookie quarterback into a star. That's the job.

At the eleventh hour, Arizona had traded with the Raiders up to the tenth pick, likely to get ahead of the Dolphins, who might have had their eye on a quarterback to eventually, or soon, replace

Ryan Tannehill. The Cardinals had an interesting set of circumstances at QB. After Carson Palmer's retirement just prior to the draft, they signed Sam Bradford with a $5 million base salary plus a $15 million signing bonus, for a total guarantee of $20 million. It's pricey but it's also the going rate for a starting quarterback. And Bradford, a former overall number one pick, has had a disappointing, injury-plagued career that never lived up to its promise. Most importantly for Arizona, the way the deal is structured, the team is not on the hook for any money going forward, once the bonus is paid. That's a perfect scenario to take the best available quarterback when your number comes up.

At this point in the draft, that's clearly Josh Rosen. He put up some big numbers at UCLA, possesses picture-perfect form, has a few issues (but who doesn't?)—an ego thing or huge self-confidence, depending on your point of view. But there's no arguing, he has a ton of potential.

In Arizona, Rosen could sit behind Bradford, hopefully shut up, and learn from him and from offensive coordinator Mike McCoy (another guy on a hot seat). If, in the meantime, Bradford breaks out and performs well, great. And the Cardinals' team overall may be the best suited to take a young quarterback, since they have a great returning running back in David Johnson (maybe second only to Le'Veon Bell), future Hall of Famer wide receiver Larry Fitzgerald, and a pretty good defense to contain opponents.

Here's Josh Rosen, UCLA, pre-draft:

NFL COMBINE: Physical: 6 ft. 4 in., 226 lbs. • 40 yd. dash: 4.92 secs. • Vertical jump: 31.0 in. • Broad jump: 111 in. •

3 cone drill: 7.09 secs. • 20 yd. shuttle: 4.28 secs. • NFL
evaluation: 6.19, NFL instant starter

There's a lot of hype around Josh Rosen. And for good reason.
After graduating high school a year early to join UCLA, Rosen was
the Bruins' first-ever true freshman opening-day starter. Rosen's
mechanics are straight out of a coach's dream tape, with his stride
and throwing motion and his good arm action with a nice high
release and bent knees. And he's probably the best QB in this class
when it comes to anticipation and timing throws; he throws when
his wide receivers are open more than any other college QB, with
accuracy and timing. He also has shown the ability to make a very
good back-shoulder throw. I'm not ready to compare him to Aaron
Rodgers, but you don't see that type of back-shoulder throw very
often. In terms of form, you could make a how-to manual for high
school quarterbacks from tape of Josh Rosen.

More pluses: He's a good tennis player, and that shows in his
footwork on the field. He has quick feet, gets to his drop quickly,
and always appears to be on balance in his drop. That means he
can elude rushers with a quick side step and be ready to throw. He
also shows an ability to "climb the pocket" when necessary and
doesn't have much in the way of wasted movements, so he keeps
the play timing on schedule. Rosen trusts his protection and keeps
his eyes downfield for the most part.

Cautions: While he does have good feet in the pocket, you'd
never call him mobile or a running threat. He is a true pocket
passer, and almost looks out of place when he's running around.
That said, you'd rather have him pass anyway. Accuracy and timing are big strengths of his game. In sharp contrast to Josh Allen,

in 2017 Rosen threw with 63 percent accuracy when blitzed. And if you dig deeper into the stats, you see his overall percentage was hurt by thirty-one drops by pass catchers. (NFL receivers are going to hang on to the ball better.) So, while people were creating excuses for Allen's weak completion percentage, Rosen, competing in a tougher conference, was consistently at or above 60 percent.

Being a West Coast guy, he has time both under center and in the gun. So we get plenty of tape to digest in play action and with his back to the defense. Rosen can give a good shoulder fake, or pump fake, to manipulate the defense.

Reality check: He's not a cannon like the other Josh. His arm strength is average to below average, and he sometimes struggles to drill a hard strike to the boundary lines.

Worries: His freshman year was easily the most impressive of his three years at UCLA. He threw for 3,668 yards, 23 touchdowns, and only 11 picks, with a 60 percent completion record. The following season, he had only six starts before injuring his throwing shoulder and missing the rest of the season. Even in those six starts, he had ups and downs. Up: a 400-yard passing game. Down: Against Texas A&M, he threw three picks. He finished the short year with 10 TDs to 5 picks and dropped under 60 percent in completions. But he started out his junior year on fire: an opener with 491 yards, completing 35 of 59 passes, for 4 touchdowns and a 34-point comeback, followed by revenge against Texas A&M, then a career-high 5 TDs against Hawaii. After five games, he led the country in passing yards, offense, and TDs, and was projected in a mock draft to be the Browns' number one pick. Then he got hurt again. This time it was a concussion, or two, or more. He came back in a tough loss to USC and Sam Darnold. Then, after UCLA won a slot at the Cactus Bowl, Rosen wasn't medically cleared to play in the game.

Fair or not, injury concerns are a legitimate caution. Some players get hurt more than others. You might say concussions aren't a measure of overall toughness, but in Rosen's case, his slim build makes him vulnerable, and his injury history goes all the way back to his high school days.

Comps: I'd liken him to Matt Ryan as a prospect—similar build and mechanics, with a true presence in the pocket for a passing game—but Ryan had to develop skills outside of the frame of the offense to really flourish. Right now, Rosen needs almost everything in the play to be "on schedule" (meaning "as planned") for it to work. He lacks the on-field creativity you need sometimes. In college, Rosen often passed over early open reads, ones that he will need to take on early downs in the NFL. And I'd also compare, or rather contrast, him to Jay Cutler, another highly touted quarterback who fell in the draft. (More on that below.)

Bottom line: His personality, character, style, whatever you want to call it, is the big question mark. Jim Mora, Rosen's college coach, is on record saying that the Cleveland Browns should draft Sam Darnold as the number one QB in this class, not Josh Rosen. Pretty tough indictment from your own coach. Then Mora wrapped a bow around it by suggesting that Darnold was a better personality fit with the city of Cleveland: a grittier Cleveland blue-collar type of player. With friends like that...But Mora isn't alone. One of my colleagues confided in me, "I remember being at UCLA and watching Rosen throw the ball and I'm thinking... he's the best passer of all these guys, but I couldn't get anybody to really vouch for the kid. Nobody, even coaches, really thought well of the leadership of the kid. Nobody vouched for his personality with teammates." The more you read about Rosen, the more you heard scouts and coaches talking about how difficult he was to coach, more outspoken than some would prefer, and even perceived as too casual about football, all unfortunately feeding into the stereotype of the privileged California kid.

"With the tenth pick of the first round, the Arizona Cardinals take Josh Rosen..." The Cardinals need a quarterback; they have a respectable starter to mentor the next quarterback; the coaching staff is in sync on their plans; the team has a solid roster to support a new quarterback—as positive a situation for a rookie QB as there could be. It's all good...except for Rosen himself. After "falling" to the tenth pick, Rosen stayed true to his petulant character...that ego thing. Rather than show gratitude to Arizona for taking him, he vented, saying, "I dropped and I was pissed." He acknowledged the chip on his shoulder, tweeting, "There were nine mistakes made ahead of me." And in case we missed the point, he soon elaborated: "And I will make sure over the next decade or so that they will know they made a mistake." He just put an even bigger monkey, or target, on his own back and on his team.

That takes me back to my comparison to Jay Cutler, no offense to Jay. Despite a lot of record-setting in his college career at Vanderbilt, Jay Cutler fell to the eleventh spot in the 2006 draft and went to Denver. But ahead of him Vince Young out of Texas was taken third overall by Tennessee, and Matt Leinart from USC went tenth to the Cardinals. Both were Heisman Trophy winners but both had brief careers, with Young being declared one of the biggest first-round busts in history, and Leinart lasting only six seasons. There seems to be something—not something good—about being taken between number five and ten in the draft in the last twenty years: Sanchez, Leftwich, Tannehill, Locker, Gabbert, Leinart—all good, none great. Patrick Mahomes, also at number ten, is the big exception. When teams pass on a quarterback, it's usually for valid reasons. Then some other team takes that guy out of "need," and need is a terrible evaluator of talent. It makes you see things that aren't there or things you wish were there. The point is, falling in the draft isn't always so bad. And by the way, Cutler handled it graciously. Check out the video. Getting picked for the wrong reasons is much worse.

Still, plenty of experts rated Rosen as the best pure passer coming into the NFL. If…if…if he can mature mentally, he could be a great selection for the Cardinals. My advice, which he didn't ask for: Josh, show what you can do on the field, not with your mouth. That's a far better way to shut the critics up.

So far, four quarterbacks were taken in the first round. A pretty good haul. And that was it…almost. Twenty-one more picks went by. Miami didn't take a quarterback, betting on Ryan Tannehill; nor did the Redskins, banking on Alex Smith; the Bengals stayed faithful to Andy Dalton; the Patriots—well, why would they do anything but stick with Mr. Immortality, Tom Brady; the Ravens seemed content with a now-healthy Joe Flacco; the Steelers believe Ben Roethlisberger is made of steel; the Jaguars still seemed okay with Blake Bortles…still? Nobody else took a first-round quarterback…until the *very last pick.*

"With the thirty-second selection in the 2018 NFL Draft, the Baltimore Ravens take Lamar Jackson…"

Opinions on Lamar Jackson are as varied as those on Baker Mayfield. Some think he could be a transformational player with freakish speed and athleticism. Others think he is a limited thrower who will have a tough time staying healthy at the NFL level (an athlete who happens to play quarterback versus a quarterback who is an excellent athlete). Some even said maybe he should be a wide receiver. To his credit, Jackson dismissed that idea out of hand.

In the final draft of his career, soon-to-retire GM of the Ravens Ozzie Newsome did a masterful job. He managed to get not one but two very promising players. The Ravens traded back twice to the twenty-fifth pick to first take tight end Hayden Hurst from South Carolina. The Ravens like tight ends and have a good history with them—Shannon Sharpe, Todd Heap, Dennis Pitta (lost to injury after the 2016 season), and Ben Watson (gone to New Orleans in free agency). The Ravens were in the market to replace the 86 receptions Pitta had in 2016 or the 61 receptions Watson gave them in 2017. To most observers, after taking Hurst, the Ravens appeared to be done.

But most observers underestimated Newsome and his heir apparent, Eric DeCosta. There had been chatter that Sean Payton in New Orleans and Bill Belichick in New England, both visionaries in seeing how the college-style game may be taking over the NFL, were positioning themselves to take Lamar Jackson to eventually replace Drew Brees or Tom Brady. Barstool baloney, as it turns out. New Orleans made a dramatic move up to the middle of the first round, and NFL draft analyst Mike Mayock delivered an impassioned monologue about the foresight of Sean Payton, getting ahead of the league in taking Lamar Jackson to groom behind future Hall of Famer Brees. Impassioned, but wrong. The Saints took Marcus Davenport, an edge rusher from the University of Texas at San Antonio. New England, now positioned at number thirty-one, could show the same visionary prowess by taking Jackson to succeed future Hall of

Famer Brady. Interesting, but again wrong. The Patriots took running back Sony Michel from Georgia. That left Philadelphia with the last pick of the first round, but with Nick Foles, who led the Eagles to their Super Bowl win, and likely a healthy Carson Wentz, they had no interest in taking a quarterback.

So the Eagles traded their first-round pick, even if it was number thirty-two, to the Ravens, who surprised everyone, including their franchise quarterback and Super Bowl winner Joe Flacco...

Taking the fifth QB of the first round, Ozzie Newsome was leaving the Ravens with their potential next-generation quarterback, Lamar Jackson. It was the biggest stunner of the 2018 draft. Would it work? Was it a legacy? Or just a hope?

Ozzie Newsome has had a remarkable career in the league, not only as a Hall of Fame player but also as a brilliant talent evaluator. I know; as a coach I benefited from his skills. Ozzie counts draft picks Ray Lewis, Ed Reed, Jonathan Ogden, Todd Heap, Terrell Suggs, Haloti Ngata, Marshal Yanda, Ray Rice, Joe Flacco, and C. J. Mosley among his stars, not to mention a slew of outstanding trades. But for all GMs, Newsome included, finding quarterbacks has always been a challenge. Some said Ozzie wanted to leave the team with a parting gift, and that was the selection of Jackson. Head coach John Harbaugh was second in the league in tenure (behind Belichick) but feeling the heat of owner Steve Bisciotti, who, after assuming that getting into the postseason was a given, had seen a drought in recent years. The previous season, Bisciotti had openly acknowledged he'd considered letting Harbaugh go. In case you think an owner won't do that with a Super Bowl–winning head coach, let me personally tell you different. Same job, same owner, same championship—boom, pink slip. That's a career in the

NFL—as they say, Not For Long. And veteran Joe Flacco, who had been out with a bad back a good part for of the previous year, looked strong again but was getting up there in quarterback years. No time to panic, but a good time to look ahead. And perhaps leave a legacy.

What did the Ravens see in Lamar Jackson that others may have missed? First of all, the team was not drafting out of "need"— at least, they didn't think they would have a need—which gives a team a lot of objectivity: No panic, we're okay, a quarterback would be nice to have if we can find the right guy. About-to-retire GM Ozzie Newsome said, "It's not like you're really thinking, 'Oh man, we're going to draft a quarterback in the first round.' We thought the team was going to be good enough that we would compete for the division with Joe...and you hate to use the high pick on a quarterback." But there was something special they saw in Lamar. Eric DeCosta, who was about to inherit the GM reins, said, "Looking at so much data...comparing Lamar to Baker and Darnold and Rosen all at once...what sort of gave me more confidence was some data from PFF [Pro Football Focus] [that] looked at all of Lamar's throws under pressure and...completion percentage and yards attempt-wise. And he was...at the tops of college football. It was he and Baker and then everybody else. That kind of stood out..." "Under pressure" is not a readily visible stat by itself. You have to look at real-time game film to see it in action. But it is the essence of what an NFL quarterback has to live with. Not throwing from clean pockets, but trying to keep a play together when the world is crashing down on you. If Lamar was good at that, DeCosta and Newsome knew it was a very good sign.

Eric thought hard about Lamar, not just looking at the obvious stats, but at the results behind them, what he might be able to project from what he saw. "It made me realize there was maybe a little bit more under the hood for Lamar Jackson than people really realized. It wasn't just this athlete who could run around back there and make plays."

Even though the Ravens weren't going to use their first pick on a QB, the conversations around Jackson started to get serious... and more frequent. *What would we do if we had this quarterback [Jackson]?... What will we look like?... How would we use him?... It's clear we couldn't force him into a Joe Flacco offense.* In one of the early discussions, head coach John Harbaugh said, "If you take Lamar, we'll build an offense around him." That sounds innocent enough, but it is a big, big commitment. It was a green light to take Jackson. It meant being willing to change everything. John didn't expect to have to make the change soon, but he showed he would embrace it, when and if it came. That's not so common for head coaches. Maybe he was influenced by another voice in his ear. The off-the-record word around the Ravens facility was that owner Steve Bisciotti was open to a new quarterback.

The Ravens did one other thing. Nothing. That is, nothing that showed. They liked what they saw and sensed in Jackson, so they kept it to themselves. They made it a point not to talk to him too much at the Combine, not to let on to anyone that they were shopping him seriously. The last thing they needed was for another team to get curious about what the Ravens saw and decide to take a closer look.

Jackson was the last of the top five quarterback prospects still on the board. Earlier, some had ranked him as high as the top slot or the runner-up. But his strength was his weakness. Lamar is a running quarterback. Some say he's a runner who can play quarterback. The NFL wants quarterbacks who can also run. It seems a subtle difference, but it isn't. So, right or wrong, he fell in the draft…right into the Ravens' lap.

Pre-draft look at Lamar Jackson, University of Louisville:

> NFL COMBINE: Physical: 6 ft. 2 in., 216 lbs. • 40 yd. dash: opted out • Vertical jump: opted out • Broad jump: opted out • 3 cone drill: opted out • 20 yd. shuttle: opted out • NFL evaluation: 5.91, will become NFL starter

In evaluating quarterbacks, you don't dwell on NFL Combine results. You take a quick look to reinforce what you already know. One guy is tall and strong. Another guy can throw the ball eighty yards from his knees. This one is fast. That one has good footwork. You've seen them all in real games, on tape, so you know that what you see at the Combine doesn't add much. That is, until you get a Lamar Jackson and realize what he *didn't* do at the Combine. He opted not to run the 40 because everyone knew how fast he was from his career at the University of Louisville and his winning the Heisman Trophy in 2016. In fact, he opted out of all the drills. And, despite pressure to show his stuff as a running/receiving threat, he declined to work out at wideout because he was determined to be seen as a quarterback. He did not hire an agent; he relies on his most ferocious advocate, his mother. But—and this is important—he gave the most impressive, honest, open, powerful interviews at the Combine. He showed potential leadership in his demeanor and his words. Intangibles can be critical.

Now, about his abilities: Jackson's TD-to-INT ratio was a solid 30 to 9 as a sophomore, 27 to 10 as a junior. But much like Josh

Allen, the completion percentage just wasn't there—56 percent as a sophomore, 59 percent as a junior.

Nonetheless, Jackson can be explosive. In his first game as a sophomore starter, against UNC Charlotte, he hit a career-high eight touchdowns, all in the first half. Then against Syracuse he had five touchdowns—four of which were rushing TDs—again, all in the first half. Same stats exactly facing Florida State, all in the first half. He's such a threat on his feet, he even started one game at running back versus Auburn. His ability and willingness to run are both good and bad. He gets tackled and puts himself in danger, and he's had too many turnovers.

No question, he did get better with each college season in terms of pocket poise and presence. When he didn't see his first read, he didn't automatically give in to the temptation to pull the ball down and scramble. He got better with his eyes, looking defenders off and then throwing to his read. But there's no denying it: He's at his best—and most exciting—when the play breaks down and he has to be creative and improvise. (He has time under center but most of his play fakes didn't require him to turn his back to the defense like a traditional play fake in the NFL.) His drop and step back look almost casual on tape—not that he's playing sloppy, but that he's inconsistent, and too often gets narrow and tall so his deep ball is also inconsistent. He struggles with his touch to get the ball over the arms of dropping linebackers. It's most often flat and high when he misses—sailing—and that leads to INTs in the NFL. For a QB on the run so often, you'd like to see him at his best when throwing off-platform, but his accuracy, at least so far, is worse when throwing on the run.

Comps: Lamar gets touted as a clone of everybody from Vince

Young to Michael Vick to Robert Griffin III to Deshaun Watson. With a cannon arm—flick of the wrist, like he's barely trying, and then flinging it—plus running ability, Michael Vick is the obvious comparison. But Jackson is three inches taller and a little more polished than Vick was as a prospect. And Jackson has obvious playmaking skills. For me, his body type and big-time running ability are reminiscent of Robert Griffin III. Jackson had ten rushing touchdowns of forty-plus yards. He is literally a big play waiting to happen, but it can look a little chaotic out there before he hits the big one. With his pure speed, elusiveness, and vision in the open field, he makes it nearly impossible for defenders in pursuit. But he's vulnerable. At six foot three and 200-plus pounds, he looks like he could carry another fifteen to twenty pounds in order to take the punishing hits his style of QB will incur on a game-by-game basis. And he has not shown a natural inclination to slide in the open field. Ask RG3: That's not a good thing.

Bottom line: Lamar Jackson is the type of player who is boom or bust on every play, and that can be an ulcer maker for a coach (and we don't need any extra causes). Can you live with the two or three horrible plays in a drive, waiting for the one explosive play? For Jackson to be successful early, an offense will have to look much like the one the Texans built around Deshaun Watson in Houston: RPOs (run-pass options) and big plays mixed in with some easy throws. Jackson's success will depend on what the coach is willing to do to build a scheme around him and how that coach can live with plays outside of the design of the offense…while waiting for the magic.

The scenario seems obvious. Since handing Joe Flacco a $120 million contract after their Super Bowl win against the 49ers, the Ravens have been a .500 team, making the playoffs only once in the last five years. John Harbaugh has a team owner who almost showed him the exit, and a quarterback in Flacco who appears to be healthy again but is also playing out his final contract year. It's time to plan ahead. Because "ahead" tends to arrive sooner rather than later. Welcome Lamar. Joe Flacco is a soft-spoken man who will be polite and cordial to Jackson but will politely and cordially have zero interest in mentoring him.

More importantly and practically, this presents a dilemma for the Ravens' coaches: What kind of offense do you start to implement for Jackson? The things you want to put in an offense for Jackson have no chance of being run by Flacco. And vice versa. The Ravens contend they see another Deshaun Watson in Lamar Jackson. Watson has the brightest future of any quarterback I can recall in the NFL, having quickly matured in 2017 in a way few could have imagined. He maintained his ability to make plays outside the pocket but developed remarkably quickly and effectively as a pocket passer as well. That's what the Ravens see, or want to see, in Jackson. Great theory and plan. Here's the caveat: Jackson does not appear to have the throwing ability of Watson. Like the quarterback picks from five to ten, the ones from twenty to thirty-two over the last twenty years are also telling. Other than Aaron Rodgers and Drew Brees, they've all been total whiffs as QB picks, some clearly worse than others—Johnny Manziel, Brandon Weeden, Brady Quinn (hmm, all picked by Cleveland). These prospects either fell to this range for good reason or moved up for bad reason, because of a desperation need by teams. They probably belonged in the second round or later. Again, with the exception of Aaron Rodgers. And there will definitely be those exceptions from time to time, the hidden gems. That's what the Ravens and plenty of gurus envision in Jackson. Here's the logic/wishful thinking: Flacco was a Super Bowl MVP, just like Brett Favre was before the Packers drafted Rodgers. So a hidden gem can replace a franchise quarterback…once in a while. The Ravens have Marty Mornhinweg—a smart, seasoned offensive coordinator—and a savvy assistant coach with deep quarterback experience, Greg Roman. Lamar Jackson plays a lot like Colin Kaepernick did when Roman was getting the most out of him in San Francisco. Put all the circumstances together and yes, we have the possibility of another Aaron Rodgers–like succession. Here's the reality: There has been one Rodgers in the past twenty years. The rest of those late first-round picks have ranged from okay starters to solid backups to washouts. Lamar Jackson and the Ravens will be the most interesting of all the rookie quarterback scenarios we will see play out in the coming year. Maybe Aaron Rodgers. Maybe Brandon Who?

Overview post-draft

Each team that picked a QB saw the quarterbacks very differently; each saw someone they fell in love with, or they convinced themselves they were in love. The analogy to 2011 is fitting. That year, four quarterbacks were taken in the first round, two more in the second round. With one exception, objectively it was a good, not great group, but there was a classic NFL feeding frenzy for quarterbacks because of "need." Cam Newton, the overall number one pick, was the exception: Rookie of the Year, an MVP, four postseason finishes, and a Super Bowl appearance. But many did not rank him as the top QB in the 2011 draft. The so-called experts put

Newton behind Jake Locker, who went at number eight, and Blaine Gabbert, picked at number ten. Locker's NFL record: four seasons, multiple injuries, mostly as a backup, win-loss stats of 9-14, and retired. Gabbert's record: rookie-year bust, injured, traded, traded again, released, and signed with his fourth team, overall 11-34 win-loss stats. Then came Christian Ponder at number twelve: four seasons—all losing—then traded, traded, traded, and retired. In the second round, Andy Dalton and Colin Kaepernick were picked at thirty-five and thirty-six respectively. Arguably, Dalton and Kaepernick had careers better than all but Newton, with Dalton taking the Bengals to the postseason four times and Kaepernick—before his kneeling controversy—leading the 49ers to a Super Bowl. The whole process shows that "beauty is in the eye of the beholder"—or the eye of the wishful thinker.

In 2018, you could say each team that drafted a quarterback got the one (or one of the two) they wanted all along. Cleveland is obvious: They had the first pick. They got Mayfield, and despite internal squabbles, the powers that be wanted him. The Jets, if you were playing the odds, were likely one of the seventeen teams that had Darnold ranked number one, so they were thrilled to get him. Similarly, Allen could very well have been the Bills' top choice, given his arm strength and what it takes to play QB in the weather conditions of Buffalo on a regular basis. Rosen, who some say is arrogant and some say is confident, but who all say has talent, fell a little, which had to make Arizona happy. And Jackson was a masterful/hopeful stroke on the part of the Ravens. Now it's time to put the laboratory hypotheses to the test: the metrics and real-world games of the NFL.

II

What Is It About Quarterbacks?

Definition of *quarterback*—noun
1. an offensive back in football who usually lines up behind the center, calls the signals, and directs the offensive play of the team
2. one who directs and leads

Merriam-Webster's Collegiate Dictionary

We know what a quarterback *is* and what a quarterback *does*. So it should be simple to find one, right? Impossible is more like it.

Predicting quarterback success, to state the obvious, isn't obvious. You're looking at stats like completion percentage, adjusted total yards, and TDs to INTs, as well as assessments like level of competition, program style, throwing style, physical size, and intelligence. But you're also looking for subjective characteristics that are much harder to quantify. *Leadership*: What is that? Brash and loud or quiet and steady? Cool under pressure? Charismatic? *Decision-making*: Fast and instinctive or patient and unflappable? When things go right or go wrong? Seeing the whole field? Reading threats? Adjusting on the fly or sticking to plan? *Command*: Fearless or measured? Total self-confidence? Follow-me-into-battle style? Selective amnesia—forgetting setbacks and moving on? Demanding or understanding? The fact is, it all depends. Different styles work for different people. With different teams. In different circumstances.

To get a little closer to cracking the code, to finding the Q Factor if there is one, we're not only putting the 2018 quarterback draft class under the microscope; we're also re-examining *the way* we appraise quarterback potential and success—evaluating the evaluators, separating the data that matters and the data that doesn't, the metrics and the magic. If we can refine the search process even a little, fractionally or incrementally, it may be enough to spot the difference between good and really good or maybe even great, between precious salary cap dollars well spent and money burned, to result in a few more leaders and a few fewer washouts. For the next class. And the one after. Maybe we'll even find a formula that provides a slight edge in spotting "quarterback types" in fields beyond football. Remember: You don't have to double the S&P index to get rich; you just have to beat it by a few percentage points.

Prototypes

In every endeavor that demands a "quarterback," whether it's the football definition or the rest-of-life definitions, context changes, so the type of quarterback that "works" changes too. Those factors of leadership, decision-making, and command look and feel very different depending on the style of the individual, the times, and the circumstances. Sometimes you need a growling, gruff George Patton and sometimes a stoic, steady George Washington; sometimes a stirring, eloquent Winston Churchill and sometimes a pious, pacifist Mahatma Gandhi; a headstrong, egotistical Steve Jobs or a low-key listener Bill Gates; an inspirational, nonviolent Martin Luther King Jr. or an inspirational firebrand Malcolm X; a self-effacing, saintly Mother Teresa or a visionary stalwart Margaret Thatcher. It's no surprise that we see the same "sometimes" situational variations in football. Sometimes you need a cocky "Broadway Joe" Namath and sometimes a Joe "Cool" Montana, sometimes an improviser like Peyton Manning, sometimes a Zen master like Tom Brady. You *never* need someone with self-doubt, who doesn't live for battle, who might even prefer that someone else give the orders.

If everyone is looking for quarterbacks, in every part of life, where, when, and how do we find all these quarterback types? What's the pedigree? If only we knew. Do we look for advanced degrees or street smarts—MBAs or prodigies, Heisman winners or hopefuls who declare early? The same enigma applies in business. Just like the promising QB prospects who enter the draft after their junior year, big-idea entrepreneurs often drop out of college to launch their start-ups, rather than wait until they're more seasoned. Bill Gates quit school to found Microsoft. Steve Jobs left to create a little company called Apple. And Mark Zuckerberg walked away from Harvard to found Facebook and become the world's youngest billionaire. And it applies to other sports too. Most major league baseball players skip college and go to the minor leagues. LeBron James was the number one draft pick in the NBA at age eighteen. We expect great "quarterback types" to come out of Harvard, Penn, Stanford business programs, NCAA Division I football, the Final Four, West Point, or the Naval Academy...but some don't. Some just come on their own, from their parents' basement, from high school, from backyard pickup games. And somehow we have to be able to spot them all.

We know that quarterbacks and quarterback types are critical to success...of teams, of companies, and of ideas. We know how literally game-changing the results can be when we find the real deal. And what a bust it is when we miss. No wonder we're in a constant search to discover a better way to find them. If and when we do, it may not only change football, it may change the way we hunt for leadership across the board.

Beyond football—the other quarterbacks

When you build from football to parallels in other fields, can you evaluate the potential and ultimate success of "quarterback types"? How do corporate headhunters and boards of directors size up CEOs to compete, innovate, and deliver high profits? How about military leaders? Generals and admirals are a lot like quarterbacks. Only the stakes are higher. Does the prestige of an MBA program/level of play predict business success—is Harvard or Wharton or Stanford like the Pac-12, the SEC, or the Big 12? Or are public university students hungrier? In a study a few years ago, it turned out that more CEOs came from the University of Wisconsin than from the Ivys. Do the best military minds come from the academies or from the ranks? From combat simulations or the actual battlefield? Or are there no patterns at all?

How we search

We're looking for a needle in a haystack...with high-powered magnifying glasses, night goggles, big data, and Ouija boards. We use all the tools we have—stats, films, more stats, coaches, awards, bowl games, more stats, and the Combine—plus anecdotal evidence (behavior on the field and off), plus our instincts (good and bad), plus all the proven and self-appointed experts. And we count on the draft process itself to push the best candidates to the top and let the others fall. It works...mostly...sort of. The draft usually does tell us who is good. But it does not tell us who will be great, who will become that elusive being, the franchise quarterback. If only it did. But in the process of spotting the good ones, can the draft actually miss great ones? Sure. Maybe.

Didn't the draft miss Tom Brady? Or did we, the coaches, GMs, and scouts, miss him? First, consider the year 2000, Brady's draft year. Clearly the "need factor" for quarterbacks was not dire that year and/or the class was not seen as being very rich in QBs. The Browns' number one overall pick went to defensive end Courtney Brown...and he was called the biggest draft bust in Cleveland history (which is saying something, considering the Browns' other misses). That year, lots of outstanding players were taken early—running back Jamal Lewis, wide receiver Plaxico Burress, linebacker Brian Urlacher—but no quarterbacks were selected until Chad Pennington at number eighteen by the Jets. And then no more in round one, none in round two, and finally a couple more in round three. That year, need didn't drive quarterbacks up the ranks.

As for Tom Brady, his stats in college were actually very good, but they were sparse. He didn't start his first two years at Michigan, and in years three and four, he had to split time with Drew Henson as a starter, so Brady played fewer games than scouts like to see. University of Michigan coach Lloyd Carr would often play Brady in the first quarter, Henson in the second, and then decide who would play the second half—a strange coaching method, to say the least. Ultimately, Brady became the starter, posting a 20-5 record over two seasons, beating Ohio State (a big deal in the Big Ten), and beating Alabama in the Orange Bowl (a big deal everywhere). Brady had a 300-plus-yard passing game and led Michigan to several fourth-quarter rallies, earning him the nickname "The Comeback Kid." For his starting years, he had better than a 60 percent completion record. (For comps, that's higher than Dan Marino, about the same as Peyton Manning, and slightly lower than Ben Roethlisberger.) The difference is, Brady not only played too few games, but when he did play, he was in a program that doesn't like to throw the ball. Although he's known as a great decision-maker in the NFL, it seems Brady may have made one bad decision. His college choices came down to Cal or Michigan, one a passing team (Aaron Rodgers and Jared Goff came out of Cal), the other a grind-it-out running team, and he picked Michigan. That, plus Carr's odd coaching style and starting only two of four seasons so his stats were thin, camouflaged him in the draft. It may be that he's not a miracle but that we coaches and GMs didn't do our homework and just missed him. The word is that young Tom chose Michigan over Cal in order to put some physical distance into his maybe overly dependent relationship with his father. Good plan, but he might have considered Ole Miss, Tennessee, Florida, or any number of passing showcases. Michigan was a good team but hardly pass-happy. And they had that bizarre alternating-starter system. No, this was not an ideal platform for the potential of Tom Brady.

What if we looked harder and smarter?

Can't we improve the evaluation process? Even a little? A little could mean a lot. If we could up the outcomes, even by an incremental amount—if we achieved a 5–10 percent plus factor—we could literally alter the fate of teams. Imagine if there was a better way to gauge "leadership." What if we looked harder at a player's character and behavior and values on *and* off the field, in the locker room, in the classroom, at home with his siblings, with his girlfriend, or the boss from his summer job. People can't hide who they really are. But coaches and GMs tend to minimize what they don't want to hear or know, and we talk ourselves into players. We may not be psychologists but we should be able to read people pretty well, pretty objectively, or we don't belong in these jobs. We need to look hard at players and face reality. *Yes, this guy can throw the ball the length of the field, but he's immature and shows no signs of growing up ... Hey, that guy was always the first one in and the last to leave, and he got better and better ... Players like playing for that guy ... This one is moody ... That one is a loner ... This guy can't stay out of trouble.* Wishful thinking will get you nowhere ... nowhere near the playoffs, for sure. What if we could examine certain situational behavior—is he better when he's ahead or behind, early in the game or late, under pressure or freewheeling? What if we assessed decision-making—sticking to the call, or improvising, or throwing the ball away? What about pure execution or outcome— making something happen even when things are going wrong? We could perhaps eliminate 5–10 percent of the draft busts, or maybe find 5–10 percent more stars. Imagine. Franchise quarterbacks instead of expensive backups. Bonuses paying off instead of being written off. Losing teams turning around in a season or two.

Data versus gut—brains versus beer

Not a tough choice: quant geniuses examining granular input to arrive at mathematically projectable outcomes or a bunch of fat scouts lying to each other over flat Buds about who looks like/walks like/smells like a quarterback. In the past few years, data analytics combined with science have caused us to re-examine so much of what we thought we knew. *Freakonomics* and *Moneyball* became best sellers because they turned conventional wisdom on its head and used data in whole new ways—digging deeper to explain successes and failures in sports, politics, social issues, and business. We've learned to measure things we thought were immeasurable—attention span, multitasking limitations, brain-side dominance, ethnic heritage, sleep deprivation effects, thinking speed, even artificial intelligence. Genetics can predict the sex, eye color, and hair color of a baby. Netflix's and Amazon's algorithms can tell us not only what we watch but what we will *want* to watch. Facebook shows us the ads we *will* like. VORP—value over replacement player—helps establish baseball players' real worth. They're not perfect indicators but they're right more often than they're wrong. Why not predictive data for a rookie quarterback's NFL performance—how he *will* do? Why not a predictor of how quarterback X or Y will perform against a pro-style nickel defense? Or at the very least, could we cut down the tendency to rely on misleading, mythical gut indicators? *He looks like a quarterback…* *He gives a good interview…He has a cannon for an arm…He's got the "it" factor.* We humans are attached to the idea that there are intangibles, things that calculators can't calculate. That's how we keep our jobs. Personally, I don't think a computer can pick a quarterback better than I can…yet. But there has to be a better way than informed guessing.

Quarterback gurus

The first place to look to unravel the formula, or crack the code, is the people with good quarterback track records. The experts range from GMs and head coaches who have spotted and developed, albeit inconsistently, NFL franchise quarterbacks, to the specialist coaches who have worked one-on-one with the best in the game. They're aided and/or hammered by the sharp-eyed, sharp-tongued sports media commentators who move players up and down the draft board as if it were their money and their teams. And now there are the fantasy football geeks who use analytics to assemble pretend teams that are better than any real teams, and the big-data whizzes who study football as a break from solving the world's real problems.

The guy who wrote the book, literally

Probably the first quarterback "professor" was Bill Walsh, head coach of the San Francisco 49ers, who drafted Joe Montana in the third round of the 1987 draft and traded second- and fourth-round picks to Tampa Bay for Steve Young, landing two Hall of Famers. As a team assistant, I literally studied under Bill and he knew more about quarterbacks, or football for that matter, than anyone I've ever known. (Okay, like almost everyone else, he missed Brady in 2000.) With Walsh, I co-wrote his definitive football book, *Finding the Winning Edge*. His insights on QBs were, and are, very telling. At the time it was written, the three top quarterbacks in the NFL were Troy Aikman, Brett Favre, and Steve Young, each with very different physical and mental makeup. Here are some of the observations Bill and I made:

"...A logical argument can be made that no position on an NFL team is more important than the quarterback."

- To make success at the position even rarer, only some of the abilities demanded can be taught; the others are God-given.

"One of the most obvious requirements for a quarterback is the ability to pass."

- Obviously, a quarterback who is a poor passer has virtually zero chance to make it in the NFL. But "arm strength" and passing success are, or can be, miles apart, pun intended. Some players can heave a ball almost the length of the field, but can't hit their targets, close, far, or in-between.
- Passing has three essential elements: accuracy, timing, and "touch"—that is, making the throw "catchable."
- And the quarterback must have a quick delivery—not hurried, but smooth, without excess motion. It can be refined through practice, but it helps to have been born with good

"motor skill." Every play is basically a race between the QB's motion and the defenders' time to stop him.

- What is "touch"? On most passes—not quick flips or long bombs—the ball has to be thrown in such a way that the receiver can pull it in without breaking stride, so he can grab it on the run and get the maximum gain. Walsh knew that well since he worked and won with probably the best touch passer in the game, Joe Montana.

"Successful quarterbacks also have the ability to read defenses."

- By and large, quarterbacks don't learn that skill in college ball. To make matters worse, defenses in pro ball are bigger, faster, and smarter.
- But looking hard at a prospect's game tapes sometimes uncovers the rare kid who can spot not just his primary receiver but his secondary, or even third/emergency guy... fast. That kid might be NFL material *if*...
- ...he can avoid an NFL-level pass rush. That requires mobility and a sixth sense. A quarterback under pressure in the pocket must move and still keep the play intact.

"...Because of the dynamic role that a quarterback plays...he must have physical, mental, emotional, and instinctive traits that go well beyond his ability to pass the football."

- He has to be competitive, not just a guy who likes to win, but a guy who *has* to win, who lives and dies with every game. And he has the guts/moxie/courage to get it done.

- His team and his coaches have to believe in him; they have to believe he can do just about anything. Especially in the face of pressure, especially when behind, especially when the game hangs in the balance.
- The quarterback's "intestinal fortitude" has to supersede doubt. Walsh would often cite two of the best as examples of this, Bart Starr and Bob Griese.

"A great quarterback also has excellent instincts and intuition."

- He has to have a "feel" for the game—another example of an intangible but mandatory quality for a quarterback. It's not just the plays, the Xs and Os, or the shorthand written on his wrist card. It's a lot more.
- It's nuance—the subtleties of reading a defense, a slight shift, an audible, a step back, even a look. Great quarterbacks seem to come out of the womb with that intuition. Coaches can't teach it.
- Walsh called it "instinctive genius"—when a great quarterback just makes "the right call at the right time."

"Finally, quarterbacks must have the ability to function at an appropriate level while injured."

- NFL players get hurt. It's a rougher game than college. And the season is twice as long, doubling the chances to get hurt.
- With bigger, better, tougher defenses than in college, quarterbacks face more punishment and bodily abuse, but are expected to withstand it and still play.

As brilliant as he was, Bill Walsh didn't give himself a lot of credit for his quarterback success; he gave it to the quarterbacks. He said he was "extremely fortunate" to work with the likes of Greg Cook, Virgil Carter, Ken Anderson, Guy Benjamin, Steve Dils, Dan Fouts, Joe Montana, and Steve Young. For the record, and record books, that's two All-Americans, four NFL MVPs, and three Hall of Famers. I'd give Bill some credit.

Mentors, sages, and whisperers

There are a handful of experts who have had notable success with quarterbacks, among them David Cutcliffe, who coached Peyton Manning at Tennessee and Eli Manning at Ole Miss and recently Daniel Jones at Duke. He worked personally with Peyton on his comeback after neck surgery, preparing him for his return to pro football and a Super Bowl win for the Broncos. Quite a record of nurturing quarterbacks. As far as finding a high-level QB, he did recruit Eli Manning to Ole Miss. But he's never been an NFL coach or a GM, so he's never had to draft a pro QB. That's a whole other level of pressure.

Quarterback "whisperer" Bruce Arians worked with Peyton Manning at the Colts, Ben Roethlisberger at the Steelers, returned to the Colts and coached rookie Andrew Luck, then moved to Arizona, a last hurrah (almost) and a comeback for Carson Palmer. At the end of the 2017 season, at age sixty-five, Arians retired from the Cardinals. Then he "unretired" to try to work his magic at Tampa Bay with Jameis Winston, their promising but as yet disappointing 2015 number one draft pick.

In his career, Arians is given credit for inspiring a young Peyton Manning to go no-huddle to get over his case of nerves, with getting Browns journeyman quarterback Kelly Holcomb to play like an All-Pro for at least one season and one postseason, and with coaxing one more "up" out of the up-and-down career of Carson Palmer. That's some résumé with quarterbacks. How will he do with Winston? In a peek ahead to 2019, so far, it's been a struggle— lots of yards passing (5,100) but way too many interceptions (30). But taking chances is part of the Arians playbook. His signature phrase is "no risk it, no biscuit": Play aggressively; give the quarterback two plays on every snap; create trust between quarterback and coach and team. Break down the coach-player wall, relate as peers, and have a drink—he says he learned his most important lessons in human nature while bartending.

There's no argument; he's brilliant. But he never drafted a quarterback. He worked with what he got, but he didn't pick them. What can he teach us? A powerful quarterback track record, but as for draft success, it's hard to say, since Arians retired from the Cardinals after going 8-8 in 2017, before Arizona had to make a 2018 QB draft pick.

So, there are clearly some guys who know how to groom and nurture quarterbacks, but does anybody really know how to find one?

Well, there's Ron Wolf, the GM of the Packers who in 1992 traded a first-round pick to Atlanta to get their backup, a guy named Brett Favre, who became a three-time MVP and an eleven-time Pro Bowler, with five NFC Championship games and two Super Bowl appearances. That was an inspired, brilliant move. Wolf knew talent when he saw it. But just to be safe, Wolf drafted a quarterback in seven of the next eight drafts. That's right. He had Brett Favre as his starter and he kept looking for quarterbacks.

Four of his picks started for other teams, including Mark Brunell, who became a three-time Pro Bowler for the Jaguars, and Matt Hasselbeck, who did the same as a Seahawk. Ron was unquestionably good at picking quarterbacks, although Wolf himself acknowledges his whiffs. In 1994, he was confident Heath Shuler out of Tennessee (third overall pick by the Redskins), was going to be great. Was he? Well, suffice to say, he made far too many "all-time busts" lists (but fortunately went on to a more distinguished career as a U.S. congressman). And of course, Wolf, like most of us, missed Tom Brady in 2000.

What did Ron look for in a QB? In the end, as Wolf said on SI.com, "It's blind luck. If I knew how to put together a quarterback, I'd have my own island somewhere." He may be a bit humble, but his combination of analysis, experience, and yes, some luck, did better than most. Ron Wolf's mentee, John Dorsey, who worked under him in Green Bay, has a pretty good record too. As director of college scouting, he helped the Packers spot Aaron Rodgers, who was falling in the 2005 draft; then as GM in Kansas City, Dorsey traded picks to the 49ers for Alex Smith, and in 2017 traded up to number ten to get Patrick Mahomes. Dorsey moved to Cleveland as GM, traded picks to Buffalo for Tyrod Taylor, and in 2018 drafted Baker Mayfield as the overall number one. Dorsey seems to know how to draft quarterbacks. But he doesn't seem to stay with the teams once they take that quarterback.

Fantasy football and PhDs

Maybe the fantasy football geeks and math nerds know better than the scouts, coaches, and GMs. They don't have their careers riding on their prognostications, so maybe they can be dispassionate and clinically accurate. Fantasy football runs entirely on stats and has become almost as large an industry as the NFL. And ever since nerds became the new cool kids, building mathematical predictive models has become one of the great avocations of professors who love data and sports. Like the rest of us, on Sundays they need a diversion, in their cases, from economic forecasts, population and mortality tables, and other dry but more important stuff.

Functional mobility—formula for prediction?

Lots of studies have been done in an attempt to analyze quarterback success *after the fact*—did they live up to their hype? Few have successfully forecast future performance. Math professor Alexandre Olbrecht (executive director of the Eastern Economic Association at Ramapo College, New Jersey) and grad student Jeremy Rosen (Georgetown University) have come up with a methodology that attempts to predict each draft pick's likelihood of success in the NFL, based on a skill set called "functional mobility." "Functional mobility" is a phrase they credit to Doug Farrar in an SI.com article, in which he explained it this way: "When we talk about functional mobility, we're not talking about quarterbacks running to run...Instead, functional mobility can better be summarized as the work a quarterback does in and just around the pocket—the boxing ring–sized area in which the truly great passers do much of their work."

Rosen and Olbrecht took Doug's initial observation and turned it into a metric. Using each prospect's college stats, they have devised a formula combining a quarterback's (a) run-completion ratio and (b) yards per rush, to come out with a projected (c) average net yards gained per passing attempt (ANY/A). If the (a) ratio is low, meaning less tendency to run, that usually correlates with a higher completion percentage, and if it is then combined with a high number of yards per rush (b), it means the prospect is inclined to pass, is accurate, but *can* run when necessary, resulting in (c) higher average yards gained per play by that quarterback. If his tendency is to run, though his yards per rush may be good, it *can* mean his completion and accuracy numbers in the NFL will not be not so good. Previous assessments have relied heavily on completion and/or accuracy but ignored the value of rushing when needed. How good are the math guys? Here's a snapshot of their predictions: Adjusted Net Yards per Attempt, at the end of March 2018 (in the context of PI or Predictive Interval, the range of career-long ANY/A). Most telling are their comments and evaluations that follow.

2018 Predictions			
Quarterback	Our ANY/A	95% PI, Low	95% PI, High
Sam Darnold	5.93	4.05	7.81
Josh Rosen	5.32	3.44	7.20
Baker Mayfield	5.27	3.42	7.13
Josh Allen	5.02	3.15	6.90
Lamar Jackson	4.97	3.06	6.88
Kyle Lauletta	4.91	3.04	6.79
Mason Rudolph	4.80	2.93	6.67
Luke Falk	4.65	2.77	6.53

"Sam Darnold receives our highest projection...Since he is good in both categories—that is, a pocket passer who can run well when necessary—he would receive our highest projection even if we didn't consider scouting grades. On the other hand, Josh Rosen's high scouting grade is the main reason he comes in second. While he has the lowest run-completion ratio of any quarterback this year, only Luke Falk is a worse runner. But most scouts believe Rosen's exceptional passing talents are enough to overcome his lack of mobility. Although Baker Mayfield is less of a pocket passer than Darnold, he is an above-average runner, and he has this year's highest completion percentage. His performance-based statistics are more impressive than Darnold's, but...we prioritize functional mobility over those statistics...On the other hand, scouts like Josh Allen better than we do...Allen's low completion percentage gives him this year's second-highest run-completion ratio, and he is not a good enough runner to make up for it...In fact, without scouting grades, he would get our lowest projection...

"Of the remaining quarterbacks, that is, those with lower scouting grades, we like Lamar Jackson best...Jackson is a dual-threat quarterback with more rushing attempts than completions and many more rushing yards per attempt than his peers. While he struggles with accuracy, he is a good enough runner to make plays in the NFL provided he stays healthy."

A little better is worth a lot

How did Rosen and Olbrecht do versus reality? How valid is functional mobility? How predictive? Spoiler alert: As the next two seasons show, and as we analyze in this book, it looks like they came out about fifty-fifty, maybe a little better—that is, a little better than half right and half wrong. And *the ways* in which they were right are important. *Being mobile and functioning well while mobile is a credible label for what works, or breaks down when not working, in the NFL.* What quarterbacks do within the confines of the pocket, or when forced or purposely moving out of the pocket, the combination of running and passing, the ability to keep plays alive and advance the ball no matter how, were the critical factors in each of these quarterbacks' successes or failures.

The lesson—the glaring lesson—is that as hard as we work, or think we work, to analyze/prognosticate/divine/wish/pray who will be the next golden boy, we could do better. We could apply more discipline and less sheer hope and desperate need. We could force ourselves to be more objective and less emotional, to really see and hear and learn. More discipline, more study, more objectivity, more film, more listening (and less talking to ourselves), more reality, more trends (and fewer highlights), may not make the outcomes quantumly different. But it all may add up to making the outcomes statistically different—a better draft pick or a lesser one left unpicked, fewer lost salary cap dollars, one more win, one less loss—because remember, teams get into the playoffs by win-loss ratios; that is, statistics. The team that gets a wild card spot is only one game better than the team that just missed, and that wild card team only had to put up one more point than the team they beat, which may have come from one more first down, from one more good play—a slant pass or scramble or designed run or Hail Mary—from the quarterback they chose over the one they passed up. And by the way, ten wild card teams have made it to the Super Bowl, and six have won it. I know; I got to hold up the trophy in 2000 with the Ravens. Statistics. A little better is worth a lot.

Now let's take a candid look at how we've been sizing up quarterbacks, and maybe how we could view them more honestly and more accurately, and make better picks.

III

Billick's Extrapolations: Observable, Projectable Trends... Not Wishful Thinking

Which, if any, analytics or evaluation or crystal ball can we apply to the process of drafting a future franchise quarterback or evaluating a rookie to up the outcomes even a little, since a small improvement over the norms can mean a lot? What methodology can help us get closer to the elusive Q Factor, if there is one? *Extrapolation.* For me, after years of living and breathing the game, assistant coaching, head coaching, studying other coaches and countless players, watching and rewatching games, dissecting plays, going to the Combine, interviewing, winning, losing, learning from success, learning more from failure, the answer is extrapolation. By dictionary definition, it means "forming an opinion or reaching a conclusion through reasoning and information." What it means to me is *using what you know to help tell you what you don't know.* The data available and the trends in the data are trying to show what is likely to happen, but we tend to ignore what we see. And it is *likely* to happen. Not certain. Likely or probably is different than for sure. That's why we have probability, not for-sure-ability.

Hey, what about instinct? Am I supposed to ignore what my instinct says? No. Data and trends are not the opposite of instinct. On the contrary, they're what inform instinct, or should. Instinct is not a shot in the dark, hoping for a miracle. Good instinct is nothing more than an accumulation of your experiences. *I have seen this before, and it did/did not turn out well... I know this formation; this is what's going to happen... I was fooled by this once before, but not again.* To borrow from Colin Powell and his Thirteen Rules of Leadership, Rule 6 is: "Don't let adverse facts stand in the way of a good decision. Superior leadership is often a matter of superb instinct. When faced with a tough decision, use the time available to gather information that will inform your instinct." He also believes in the 40-70 principle of decision-making. Get at least 40 percent of the information available before you make a decision. But... if you have 70 percent of the data, don't get paralyzed into indecision and lose an opportunity while you're trying to gather the other 30 percent. No amount of data will make the decision for you. You have enough. Strike now. Your competitor isn't going to wait.

You reach your conclusions based on hard observation, on what you've learned, on what you know, not on what you hope for, not on what might happen once in a while, sometimes, when the wind is blowing just right and the stars are aligned. Here's a guy who has thrown a lot of picks. Every year in college. He won a lot of games but he has an accuracy problem. That isn't likely to get better. On the other hand, here's another guy who threw a lot of picks in high school—kids do that—but then threw fewer his first year in college, but still too many, then fewer still by his senior year. And he also won a lot of games. That extrapolates to a positive trend or direction. Not enough, by itself, to draft him high, but enough to keep him in the running, to look at along with other factors and then extrapolate further.

Everything takes you back to the film

Stats, analytics, scouting reports, hearsay, and the Combine are good indicators, but the truth is told in the game films. Not highlights or one great game, but hour after hour, game after game.

If a guy is good, it keeps showing up. If a guy has a weakness, it keeps showing up. If you look hard enough at the evidence, without emotion if possible, you can extrapolate from all of the relevant components. Not just the physical attributes or game stats, but even decision-making, maturity, and leadership. You have to watch endless hours of film on a prospect, play after play—routine plays, broken plays—down after down, good and bad, not just glory moments supplied by his parents or old coach or new agent. You want to see him when things go well and when they don't.

The same goes for his behavior. If a kid got in trouble off the field in high school but seemed to rise to the occasion in college, that's a good sign. Kids get in trouble and kids grow up. But if you see a kid, no matter how talented, how athletic, how accurate, how good on the field, who is bad off the field, year after year, warning after warning, run from that kid. He may tell you in an interview that now he's ready to be a model citizen, but the trend isn't there. Could he do an about-face? Sure, it happens. But can you afford to bet a high draft pick and a pile of money on it? No. It doesn't extrapolate. Don't misunderstand me. Kids change, and I am the greatest believer in the world in second chances, even third and fourth chances. But you need some evidence of change, of progress in the right direction. If you see signs that a positive pattern is emerging, by all means extrapolate from it. Carefully.

Data alone is dangerous

Way back when I worked for Bill Walsh at the 49ers, we knew enough to pay attention to data, but to not become slaves to it. We knew it was hard to resist. But sometimes more data, instead of being good, is the opposite. Or, as we warned ourselves back then, "When a certain critical mass of data accumulates to support a course of action, that course of action becomes inevitable whether or not it makes *common sense.*" We didn't call it extrapolation. We called it common sense—gather the *relevant* data and put it together with experience and judgment, and then decide.

Today I say, "Look at all the data, the stats, the film," and I add, "Do it as dispassionately as you can. Conclude from the cumulative evidence you see." I repeat: not what you want to see, but what you do see. I'm the first to confess, I didn't always do that when I was coaching. Maybe I had too much information. Maybe I should have reminded myself of what I learned with Bill Walsh, what I later coined as my own phrase on the subject, "The seduction of information grows in direct proportion to the amount of information available." Or maybe I was swayed by other people whose enthusiasm or optimism could be contagious. I wanted/needed a quarterback so bad, I sometimes got exactly that, a bad quarterback. Maybe I didn't go back to the film as much as I should have. Or maybe I turned a blind eye to what the film was trying to tell me and saw only the evidence that supported what I wished for. *Forget those passes he over- or underthrew. Forget the open receivers he didn't see. Forget how many balls he had to throw away. But look at this one picture-perfect completion.* I didn't extrapolate as much as I should have. Extrapolation works. How well? Better than pure data in a vacuum ignoring trends. Better than wishful thinking. Better than a lot of picks made these days. Not perfect. Better.

"Those managers best able to sift quickly and insightfully through the vast debris of data—let's call it the *infolanche*—will be winners, while those who keep wanting more for its own sake will end up paralyzed." I learned that from Bill Walsh a long time ago. I need to reread it from time to time.

The opposite of synergy

Don't get me wrong. Data is important. It tells us a lot. Wins and losses, pure completion percentage, height, weight, arm strength, yards per catch, passer rating—they're all valuable individual stats. Obviously, a guy who has a strong arm is better than a guy who has a weak arm. But there is a phenomenon we fall prey to that I call the opposite of synergy—or the danger of data-only.

First let's go back to synergy and what it is supposed to mean: *The whole is greater than the sum of the parts.* For instance, you put together a bunch of parts like cylinders and pistons and rods and belts and batteries and fans that individually can only perform limited functions, but assembled properly create a combustion engine that can power a four-thousand-pound automobile.

Conversely, one of my favorite phrases describes what I learned the hard way: *Sometimes the whole does not equal the sum of the parts.* I apply it to quarterbacks who possess a lot of good traits and stats but somehow they don't add up to a total quarterback.

When I was head coach of the Ravens, I saw it with one player in particular—Kyle Boller—but I realized it applies to so many. Boller came out of high school passing for almost 5,000 yards and 59 touchdowns. At Cal, he passed for almost 8,000 yards and 64 touchdowns, the second most TDs in school history. He was six foot three, 220 pounds, smart, engaging, and California handsome. He looked like a quarterback; he acted like a quarterback; he threw like a quarterback—practically the length of the field as a demo during the Combine; and he set records. What could go wrong? What was missing? Well, trends. A closer look at his stats reveals that he actually had only one great year in college, his last. The other three years ranged from poor to okay, with way too many interceptions (number eleven all-time in the Pac-10). His completion percentage was similar, from poor to fair, with one acceptable, not outstanding, final year at 53 percent. We looked at the good numbers—total passing yards and total TDs, his body, his arm. We talked ourselves into believing that one good college season was the beginning of a new trend and not an aberration in the older, established one. We talked ourselves into chalking up his accuracy issues to a lack of quality receivers. We gave in to wishful thinking. We weren't alone. The draft experts had him touted to go early to mid-first round. The Bengals, Jaguars, and Bears were all hunting for quarterbacks. We grabbed Boller at number nineteen. Unfortunately, when he got to the NFL is when the real trends emerged. He was plagued by injuries, but when he did play, his TD-to-INT ratio was either upside down or nearly one-to-one at best. His completion percentage hovered in the fifties and his passer rating in the seventies.

Since then, I've seen it happen over and over with all kinds of players, but mostly with quarterbacks. It may sound counterintuitive since probably no position is measured by as many stats, but quarterback is the least quantifiable position on the field. The numbers are there and they matter...but they don't determine. They point but they don't promise. Pay attention, but don't overpay. That's what makes arriving at the Q Factor so elusive.

Too many quarterbacks possess good individual parts, but when assembled, those parts don't make an engine. Why? Well, we could say a guy was missing the great intangible, the "it" factor, but the truth is, we—the scouts and coaches—looked at the pieces, especially the pieces we liked, but we didn't always dig deeper for the worrisome patterns or the absence of positive trends. We saw what we wanted to see and/or we made excuses. We didn't extrapolate.

A tale of two Russells

Two classic examples of *not* extrapolating properly were JaMarcus Russell and Russell Wilson. Actually, Russell Wilson's 2012 quarterback draft class is a study in itself.

But let's start with LSU quarterback JaMarcus Russell, the top pick of 2007, who also has the dubious honor of being one of the all-time (as in, worst) draft busts. In a class that included talent like Calvin Johnson (six-time Pro Bowl wide receiver, NFL single-season receiving record—1,964 yards), Joe Thomas (ten-time Pro Bowl offensive tackle), Adrian Peterson (seven-time Pro Bowl running back, NFL single-game rushing record—296 yards), Patrick Willis (seven-time Pro Bowl middle linebacker), Marshawn Lynch (five-time Pro Bowl running back—10,000-plus rushing yards), Joe Staley (six-time Pro Bowl offensive tackle), and Greg Olsen (three-time Pro Bowl tight end, over 8,000 receiving yards)…among all of those future stars, JaMarcus Russell was taken number one overall by the Oakland Raiders. Why? Because as much talent as that draft class had, what it lacked was a distinguished group of quarterbacks. Brady Quinn was the only other first-round quarterback pick (number twenty-two), playing four seasons for five different teams.

Just because the talent pool is thin doesn't mean the demand for quarterback talent isn't high. No rule says talent coincides with need. So a team desperate for a quarterback could hardly be blamed for reaching for JaMarcus. Especially considering Russell's seeming pluses: He had a stellar high school career, was awarded an honorable mention in *Parade* magazine's All-America football team, was heavily recruited for college, physically looked like a quarterback at six foot six, went to LSU, and was highly productive at a major program. He had college career completions of over 60 percent, a ratio of 52 TDs to 21 INTs, and a final year of over 3,000 yards and completions at almost 68 percent. He led some breathtaking comebacks—one against ASU, one against Alabama, and another against Tennessee, that one capped by a fifteen-play, eighty-yard drive and a final touchdown throw with under ten seconds on the clock for a 28–24 win.

Oakland was not alone in swooning over Russell. Almost every team in the league saw him as a can't-miss pick. (Boy, there's a dangerous expression—can't-miss pick—it almost begs to backfire.) I was with the Ravens, and I confess, we had him rated higher than any other quarterback in my nine years there.

How did Russell do with the Raiders? Well, how did Russell Crowe do at singing his way through *Les Misérables*? A famous actor—handsome, macho, great box office draw—and here comes a juicy role. What could go wrong? Everything. No one extrapolated that Crowe had a great range in acting but zero in singing. And no one extrapolated that as much God-given talent as JaMarcus Russell might have had, he wasn't driven, disciplined, obsessed enough to play football at the pro level. You have to want it bad because, if you don't, there are guys just waiting to take your head off, cut your legs out from under you, disrupt your game plan, pick off your passes, and toss you to the ground like an empty bag. (They don't call it a sack for nothing.) You have to want it bad because there's a guy waiting to take your place the moment you stumble. You have to want it bad because they pay you a lot and expect you to give up your body, mind, and soul to earn the money. To state the obvious, it's hard.

Russell played only three years in the NFL, and really not much during those seasons. The word was that he just wasn't motivated enough. He was plenty motivated to land a big contract, holding out on the Raiders long enough to miss the first game of the season, eventually signing a contract with an upside of $68 million and $32 million guaranteed. (Compare that with Cam Newton's or Andrew Luck's rookie contracts, each a little over $20 million with $14-plus million in bonuses.)

JaMarcus was used to having success come easy but lacked the work ethic demanded in the NFL. He was constantly out of shape, overweight—by as much as fifty pounds—and mentally unprepared. All in, Russell had a 31-game NFL career, with an upside-down TD-to-INT ratio—18 to 23. Cut loose after 2009, he never played another snap. He tried some comebacks but they all fizzled. Teams worked him out but none were convinced he had the stuff to play.

Weren't there any early warning signs? Had we all misjudged him? Had success come so effortlessly that he could skate by in high school and college without discipline? Or had he been disciplined back then but lost it later on? There was one clue that we all should have noted. Lions GM Matt Millen interviewed JaMarcus Russell and said the whole time they talked, Russell kept looking at his watch. Millen finally asked him if he had to be somewhere else. Russell said no and seemed, for a moment, to pay attention. Then, a few seconds later, during the next round of questions, Russell was looking at his watch again. Millen had seen enough. Draft prospects take these interviews seriously, or should. They're auditions. There's a lot at stake: They have five or ten minutes to put forward their best selves—dressed up, prepared, polite, up on the team they are visiting, sharp and focused. Russell was sending all the wrong signs. Millen told him they were done. He then picked up the phone and told Lions head coach Rod Marinelli the team should use their first pick to take Calvin Johnson and not waste it on this kid whose head wasn't in the game, which turned out to be a good move for Detroit. Millen even tried to warn Raiders owner Al Davis. But instead of extrapolating, the Raiders let need overrule observation.

How about the other Russell, Russell Wilson? The situation is almost the diametric opposite. Russell was an accomplished college quarterback at North Carolina State, then transferred to become a star at Wisconsin. But he was the seventy-fifth pick (third round) in the 2012 draft. Why was he missed? To begin with, this quarterback class was a pretty rich one—enough to satisfy the QB appetites of a lot of teams. Eight quarterbacks became eventual NFL starters, four from the first round—Andrew Luck, number one; Robert Griffin III, number two; Ryan Tannehill, number eight; Brandon Weeden, number twenty-two. Why did they all go well ahead of Wilson? Must be the stats, right? Luck had lights-out numbers—9,400 passing yards, 67 percent completion, 82–22 TDs to INTs, and 950 rushing yards. No argument, he was the top guy. Griffin also had great numbers—10,000 passing yards, 66 percent completion, 78–17 TDs to INTs, and almost 2,200 rushing yards. Tannehill, who had gone from wide receiver to quarterback, only had one full season under center—3,700 yards passing, 61.6 percent completion, 29–15 TDs to INTs, and 306 rushing yards. Good numbers for a single season but not much to extrapolate from. Brandon Weeden—two full seasons at quarterback with 9,200 passing yards, almost 70 percent completion, 71–26 TDs to INTs, and a net negative 150 rushing yards. Okay, don't run, Brandon. All impressive stats.

So maybe it's no wonder Wilson fell in the draft. Maybe he didn't measure up. What were his numbers? He had 11,700 total college career passing yards, with 8,500 in three years at North Carolina State and 3,100 at Wisconsin. He also hit almost a 73 percent completion rate once he got to Wisconsin and far better receivers than at NC State. Over his college years he had 109–30 TDs to INTs and 1,400 rushing yards. Hold on! He had more passing yards than any of the others, comparable completion percentage, a better TD-to-INT ratio, and rushing yards exceeded only by Griffin. But he went at number seventy-five in the third round? Why? Well, we didn't extrapolate what we should have and we did extrapolate what we shouldn't have. Wilson showed that he could play quarterback brilliantly, not for a season or two, but for four years. He showed he could do it in a good program at NC State and a better program at Wisconsin, with a better receiving corps around him. He did it with his arm, notching big passing numbers. And he did it with his legs, racking up a lot of rushing yards. But—here's the but—he was only five foot eleven. Quarterbacks are supposed to be six four, six five, six six, so they can throw over the rushing linemen and other defenders. Does that make sense? Sort of, but only at the extreme. There's probably a height that's too short. Like Doug Flutie, who was highly talented but only five foot nine, or arguably five ten (and people did argue about it). In the end, Flutie was good but not great. Was it his height or other factors? Did we extrapolate the right stuff on Flutie or the wrong stuff? Did we decide it was his height that kept him out of the Super Bowl when it might have been those other factors? He was only recruited by one Division I school, Boston College, not exactly a football powerhouse, and colleges are pretty good at assessing high school talent. At BC, he threw for a lot of yards but had a mediocre completion percentage—53 percent—and a weak TD-to-INT ratio of 67–54. But he won the Heisman Trophy. He was drafted by the USFL New Jersey Generals and went on to play for five NFL teams and a handful of CFL teams. A solid backup. One case does not make a statistic... or it shouldn't.

But most of us missed Russell Wilson. Most of us ignored the fact that he had faced a lot of big, tall monsters in the ACC and the

Big Ten and he was just plain brilliant. Somehow we, the football experts, decided he couldn't throw over the same-size guys in the NFL. But the Seattle Seahawks thought otherwise. They looked at the other numbers and extrapolated. The rest of the world looked at his height and missed and had to watch Wilson and the Seahawks in the postseason six out of seven years, and the Super Bowl twice. Jon Gruden, who at that time was an analyst for ESPN, said if Wilson were six four or more, he likely would have been a first-round pick. To say the least, he should have been.

The 50-50 rule

If you pick a quarterback from those that rise to the top of the draft, the natural process—stats, win-loss records, blowouts, comebacks, bowl games, coaches' assessments, scuttlebutt—will lift the best to the top almost all the time. ("Almost all the time" means on average, not every single time. That's statistics.) Among those at the top—the first-rounders—you have about a 50 percent chance of getting one who becomes a Pro Bowler, wins divisions and championships, and might even get into a Super Bowl…and a 50 percent chance of getting either a solid backup or an outright bust. As for your chances of getting a truly great one, "elite" as people like to say—the next Manning, Rodgers, Luck, Roethlisberger, or Brady—if you get on the good side of the 50-50 rule, at least you have a shot at it. You just need three more pieces. First, a coach who clicks with the quarterback. He doesn't have to be a great coach; he just has to have the right chemistry with the QB. If they win together, everyone will call him a great coach anyway. Second, good personnel to surround the quarterback. Great throwers need guys who can catch the ball and then run after the catch, and good running backs to grind out yards so every play isn't clearly a pass. And third, a strong defense to keep the other team's score down, so your great quarterback isn't trying to perform miracles every Sunday.

The coach-quarterback match is also subject to the 50-50 rule. It's not just a matter of having a good coach and a good quarterback. It's having a good, smart coach who knows how to coach that particular quarterback, and a quarterback who responds to that kind of coach. It's chemistry. Like dating. Smart, beautiful girl meets smart, handsome guy...and they fall in love...or they hate each other. Take these two cases: Andy Reid, acknowledged to be one of the best minds in football, drafted Donovan McNabb out of Syracuse with the number two overall pick, and was slammed by the critics and Philadelphia fans for missing Tim Couch at number one, Akili Smith at number three, and maybe Daunte Culpepper at eleven. Those three he passed up had careers in the NFL that are hardly noteworthy. Reid and McNabb, capitalizing on the quarterback's running and scrambling, with enough passing to get by, had seven of eleven seasons with ten or more wins, and a Super Bowl appearance in 2004. Then, in the next few seasons, the same coach couldn't quite find a match, including Michael Vick near the end of his career, and Reid was fired. Fifty percent good with McNabb, 50 percent not good with the others. Then Reid went on to Kansas City, eventually got Patrick Mahomes in the draft, and found what seems like a match made in heaven, back to the good side of 50-50.

Then there's the case of Jeff Fisher, head coach of the Houston Oilers/Tennessee Titans, who drafted Steve McNair out of Alcorn State as the third overall pick. It was a thin year, with Kerry Collins the only other first-rounder. McNair was one of those labeled—for good or bad—a running and passing quarterback, which Fisher saw as good, and together the Titans had four seasons of ten or more wins, and a Super Bowl appearance. The good 50 again. Then, Fisher drafted Vince Young, third overall, the sure-thing pick out of Texas. The only thing sure about Young's career is that it was a disappointment, with six years in the league, under 60 percent completions, an upside-down TD-to-INT ratio, and too many losses. The bad 50.

Was it Fisher or McNair that worked? Was it Fisher or Young that didn't? Was it Reid or McNabb that worked? Was it Reid or the others that didn't? It was the marriage. I believe the stats on divorce are about the same.

Billick's extrapolations #1: Completion percentage

Completion percentage matters in college and it matters in the pros. In a quarterback's arsenal, there are only two offensive weapons: running and passing. Generally, passing has the potential to gain more yards on a single play. So the quarterback better be able to complete his passes most of the time. "Most" means over half the time…well over. The magic number is 60 percent and with each year it seems to go up. Look at his completions year by year in college. Which way are they going? Flat or down, regardless of TDs and wins—those are not good trends. Up, even little by little, is good. If he breaks the 60 percent barrier, that's even better. It's rare to see a college quarterback's completion numbers go up in the NFL. Yes, the receivers are better in the pros. But the defenders are better, stronger, and faster; they read the quarterback's eyes and footwork; and they've seen everything you can throw at them.

They feed on picks. If a prospect completes 55 percent or fewer of his throws in college, even if he can throw the ball eighty yards like a bullet, even if he is so big it's hard to sack him, even if he can run like a halfback, even if he's the smartest guy on the field, if his completions are well below 60 percent, scratch him off your list. Do not, I repeat do *not*, get deceived by his other skills. If he can throw that far and that fast, maybe he should be a major league pitcher.

Extrapolation #2: TD-to-INT ratio + percentage

The TD-to-INT ratio is important, but not in a vacuum. This one should be coupled with TD and INT *percentages*. At first glance, it looks like the ratio stat should be a good indicator by itself. After all, it's better to throw more touchdown passes than picks. But it's precisely the ratio part that can throw you off. I'll use an exaggeration to illustrate: If a conservative quarterback throws ten touchdowns all year and no interceptions, his ratio is perfect. But his team isn't scoring much. And he may be throwing hundreds of incomplete, uncatchable passes, even if they're not intercepted. One more shortcoming to the ratio: It counts negatively the passes that should have been caught but were bobbled by a receiver... right into the hands of a defender as INTs. And if you go by ratios only, there are flukes. In 2013, Josh McCown, the ultimate journeyman quarterback, who has been with nine different teams, put up a 13-to-1 TD-to-INT ratio for the Bears, third in the all-time rankings. An undrafted guy named Damon Huard posted an 11-to-1 ratio in 2006 for Kansas City. Both of them threw far fewer passes than the leaders, and it never happened to either of them again. Neither makes the career list of TD-to-INT ratios, led by

Aaron Rodgers at 4.36, Russell Wilson at 3.31, and Tom Brady at 3.03. No one on the all-time list is in double digits. That happens once or twice in a career. Brady hit 14 to 1 and Rodgers posted a 12.5 to 1 . . . once each. So, looking at only the ratio, and only at a year or even two, makes for good examples of the danger of not extrapolating.

It's better to look at the ratio along *with* hard percentages—TD and INT percentages: How *often* does this guy throw touchdown passes? Let's say it's 5 percent or more. That's good. Look at the historic leaders: Brady at 5.4 percent; Brees at 5.3 percent; Roethlisberger, Marino, and Montana at 5 percent. The outliers are Favre at 4.9 percent, Elway at 4 percent, Aikman at 3.4 percent. In the modern game—that is, more passing—at the top of the touchdown percentages are Aaron Rodgers and Russell Wilson, each with 6.0-plus percent of their passes going for TDs. Early in his career, Patrick Mahomes has a TD percentage of almost 7 percent. And Lamar Jackson, after a season and a half, is at 7.4 percent. It's unlikely they can keep those numbers up, but they will definitely have to be above 5 percent to stay at the top of the game.

Think about that 5–7 percent though. Consider all of the five-, ten-, twenty-yard passes the QB throws that move the team up the field from, let's say, the twenty-five-yard line where they started, and over 5 percent of those total passes go for six points. That's meaningful. Now, how often does the same guy throw interceptions? In an earlier, less aerial game, quarterbacks like Staubach, Montana, and Elway could get away with higher interception rates. But today, in the pass-happy era, the pick percentage has to be low. Career-long, Aaron Rodgers (1.4 percent), Colin Kaepernick, Tom Brady, and Russell Wilson (all 1.8 percent) have the lowest percentage of interceptions. That is less than two passes in a hundred! That's meaningful too. Especially with a guy whose overall completions are better than 60 percent. So far, Mahomes and Jackson are both at 1.6 percent interceptions.

When you're sizing up a draft pick, you have to look at *both* the ratio and the percentages, separately and together, and then year by year, in order to extrapolate and draw your conclusion.

Extrapolation #3: Yards per attempt

This is a good indicator of both the coach's and the quarterback's confidence in the QB's abilities. Can he keep drives alive with passes long enough to move the chains? His throws don't have to be super deep but they can't just be dump-offs to avoid a sack. They have to indicate that the quarterback is seeing the whole field, adjusting to the defense, spotting open receivers midfield or downfield. Yards per attempt doesn't just show whether he's a passer; it can show that he's an aware quarterback. It reveals judgment. And yards per attempt, by definition, is an extrapolation. It isn't a measure of longest pass, or total yards gained by passing; it's an average of a lot of passes—short, long, and medium—to arrive at the depth of throw he can make reliably. Again, you can't look at it without completion percentage or TDs-to-INTs, but in concert, you can start to see a picture of the future.

Extrapolation #4: Pocket presence and decision-making

These combined elements are critical, but admittedly hard to quantify and project. There's no pocket-presence metric or percentage.

He's 52.56 percent effective when giant monsters are trying to kill him...When the play falls apart, he throws the ball away 14 percent of the time...His ratio of panic to cool is 1.4 to 3.5. Unfortunately, no such numbers exist. There's no calm-under-fire metric. Even the definition of pocket presence varies depending on who you ask. The consensus is that pocket presence is the ability—the presence—to see and feel where the pressure is coming from, how fast, how long you have, and then adjusting your play to avoid or beat the pressure, reacting but not overreacting, and still making a play. My personal definition of pocket presence is: *finding opportunity in the midst of chaos.* Every snap for a quarterback is a plan versus a hundred ways to wreck the plan—shifting packages, blitzes, man coverage or zone, you name it.

This is the way Joe Montana put it: "Standing in the pocket in the face of a heavy rush has been compared to auto racing, and that's not too far off. Personally, I always thought it was more like standing in the middle of a freeway."

Decision-making is what the quarterback does in the midst of that chaos: (1) read the defense, (2) stick to your play or call an audible, (3) see the whole field, 270 degrees, sometimes 360 if they're coming up behind you, (4) adjust on the fly, and readjust, (5) hand off or keep or roll out, (6) find the first-read receiver(s), (7) check down to the second read, (8) throw the ball, and (9) don't throw an interception, (10) or get sacked, and (11) somehow pick up a first down...in less than three seconds. When he can do that under the worst circumstances, that's pocket presence. When he can't, that's when bad decisions are made.

So how do you evaluate pocket presence and decision-making in a quarterback prospect? Watch film of the kid in college, but *do not* watch only plays that go according to plan. As Kevin Stefanski, who has held almost every offensive coaching position there is at the Vikings, said not long after being named new head coach of the Browns, "Most of the game is played 'off-schedule,' when there's nothing there. Then, can you make a positive play when you have no right to?" A wise observation. And he'll need plenty of that wisdom at the Browns next year. Plenty will happen off-schedule.

So no, do *not* watch the sizzle reel: The kid takes the snap, drops back, gets good protection, spots his receiver cutting across the middle getting separation, hits him with a quick strike for ten yards, gains another five on the ground, and it's first and ten at the other team's forty. Nice but not so relevant. Find as many plays as you can that went bad. Not disastrously bad, just not picture-perfect. With a stopwatch in hand, study snaps where the defense reads the play, comes crashing through the O-line, arms waving, blitzing and mauling; the receivers are covered like blankets; the blocking backs are trampled; linebackers are hanging on the quarterback's shoulders…then watch what happens. What did the quarterback do? Run the play over and over, with one eye on your stopwatch. Give the kid one…one and a half…two…two and a half…three seconds. Freeze the film at each second or half second. What's he doing? Is he still looking for a play? Is he stepping up instead of stepping back, looking for opportunity instead of taking cover? If the defense is all over him, the only good news is, some receiver out there has been left uncovered. Does he see a tight end who shook free? Is he looking for a running lane? Or is he throwing the ball away? Or curling up for the sack? Or worse, throwing the ball into Pickville? Hit the play button. In the next second you'll see whether the kid has pocket presence. Remember, he's only got 2.5, maybe 3.0 seconds, at most.

Find ten or fifteen plays like that, from each year he played in college. You can't judge by one or two plays—every quarterback gets clobbered. It's what they do after they've been hit over and over that matters. It's like Mike Tyson's famous quote: "Everybody has a plan until they get hit in the mouth." That's what you're studying. Go through each play, second by second. Assign him a number grade for every second, let's say on a 1–10 scale, so a perfect score for one play that lasts three seconds would be thirty. Then take the total score of all the plays and divide it by the number of plays, to come up with his average score per play. A very good number would be in the mid-twenties. Low twenties could be okay. Below twenty, there's trouble. Then compare the scores he got per year. Are they getting better, staying the same, or getting worse? The same method works for grading a rookie, but then it's even more accurate. Now, instead of trying to figure out if a kid should be in the NFL, you're judging a quarterback in the NFL and deciding if he belongs there, maybe even how long he'll last.

The NFL doesn't have a decision-making metric, nor does any major statistics source. But they have assembled some indicators of what a quarterback does, why he does it, and whether there's a pattern emerging… *if* you read them as trend lines. First, there's the list of the twenty most improbable completions; that is, the twenty toughest completed passes in the entire NFL, over the full season, who completed them, and how difficult they were—ranked from 1 to 20, with number 1 being the hardest pass to complete. It also tells us, by omission, who *didn't* throw as many tough passes but may have been completing smart, good passes game after game. It reveals both talent and desperation. In another fast-forward, look at the 2019 real results: Ryan

Tannehill threw the single most improbable completion, a 47-yard pass to A. J. Brown, but it was the outlier in an otherwise remarkably steady performance that put the Titans in the playoffs. Tannehill was nothing if not consistent, relying on midrange passes (average 9.6 yards), with a 70 percent completion rate, and the league's most productive red zone offense (88.6 percent TD result.) On the other hand, Baker Mayfield completed the sixth most improbable pass, but unfortunately threw too many others that were equally improbable but not complete. Then there's Russell Wilson, who threw number 2, 8, 13, 14, and 24. That tells us a lot. Russell Wilson can consistently throw and complete passes in awful circumstances. Tom Brady completed exactly one of these miracle passes, number 19 on the list, which is consistent with Brady's reputation for wise decisions. Sam Darnold was equally conservative, with one such pass. Among our other 2018 draft quarterbacks, Josh Allen and Lamar Jackson didn't make the list, which may well be a good thing. That's good decision-making too.

Another insight into decision-making in the NFL data set is "completion percentage above expectation" (expectation is a number arrived at through other aggregated data). Again, looking at 2019, Ryan Tannehill was at the top, with a 70 percent completion rate, 8.1 percent higher than expected, which fits with his unexpected comeback year and his heavy reliance on the run game. Drew Brees at 74 percent was 6.3 percent better than expected as an elite quarterback who often tends to outperform expectations. Among our draft group, the ranks were: Lamar Jackson at 66.1 percent, which was .08 percent above expectation; Sam Darnold at 61.9 percent, or .03 percent above expectation; Baker Mayfield at 59.4 percent, or -3.5 percent; and Josh Allen at 58.9 percent, or -3.7 percent. Josh Rosen was not a starter in 2019 so he was not listed.

Those numbers don't tell you exactly how the season went for a quarterback. After all, Drew Brees and the Saints didn't survive the wild card round. But they do give a good picture of how each QB did. Jackson—good. Darnold—so-so. Mayfield—up and down with too much down. Allen—better results than the numbers show.

Since making decisions gets harder, and more telling, when plays threaten to break down, the NFL's Next Gen Stats compiles one of the more revealing data sets—quarterback performance under pressure—whenever a pass rusher gets within two yards of the quarterback near the time of the pass. For the 2019 season the results were both instructive and predictive: Again, Tannehill and Brees top the list of getting it done when the heat is on, one for his surprise season, the other for his likely Hall of Fame career. But let's look at our draft group in order (again, excluding Rosen for '19): Lamar is number four, completing almost half of his passes under pressure and averaging seven-plus yards per play. Josh Allen isn't far behind at number nine; then we drop to Mayfield at number twenty-five and Darnold at twenty-nine.

All three analyses are more than snapshots of what happened. They can be extrapolated into what is likely to happen. Russell Wilson is probably going to keep completing difficult passes. He's that good. Conservative QBs are going to keep *not* throwing those balls. Desperate quarterbacks are probably going to get more desperate. Completions above expectations may reinforce success—as with Brees—and maybe offer some new guidance: Tannehill could continue to surprise; Lamar Jackson is on the rise; Darnold is a maybe; and we should worry about Mayfield and Allen. When it comes to pressure play, the same pluses hold for Tannehill and Brees, but here it looks like we're seeing more good indicators for Jackson and maybe for Allen, and more concern for Mayfield and Darnold. Put the data together and there's a decision-making pattern...if we pay attention to it. Lamar Jackson is a yes, Allen is a probable yes, Darnold and Mayfield are somewhere between maybe and no, and with Rosen not on the charts, it looks a lot like 50-50 so far.

Vision—a critical subset of pocket presence and decision-making: Vision is the ability to see the whole field. All at once. Fast. Fighter pilots are tested for their "vision"—that is, how much information they can process—in their near or short field of vision for instrument readings, and their far or long field in a 180-degree sweep for approaching aircraft and/or weather, and then amalgamating and processing all of the input and determining a course of action in a matter of seconds. For a quarterback it means seeing the short field—approaching defenders, blitz packages, edge rushers, and maybe an open running lane—as well as the long and wide scope—pass coverage, receiver routes or broken routes, and possible open targets...all in less than three seconds. The fighter pilot has a lot more on the line than the quarterback, but the similarity in skills is clear. If you have that ability to see more and process more and do it fast, you make better decisions. If you can't, you get sacked, or shot out of the sky.

A study published by the National Institutes of Health on pilot performance showed very clearly that, to state what may seem like the obvious, vision matters. A team of international experts in kinesiology—the study of the mechanics of body movement—looked at the relationship between key pilot attributes, which they categorized as expertise, performance, and gaze behavior—what you look at and for how long—in detecting errors in complex cockpit tasks. They studied twenty-four pilots and, as a control, twenty-six non-pilots, all of whom watched videos from a pilot's point of view, and all of whom were asked to look for malfunctions on the instrument panel. Pilots did better, substantially better, than non-pilots. Pilots actually spent less timing "staring" at the instruments, but seemed to absorb more, faster. They are superior at shifting attention from "global"—big picture—to "local"—cockpit—information. In football terms, it means the pilots could see the blitz and the pass coverage and meld both into a decision. All of which should give us some comfort next time we fly.

On the football field (and in the air), what vision translates to is anticipation, the sense not just of what is happening, but what is *going* to happen. All great quarterbacks have vision and anticipation. It's a difficult quality to evaluate because it can be judged best by actual success. It's particularly hard to spot in college quarterbacks, again because we don't have a metric to measure how much the QB sees and how fast he processes it.

But there are attempts to teach this type of vision. IMG Academy runs a program for NFL and Major League Baseball players in "vision training protocol," based on Air Force Academy pilot training. Some quarterbacks have used it to prepare for the Combine, some receivers to improve their anticipation skills. Can "vision" be taught or is it God-given? It's hard to say, but measuring it, and then trying to train or refine it, can't hurt. IMG staff are convinced they can improve the speed and results of the brain processing input, and then the quality of reaction. You often hear the phrase "the game slows down for a quarterback" after a while. Obviously the game doesn't actually slow down, but a good quarterback begins to see things and, more importantly, interpret things more quickly, and clearly that leads to better decisions.

With regard to rookie quarterbacks, I've often said they can only throw what they see. If a receiver is wide open, they can usually fire the ball in with great accuracy. In college there tends to be more separation between receiver and defender, so it's easier to spot a player who is open or is going to be open. In the NFL those margins are not as big, and a rookie quarterback may not "see" a player as open, while an accomplished, experienced quarterback can see that a receiver is open or, based on his experienced eye, is going to be open at a particular point.

Interestingly, when you're facing a young quarterback, the instinct of the defense and the defensive coordinator is often to blitz and pressure, with the goal of making the game feel faster and more confusing to the novice. In fact, that may actually make things easier for the QB because the defense unfolds quickly and clearly: blitz package, man-for-man coverage, so that means there's likely an open receiver. Of course, if the QB is swarmed by NFL linemen, he's on the ground before he can process that. But if he stays on his feet, he has a chance. Sometimes the smarter way to go after the kid is to play different zone coverages so the quarterback ends up holding the ball, trying to sort out what he's seeing—who's covering who, shallow or deep—so he's taking too much time and is less confident in making the throw. Vision isn't just seeing it all; it's processing it, not being overwhelmed by it. I remember talking with Tim Tebow at a game when he was a rookie, and he said, "Coach, I swear at times there are twelve guys out there."

Unfortunately, unlike some other traits, there are no stats (yet) for extrapolating vision for the college prospect. If only there were… You can try to assess game footage when the quarterback is pressured and see how often he's able to make a good play, but you're never quite sure if it was because of his vision or other factors. Because the thing about vision is it does *not* mean moving your head left, right, and center, looking up and looking down. That's what the kinesiology experts learned—the best pilots move their head and their eyes less but take in more, and do it faster. It's almost the opposite of movement. It's what you can see almost all at once, from one vantage point...like a pilot.

But when you're looking for signs of "vision," you can look at results—plays that went right or wrong, completions or interceptions, sacks or escapes. You can study the college plays and replays for outcomes. Even though good results won't always indicate he has vision, enough good results may at least tell you that the quarterback doesn't *lack* vision. He doesn't process information one frame at a time—safety blitzing, offensive line leaking, tight end covered, better check down to...*boom*, he's eating turf. There are lots of talented athletes who have the physical skills to play at the college level, but few also have the mental complements to survive at the highest levels. That goes for every position, not just quarterback. Linebacker Ray Lewis was the greatest player I have ever seen in the ability to see-process-react. When he added experience and then anticipation to this ability, it made him the true Hall of Famer he is.

The '18 rookies seem to cover the gamut in vision ability. The observation on Lamar Jackson is that he sees the field very well. Proof of that may be the way he describes a play after the game. He'll identify all the players on the opposing team during a given route, by number: "22 fell a step behind and 42 was heading away, 59 came across so there was a hole, and I spotted Mark [Andrews]..." He saw them, then recorded them mentally, and he made a decision. And he even remembers them after the game. That's vision. On the flip side, there are those who now question if

Baker Mayfield "sees" the whole field well enough, hence too many interceptions. Josh Allen is very effective versus man coverage and also when he gets outside of the pocket, so he can "see" a specific receiver. But when he has to operate from the pocket versus zone coverage, he seems to become unsure of himself and is not confident enough to throw the ball where it needs to go. They're all facing the same game, often the same defensive packages, but their ability to process it all and make the best choice varies widely. Vision may be teachable in a little kid. But it's unlikely to get better in an adult. Especially an adult who's being attacked by monsters.

My final verdict on pocket presence/decision-making is simple: It's binary—yes or no. Extrapolate from the year-to-year trends. If the positive indications are going up, he may be a prospect. If they're flat, be concerned. If they're going down, you know what to do—run. For those who do make the cut, now you have to look back at what you learned in the other extrapolations. If a kid has pocket presence/decision-making and you add that to other metrics that are strong, he's a good prospect. If his other metrics are good but he lacks pocket presence/decision-making, scratch him off the list. Do not let yourself get talked into him. I speak from experience, good and bad. No quarterback has ever found NFL defenses less pressuring, less threatening, less intimidating, shall we say kinder and gentler, than in college. Ask Tim Tebow, Johnny Manziel, Ryan Leaf…there's not enough space for this list.

Extrapolation #5: Maturity/Leadership

Once I interviewed a kid at the Combine whose draft summary looked good on the field but who was a sea of red flags off the field—school discipline, misdemeanors, probation, suspensions. I asked him, with my less-than-subtle word choice, "Young man, are you a thug or just stupid?" The kid was surprised by my bluntness, took a beat, and replied, "Coach, are those my only two choices?" I had to admit, that was a pretty smart answer. He knew his record looked bad, but I got the feeling at least he was trying to find a way to get on a better path. I couldn't bring myself to have the team take a chance on him, but he did go on to have a very good career, and very little trouble.

Maturity isn't a luxury in a quarterback; it's a must. He is the one guy on the team who absolutely must be reliable, steady, and wise under pressure, displaying good judgment and making good decisions on and off the field. No successful quarterback in the NFL has been immature or childish, at least not for very long. They either grow up fast or burn out fast. Think about the great ones, the Hall of Famers and future Hall of Famers: Joe Montana, Dan Marino, John Elway, Warren Moon, Brett Favre, Tom Brady, Peyton Manning, Drew Brees, Aaron Rodgers. Plenty had troubles—who doesn't?—but all ultimately showed the sound judgment to be guys you can trust with the keys to the car. Michael Vick had a bout with stupid behavior, but he dealt with it and showed he could learn and return to the field. Same with Ben Roethlisberger.

Athletic arrogance

Some players are confident. Some are overconfident. There's a difference. Being just plain cocky, conceited, overinflated, full of themselves, or full of other stuff comes from a kid being told that because he can throw a ball or sink a basket, he has license to get away with bad behavior. That's not confidence. That's being a jerk.

Then there are the guys who are confident because they have the goods. Joe Namath was assured, even brash. But not without cause and a plan. By "guaranteeing" his upstart Jets team could beat the powerhouse Colts, he replaced his own and his team's self-doubt with self-confidence. Sixth-round draft pick and rookie Tom Brady supposedly told Patriots owner Robert Kraft that drafting him was "the best decision" the team had ever made. A boast? Maybe. But then he made good on it. As Dizzy Dean famously said, "It ain't braggin' if you done it." Today Brady throws fits on the field when things go badly, but they may be the wisest, most strategic fits you'll ever see. *The refs are treating us badly!... We have to play harder and smarter...I threw that ball where you could catch it...I need you at your best... That guy hit me late...Get mad, get even, win the game!* He's not immature. He's a motivator. Muhammad Ali used confidence—call it braggadocio—as a tactic in his career. He had fights half won before he got in the ring. I see some of those same traits of confidence in Patrick Mahomes. He doesn't make hollow, egotistical boasts, but his natural swagger, his on-field style, and his off-the-field smile are all infectious, in a good way. His team believes, with him at the helm, they can do just about anything. And they have.

If you have the proven talent, the results, the *trends*—not just some good stats or a few *SportsCenter* clips—you have what I call "athletic arrogance." The "athletic" part means the proof—high school, college, bowl games, comebacks—and the "arrogance" part means you have the attitude—confidence, conviction, swagger, leadership—that your results have warranted. Some players achieve good results but lack the attitude to lead. Too many players lack the results but are long on the attitude. A handful have athletic arrogance.

Extrapolating maturity

Maturity may seem amorphous and hard to evaluate, harder to extrapolate than even pocket presence and decision-making, but it really isn't. Granted, we don't have a collection of stats put together by the NCAA on maturity like they produce for quarterback metrics. But we do have strong indicators. However, we often look at the wrong ones. Some people look at background or environment and think a kid from a good neighborhood is somehow more likely to be mature than one from a tough area. Some think a kid from a two-parent household is more solid than one raised by a single mother or aunt. Some place a value on economics—kids from middle-class homes over kids from lower incomes. Some add another wrinkle, with a prejudice against kids from affluence, believing that they'll be spoiled and hard to discipline. Some, whether they admit it or not, look at race. I don't have to make that case; we can just look at how many, or rather how few, African American quarterbacks we've had until very recently, despite the large number of players of color in other positions.

The real indicators are not economics or number of parents or race. They're who influenced the kid and how the kid responded. Not once, but over time. Not if he got in trouble, because almost everyone does, but how he acted afterward, what he learned—if anything—how he behaved next time. Look at the patterns. Then extrapolate.

Nine-time Pro Bowler Warren Moon came from a one-parent household where he had to choose one sport to play so he had time to hold down a job to help the family get by. You think that didn't build Warren's character, humility, and determination? For sure it did. The Manning boys came from a privileged, athletically savvy family, with father Archie a renowned quarterback and New Orleans local hero. When the parents were deciding where to send their boys to grade school, they didn't pick an athletic powerhouse, they picked an academic powerhouse. They figured if the boys had sports skills, they would show, but in the meantime, education was the highest priority. You think that didn't help form the character of Peyton and Eli? It was absolutely central.

In the 2018 draft class, we have two highly talented young men with maturity question marks. One is from a smart, successful, affluent, Southern California family—as good a background as you could find. The family raised an uncommonly gifted golden boy who has been criticized for an attitude of entitlement and an oversize ego, who is so confident he's been considered by some as hard to coach. So far, that knock has stuck on Josh Rosen.

The other question mark is on a kid from a family that faced financial reversals, going from prosperity to losing their home, from the heights to the depths, upheaval that could have resulted in personal reserve and modesty. Instead, this young man gained an early reputation for in-your-face gestures, crude stunts, and unwarranted boasts. Overcompensation for insecurity? I'm not enough of a psychologist to know. What I do know is that has become the MO for Baker Mayfield. With no apologies. Mayfield says, "Hey, that's just who I am." The critics are saying, "Yes, it looks like that is who you are."

Then there's a guy who was raised in a small town, on the

third-generation family farm, weaned on homespun rural values. He looked like a model young man, all-everything, playing multiple sports, working the family farm and restaurant. But just before the NFL Draft, racially biased tweets from his high school days were revealed. Instead of denying them or shrugging them off, he owned the responsibility, saying he had been "young and dumb," and regretted having ever done such a thing. His college teammates came to his defense. He vowed to live up to the mantle of NFL leadership. So far, Josh Allen has done that. The pattern of maturity emerged.

There's another guy in that class, a kid who came from nothing, almost literally. His father died of a heart attack when he was eight years old, the same day his grandmother died. He and his three siblings were raised by his iron-willed mother in South Florida's tough neighborhoods, known for breeding football players and/or kids in trouble. Lamar Jackson set out early to be a quarterback, and his mother set out to relentlessly support his single-minded goal. He watched hours and hours of game films even in high school. When high school coaches and college recruiters urged him to become a running back or wide receiver, Lamar and his mother never wavered—quarterback or nothing. When scouts wanted him to do run drills at the Combine, he didn't waver— quarterback or nothing. Where did he get his resolve? Not from two parents but from one with an iron will, as well as the influence of an early coach who stuck with him. And from his inner grit. From age eight to twenty-one, from youth football to high school to college to the NFL. It was a trend of maturity. So far, that has served Lamar Jackson well.

Maturity doesn't guarantee leadership, but leadership demands maturity

There are all kinds of styles and types of leadership, but every variation has one common element: maturity. You cannot lead if you aren't solid, dependable, mentally and emotionally grown up, at peace with yourself. And no one will follow you and trust in you, if you aren't mature. The others are counting on you to be their guide. If you do it irresponsibly, egotistically, rashly, they may follow you once or twice, but not for long. Leadership demands maturity.

But maturity is the one element we tend to make the most excuses for. We say a kid isn't mature because he's young. We say it will come later. *He's just a kid and he'll grow out of it.* Maybe. But probably not. Maturity tends to show itself early. It's not age; it's sage—the seeds of wisdom. We've all met fifty-year-olds who are immature and make bad decisions every day. And we've met ten-year-olds who have a pretty solid grip on things. Maturity is much more a result of circumstance and guidance than number of years. Those are the stats of maturity. Who influenced this kid? With what values? Did he get to practice on time, or even early? Did he stay late? Did he have trouble with the law? Or in school? What did he do after he got in trouble... to make sure it didn't become a habit? Did his coach or teacher get him off the hook, or did he have to pay for his mistakes? How did he affect other people around him? Is he entitled or grateful? Humble or haughty? How about his maturity... from grade school through college? Extrapolate. And do not, do not, do not assume it will all get better with age. After all, his NFL career is likely to be over before he hits forty.

Extrapolations and some Do-Not-Extrapolates

Clearly, there are some indicators I didn't include or emphasize. Yards gained passing I don't like because there are some guys who are okay but not great quarterbacks who can sling the ball with ease and pile up big numbers and still lose ball games. The passer rating I use but am cautious about because, although it was the stat officially endorsed by the NFL to evaluate college and pro quarterbacks, it correlates passing to wins but doesn't account for yards gained running. The most popular stat today, which I personally avoid, is ESPN's Total Quarterback Rating (Total QBR), a complex formula that claims to factor in every quarterback action, from passes to scrambles to rushes to sacks to penalties, even adjusting for difficulty per play, all then synthesized into what they call "Expected Points Added" or EPA. The exact formula or weighting per factor is not only complex, it's secret and ever-changing...or voodoo. According to ProFootballTalk/NBC, ForTheWin/*USAToday*, and other analysts, Total QBR has been wildly off base, including putting Ryan Fitzpatrick ahead of Tom Brady in 2015, another time ranking Brian Hoyer over Ben Roethlisberger, Matt Ryan, Philip Rivers, and Russell Wilson, and once putting Ryan Mallett over Cam Newton. Sometimes you have to just trust your eyes and the facts: the won-lost column, and postseason appearances. Brian Hoyer has never, ever been better than Ben Roethlisberger, except maybe at Scrabble. They've tweaked the Total QBR formula from time to time, but to say it's flawed is to say Swiss cheese has holes in it.

Extrapolation beyond football

The need to extrapolate is hardly restricted to quarterbacks or football or sports in general. The danger of isolated data applies to every field imaginable. If you hit oil twenty times on a parcel of land, it does not guarantee the next derrick won't come up dry. The stock market highs and lows can be tracked, but if you don't look at trends, good luck. Extrapolation is like tracking hurricanes. It isn't a sure thing. Plenty of hurricanes veer one way or another or just die out. But most don't. So you look at the data—the speed, the winds, the temperatures—but if you don't extrapolate the path, you're just hoping for a miracle. It doesn't mean it will follow the path you predict, but it means it's likely, so if you live there, pack up and get out.

The sum of the parts, the data only, without extrapolation, does not add up to the whole. What I call the opposite of synergy applies, not only on the football field but in other places as well— everyplace. Business is full of CEOs with great credentials—Ivy League degrees, MBAs, highly recruited, off-the-charts IQs. Then along comes a brash big thinker who eats their lunch in the real business world. We all know the Facebook story, how the Winklevoss twins, with golden résumés, including prep school and Harvard and even the Olympics, had an idea for an online social platform, yet it took an unorthodox rule-breaker in Mark Zuckerberg to drop out of Harvard and make it a reality. But if you looked back at Zuckerberg's trends, from his writing software in middle school to creating a network between his father's home computer and dental office, inventing instead of just playing computer games, building a music player based on machine learning that was recognized by *PC Magazine*, you'd have extrapolated that this guy was a first-rounder on the entrepreneur draft board.

Another unlikely pick by conventional credentials might have been an English art school student with no formal education in engineering who came up with the best vacuum cleaner in the world. Again, if you looked back at his design for a wheelbarrow based on a ball instead of wheels, and a boat launcher on the same principle, and even his land-sea vehicle, you might have moved James Dyson to the top of the inventor draft board. Extrapolation, whether it's with Mark Zuckerberg, James Dyson, or Russell Wilson, can lead us to a whole that's greater than the sum of the parts, instead of the opposite.

Extrapolation is not a guarantee; it's a safety rail

I have arrived at my five Extrapolations. I didn't have them early in my career. They're not perfect. They're a work in progress. If you think you have all the answers, you soon become a stat yourself—a casualty. So I will modify them if better indicators come along. For now, if I were going to draft a quarterback today, I would apply them rigidly, dictatorially, and tyrannically. The only edge I know over the 50-50 rule is extrapolation.

All the quarterbacks in our study of the 2018 class were picked with their team's combination of hard information, collective experience, and, of course, gut. Did they study the data, not just for stats but for trends? Or did they talk themselves into their picks? Did they bet on their gut? Or did they extrapolate? If your gut is golden or infallible, you can go with the gut. If you're mortal, extrapolate. Year one is over. Let's see how they did...

IV

Rookie Year Report Card: Premature but Predictive

*L*amar Jackson takes the snap, drops back, looks left, looks right, rolls out, and...is sacked. It's August 2, 2018, the annual NFL Hall of Fame game in Canton, Ohio, on the day the new members of the Hall are inducted. Typically, the teams selected to play each have a star about to be inducted. This year, it's the Ravens versus the Bears. Or Ray Lewis versus Brian Urlacher, two legendary linebackers who will receive their gold jackets. It's also the NFL debut of Lamar Jackson. With Ravens starter Joe Flacco not playing, it was a showcase for the two backups, Robert Griffin III and Jackson. While Jackson may be the Ravens' quarterback of the future, based on performance, RG3 looked like their backup for the present, going 7 for 11 in passing at an almost 70 percent completion rate. Jackson was 4 for 10, with one TD and one interception, for a 42.9 percent completion rate. He did run for twenty-five yards but even that was over eight carries. And he was sacked three times. The Bears didn't play many starters either, including quarterback Mitch Trubisky. In fact, the secret weapons of the Ravens and Bears offenses were their defenses. Final score: Baltimore 17, Chicago 16. Based on that game, you wouldn't have overly high rookie-year hopes for Jackson. You certainly wouldn't have predicted what actually happened.

The same might be said of the preseason. It gave us a closer look at all five of our 2018 QBs, but it didn't give us a prognostication of how things would go in real games in the real season. In those "pretend" games, over four contests Sam Darnold displayed the most poise of our five guys. Not the most flair or excitement, but a steadiness and comfort that you hope to find in a rookie. He played three of the four games, turned in strong numbers, made good decisions, and was held out of the last game only because it was clear he was ready to be the Jets starter. Baker Mayfield showed cool command and some big-time moments, with pocket presence and some impressive throws even without the top receivers in the games. The two Joshes were up and down, Rosen with the highest highs and lowest lows playing in only two of the four games, Allen with weak moments offset by one particularly good game against the Browns and Mayfield. Lamar Jackson had two bad games and two not-bad ones, though one of those was against the really bad Dolphins. If nothing else, playing in four games meant his first NFL game was now behind him, and the more he logged, the better.

Then, for all five young kids, the OTAs, non-contact practices, X's and O's, pre-liminaries, pre-paratories, pre-season, pre-everything were all over. It was time for the real deal.

How did the 2018 rookie quarterbacks do?

Suffice to say, one season hardly provides enough evidence to anoint anyone "franchise," but there's lots to be learned about how well the teams guessed, who looks promising, what a team can realistically expect of a new quarterback, how opponents can prepare for these new guns, and especially what front offices can learn in looking for their next miracle in the next draft class.

In 2018, all five quarterbacks taken in the first round—Mayfield to the Browns, Darnold to the Jets, Allen to the Bills, Rosen to the Cardinals, and Jackson to the Ravens—were supposedly going to sit for some period of time behind veterans to learn. None did. In the NFL today, with owner pressure, coach pressure, fan pressure, and win pressure (and instant 24/7 social media pressure to amp up all the other pressures), that rarely happens. It didn't this year. Instant gratification and impatience ruled. All five rookies became starters.

As for their performance, one might make the observation of my mentor and coach, Dennis Green: *"They are who we thought they were."* What we saw in their college years largely played out in their first NFL year. What they were good at back then, they're good at now. What were shortcomings didn't suddenly get fixed. With the exception of Baker Mayfield, the group had very rookie-like numbers—under 60 percent completion percentages and 1:1 touchdown-to-interception ratios, or sometimes worse. With the exception of Jackson, none made the postseason.

Never forget, the worst teams get the best picks

Sometimes people forget that losing records, not winning ones, are rewarded with high picks. It's the NFL's attempt at maintaining parity among the teams... *if* those losing teams are good at making draft picks. But teams that have weak finishes almost always have weaknesses at a variety of positions, on offense and/or defense. They are rarely otherwise good teams just waiting for a great quarterback. So no matter how well they draft, rationally we shouldn't expect a miracle in year one. But owners, commentators, and mostly fans do. Rationality has nothing to do with it.

One other thing: Rookie quarterbacks should come with a warning—may be hazardous to the health of coaches. When the coach and the QB aren't in sync, when the coach has been around for too many losing seasons and then fails to turn the team around instantly, when there's anything other than a miracle with the new first-rounder, coaches need to pack up their homes and post their résumés. It's not fair. It's just a fact.

Extrapolations rookie year—not the SATs, more like the PSATs

Using my "BB Extrapolations" as the measurements, here are my report cards for the rookies, with previews as to how they'll do next season and some takeaways for others looking for leaders.

Baker Mayfield—end of the curse of the Browns?

When Baker Mayfield went onto the field for the Browns, all he had to do to become a hero in Cleveland was win a game. The Browns hadn't won in nineteen games, not since 2016, 635 days ago. The team, as usual, didn't make it easy for him, spotting the Jets fourteen points before Mayfield came in for Tyrod Taylor. But Baker brought them back to win the game 21–17. A win…in Cleveland…finally. (To be totally accurate, the Browns had broken their losing streak in game one of the season against Pittsburgh, as only the Browns could, with a tie and a missed overtime field goal.) But with the outright win, the town went wild. Fans cheered from windows and porches, and car horns blared. Bars were jammed. Beer flowed. Locked refrigerators placed around the city with the promise they would open for a win were unlocked and dispensed free Bud Light. Diehard Browns loyalists partied into the night. Celebrations like that are usually reserved for a Super Bowl win, spring break in Florida, or the running of the bulls in Spain. Mayfield was immediately anointed the next Otto Graham. *Who?* Most Browns fans have no idea who Graham was or weren't even born when the Hall of Famer played from 1946 to 1955, but that's how far you have to go back in Cleveland to find a great quarterback. Mayfield was basically declared the God of Lake Erie. He brought a W to the standings, and on *Thursday Night Football*, for the whole country (or those who follow the Browns) to see. He officially took over as the starter, the Browns thirtieth starter since 1999, the year they came back to the NFL; that's more than any other team—another ugly distinction.

Baker Mayfield has beaten the odds before. He was the first walk-on true freshman to start at Texas Tech, leveraging that success to transfer to Oklahoma. Then he went on to win the Heisman Trophy. And he became the overall first pick of the 2018 draft. Now come the two "buts"—one bad, one good. Bad but: He may have had the toughest challenge of all the NFL rookie QBs, because if the best picks often go to the worst teams, in this case he went to the worst team in the NFL for years, and years, and years. Good but: The combination of Mayfield's impressive abilities and his powerful personality may make for the perfect fit, just what the team is crying out for; they were no doubt key factors in the team's decision to draft him. The Browns were betting the second "but" would outweigh the first and Baker Mayfield could transform the culture in Cleveland, no small feat.

THE Q FACTOR

Coming out of the 2018 draft, I questioned two things: (1) his completion percentage—high 60s to low 70s at Oklahoma—great, but hard to match in the NFL, and (2) his emotional immaturity (negative), which was part of his passion for the game (positive), a mixed bag at best. That positive side, the passion, evidently drew GM John Dorsey to pick Mayfield at number one over Sam Darnold or Josh Allen, or even running back Saquon Barkley. The negative side may be what caused then–offensive coordinator Todd Haley, who said, "He's not my guy," and head coach Hue Jackson to be less enthusiastic about the number one pick. But he was Dorsey's guy.

Mayfield—year one, graded on a rookie curve: pretty good

How did he do year one? By the numbers, he was by far the best of the rookies. He answered the skeptics loud and clear, living up to his Oklahoma stats even on the big stage of the NFL. His college TD-to-INT ratio was obscene, as in obscenely good, hard to maintain in the NFL. In college he had 131 TDs to 30 INTs—a 4-to-1 ratio, incredible even for today's high college numbers. I knew he couldn't match that metric in the pros but doubted if he could keep it in the pro range of 2 to 1. I have to give him great credit for doing it. Extrapolation: His 27 TDs to 14 INTs project out to 33 TDs to 17 INTs had he played a full sixteen-game schedule, virtually 2 to 1, the minimum for top-tier NFL quarterbacks. Since I like to look at the ratio along with the percentages, Mayfield threw TDs on 5.6 percent of throws versus interceptions on 2.6 percent, pretty good on the touchdowns, acceptable on the picks.

Most impressive were his three fourth-quarter comebacks and four game-winning drives. His two games against Baltimore came as close to a laboratory study in pocket presence as you could find. Facing the number one defense in the NFL, he did not give his ground; he kept calm and found ways to make plays while besieged by All-Pros Eric Weddle, Brandon Williams, and C. J. Mosley. He made decisions under duress, took the team into overtime, moved up the field, won 12–9. Study that game film if you want to see how a guy does when plays go bad, or what he does to keep them from going bad. Mayfield almost pulled the same thing off in the season finale, a must-win for Baltimore to make the postseason. He threw 23 of 42 for 376 yards and 3 touchdowns. But he also threw 3 interceptions. Again he was under attack, again by the league's most intimidating defense. Down 26–24, using the clock masterfully, Mayfield coolly moved the team down the field in what appeared to be a final drive to beat the Ravens again. Every play they were coming at him; every play he stood tall in the pocket and found his receiver, or made a checkdown, or avoided a sack. All he had to do was get in field goal position. But he threw one ill-advised pass across the middle, a pass he did not have to make. And C. J. Mosley picked it off. Game over. To me, the two games comprised a graduate course in pocket presence and decision-making—what to do and what not to do. Both were case studies in playing under duress, not beauty shots or instruction videos. Ugly, tough, what-do-you-do-when-the-heat's-on cases. Baker Mayfield did well, very well, in both. Facing the league's best defense, he showed the ability to extend plays outside the pocket, to break down the Ravens' secondary. He wasn't running the ball, but rather moving around to extend the play and finding big plays down the field. One game showed his cool. The other showed his drive. And one error, maybe indicative of ego? That throw he didn't have to make. But overall, pocket presence and decision-making grades: very good and good, respectively. The real proof: He broke Peyton Manning and Russell Wilson's previous record for rookie TD passes at 27. Pretty good first year.

The coach change and the maturity thing

The one other factor we have to consider to assess Baker Mayfield is the coaching debacle. We know how important the coach-quarterback relationship is. When it works, it can be transformational. When it doesn't work, it can be a disaster. After not being totally on board with Mayfield as the number one pick, Hue Jackson and OC Todd Haley didn't do much to improve the rapport with their quarterback. According to insiders, the tension in the locker room was palpable. After that first win over the Ravens, the Browns lost three in a row. On October 29, Jackson was shown the door, as was Haley. Gregg Williams, defensive coordinator, took over as interim head coach, and Freddie Kitchens kept the offensive reins. A few weeks later, Jackson signed on as a sideline coach for the Bengals, and during the Browns game, Mayfield did what could only be called a "stare-down" as he walked past Jackson, confirming that they were not the best of pals. Later that game, he did what was becoming his signature celebratory crotch-grab gesture to OC Kitchens after throwing a touchdown pass, and earned a $10,000 fine and a suspension. The crotch grab goes way back with Mayfield; he did it at Oklahoma and brought it with him to the NFL, not something to build a legacy on.

Eventually, to succeed, a quarterback has to mature (ideally this comes well before he's retired and looking after his grandchildren).

Mayfield explained his behavior this way: "People get maturity confused with me being 100 percent comfortable in my own skin… That's absolutely how I am. I've always been that way." (Hmm, "I've always been a jerk" doesn't seem like a good defense to me.) It remains to be seen if Mayfield can mature in the face of the Browns' history, high hopes, fans prepared for disappointment, and their readiness to give up in a split second, the moment a golden QB tarnishes. Can Mayfield become their marquee quarterback? That's a tall order for anyone, let alone a kid with an attitude, and there's plenty of skepticism over him being able to match his college numbers.

From nothing-to-lose to high expectations

What we have to watch for in 2019 is whether, as an established quarterback with a team that now has high expectations, he can deliver. Last year he could have had the mentality of Richard Gere in the movie *Red Corner* when he was on trial in China and defied the judge, asking, "What will you do? Shoot me twice?" Mayfield was playing with house money. What was the worst that could happen—lose another game in Cleveland? Now that they are expected to win, we will see if he can keep up that gunslinger mentality.

At this point I would compare him to Hall of Famer Brett Favre. That's high praise; however, it's not necessarily a compliment. Mayfield has the flair and the similar gunslinger style that were the hallmarks of Favre, but I would point out that Favre, despite his ability to win critical playoff games, posted regular-season numbers that were often less than stellar. Career-long, he had 508 TDs to 336 INTs, a 1.5-to-1 ratio, way short of future Hall of Famers—Brees and Manning (2 to 1), Brady (3 to 1), and Rodgers (4 to 1). Early on, we noted that this 2018 draft class was compared to the 1983 and 2004 classes. Favre and perhaps Mayfield compare well with those guys—Marino (1.67 to 1), Elway (1.3 to 1), Eli Manning (1.5 to 1), Rivers (1.5 to 1), and Roethlisberger (1.9 to 1). Only Roethlisberger approaches the magic 2 to 1. So Mayfield could be like Favre in a good way. Or he could be like Favre, stat-wise, in a Neil Lomax, Matt Schaub, Kyle Orton way.

The Browns will do their best to surround Baker Mayfield with offensive weapons, so he doesn't have to carry the team alone. And we can hope that he will come into 2019 a year older and a year wiser. And maybe lose the crotch grab as his signature gesture.

Sam Darnold—finally Broadway Joe's successor?

In his first game in the NFL, Sam Darnold threw his first pass for a touchdown...by the opposing team. Twenty seconds into Darnold's pro career, Detroit Lions cornerback Quandre Diggs picked off the throw and ran it back thirty-seven yards for a touchdown. But Darnold settled down and the Jets went on to win the game. Head coach Todd Bowles said in the postgame press conference, "I could sit here and tell you we planned that so he could get the jitters out, but we didn't."

That's what winning is like. Mistakes are turned into punch lines, positive clichés gush, and all is good. Until it isn't. Until a 1-0 start turns into a 4-12 season.

Spoiler alert

After four years as head coach, after getting a two-year extension to 2020, Todd Bowles lost his job in December of 2018. Then in

May the Jets fired GM Mike Maccagnan—all that losing must be his fault too. Selecting Sam Darnold with the third overall pick in 2018, the Jets had bet their near-term future on him. He was the savior. That meant if the Jets didn't win, it couldn't be blamed on Darnold or the weak team around him. It had to be the coach and maybe the GM. (In fairness to management/ownership, Bowles was 24-40 at the Jets, with three losing seasons in a row.) But let this be yet another warning that the tenure of a head coach and the drafting of a franchise quarterback must be aligned—it's all about the timing. If the timing is not in sync—that is, the head coach was already there and not winning, and a new quarterback arrives and they're still not winning—the story doesn't end well for the coach. Bowles had two losing seasons BD—Before Darnold—and another losing season AD—After Darnold. Someone has to go. And it's not going to be the new savior. That's the price of not winning right now! Thanks for your service, here's the door. The season's barely over and the team has moved on to next year, next coach, next hopes.

Harsh reality—aka the NFL

But before we look ahead, let's take a look back at Darnold's first year. Coming into the '18 draft, despite concerns about his up-and-down college performance, Sam had draft experts pointing to his USC year-two stats of 64 percent completions and 57 TDs to 22 INTs, and putting him head-to-head with Mayfield as the top pick. In fact, he was the second quarterback taken. Then he promptly beat out Teddy Bridgewater and Josh McCown and was named the Jets starter before the season even began. Did he really beat them out or was it preordained by the belief that the new hope is always better than the old hope?

That may have been the hope, but the reality was harsh. Darnold's 77.6 passer rating ranked 31st out of 33 quarterbacks, with only fellow rookies Josh Allen and Josh Rosen ranking worse. His completion percentage was a lowly 55.2, and his fifteen interceptions thrown had him tied for the second most in the NFL. In fairness to Sam, his numbers started to get better late in his rookie season. After missing weeks ten to thirteen with a foot injury, he bounced back to finish the season on a high note with six touchdowns to just one interception and a 99.1 passer rating in the last four games, and his seventeen passing touchdowns were the second most by any Jets rookie QB, only behind Hall of Famer Joe Namath. There was a glimmer of hope.

With Darnold, it wasn't just the late-season statistical improvements; he also showed signs of progress by watching the game tapes. Darnold has a quick release and often would get the ball out of his hands in under 2.5 seconds. That helped the Jets rank in the top third of the league in sacks given up. But his quick release is only as good as his ability to dissect the defense and know exactly where he wants to throw the ball, based on the looks he's given by the defense. Those four weeks he missed due to his foot injury may have given him a chance to sit back and learn from himself— to self-scout the tapes and see what defenses were doing to him and where he needed to adjust. He gave himself a tutorial in pocket presence. Darnold watched his own film carefully, second by second, play and freeze, and he saw what he was doing when the pressure was on (which was almost always), what he did wrong, too fast or too slow, the openings he may have missed, his decisions.

And he must have processed it all in a positive way, because when he came back, he got better. That's what separates the average guy nursing an injury from the gym-rat/tape-rat/do-or-die jock. The former waits to get better. The latter spends every day *getting* better.

BB Extrapolations: Obviously, not good. Late progress. Question mark for next year. Takeaway lesson: Get your coach and quarterback on the same page.

Help wanted

The season had gone badly, but not unexpectedly. The question was, What would the team do to make the following season's story turn out differently? First, the Jets handed the keys over to new head coach Adam Gase, fresh from Miami with a history of turning quarterback hopefuls into performers.

Then the front office went on an off-season shopping spree. The Steelers' super running back Le'Veon Bell famously sat out game after game in 2018 waiting for Pittsburgh to pay him what he and his agent thought he was worth. They never ponied up the dough and he missed the whole season. But the Jets opened the vault and signed him. And let's not overlook what a revamped rushing attack can do to support the progression of the quarterback, especially a running back that has the receiving ability of Bell coming out of the backfield. Bell's patience allows him to pick holes created by another off-season acquisition, one that may be just as important, offensive tackle Kelechi Osemele. Osemele gives the Jets a presence along the offensive line and a leader for that group, since he's been one of the best at his position over the course of his career. Bell and Osemele are an obvious upgrade to a unit that ranked 26th in rushing yards. Here comes a guy who opens big holes and a guy who knows how to run through them. Additionally, Bell can be the outlet or checkdown pass catcher, a mismatch nightmare for the defense and a true weapon for the Jets. In his last three complete seasons (2014, 2015, 2017), Bell averaged 81 catches per season. Compare that to the 21 catches running back Isaiah Crowell had for the Jets in 2018 and you clearly see an advantage to the 2019 offense. The presence of the Osemele-Bell combo will only help take the pressure off of Darnold's shoulders.

Then the team went receiver shopping. They landed deep-threat wide receiver Jamison Crowder from the Redskins. They figured/hoped/prayed that those pricey additions, along with the proven production of wide receiver Robby Anderson (an undrafted free agent who beat out all the veterans), could combine to translate into the growth you love to see between your franchise quarterback's first and second years, albeit in an entirely new system. And never underestimate the adjustment to a new system. It's either the formula that makes everything click, or it's trying to master a foreign language that has no vowels. The Jets were figuring/hoping/praying the equation of Darnold + Bell + Crowder + Anderson + Gase and his system = winning. There was a sudden injection of confidence into the team and into Darnold himself. How much confidence?

Prior to the 2019 season, the Jets have in-house expectations of competing for a division title and a playoff spot. Darnold is quoted as saying that winning the AFC East is "absolutely realistic." But the boost in confidence must translate to a boost in production and, most of all, wins. It can't just be a warm feeling of self-assurance or an overdose of cockiness—*I feel good so I must be good*. It has to be the real deal. Because the Jets offense was abysmal across the board in 2018. They ranked 29th in total offense and 23rd in scoring while finishing in the bottom five in third-down conversions, turnovers, red zone production, and big plays. Those are all key offensive stats that must improve drastically if the Jets really are to have an "absolutely realistic" chance at making the playoffs in 2019.

Change in mentor

If there is a coach who can make those improvements, it's Adam Gase. From Peyton Manning to Jay Cutler to Ryan Tannehill, Gase has shown that quarterbacks make improvements with him as either their head coach or offensive coordinator. His quarterbacks have historically added three points to their completion percentages, nearly fifteen additional passing yards per game, a better TD-to-INT ratio, and a passer rating increase of nearly ten points. Those numbers can be the difference between winning and losing. In 2015, Tannehill had a 61.9 percent completion rate, but working with Gase in 2016, it went up to 67.1, a five-point gain, and the Dolphins, for the first time in a long time, were in the playoffs. Those stats are exactly the areas that Darnold needs to improve the most—completion percentage, TD-to-INT ratio, interception percentage, and overall passer rating. All the stats that showed signs of improvement after he came off the injured list.

The added off-season talent, Darnold's momentum, and a dose of Gase's QB medicine have Jets fans, Jets front office, and even some in the media encouraged that Darnold really can be the franchise quarterback worth the number three overall selection.

If…if he can make the jump from year one to year two. We saw it with Jared Goff, who went from 0-7 in games he played in his rookie year to the Super Bowl the next year. We saw it with Mitch Trubisky, who had god-awful numbers in year one—a passer rating of 77.5 compared to Darnold's 77.8—but improved enough the next year—95.4—to take the Bears to the postseason and earn himself a Pro Bowl slot. If Darnold can do likewise, he's on his way.

Rookie-to-veteran is the most telling, difficult, and sometimes career-busting transition for a quarterback. No gentle progression; no gradual easing into it; just *boom*—now. So it shouldn't be surprising that it's daunting. It's a big step. It's hard. And it's scary. The same kind of thing happens in every part of life when you're supposed to suddenly "grow up." How tongue-tied were you the first time you asked someone for a date? How badly did you do on that first exam in college? New hires in business can't find the bathrooms. Freshmen in Congress don't open their mouth for fear of putting their foot in it. Even CEOs need time to find their ground, learn the competition, and watch out for internal politics. But the good ones, in every endeavor, do it. And they do it fast. Especially quarterbacks. In year one he got hit, sacked, picked off, three-and-outed; he looked up at some ugly scoreboards and got savaged by sportswriters—*He's a bum, never should have drafted him.* But a year later, when the three-hundred-pound linemen attack, the safeties blitz, and the pocket collapses, that quarterback can now sense what's coming, maintain his poise, look off the covered receiver, check down to the open man, and thread a twelve-inch window forty yards away. That's the difference between a rookie and a veteran. He's seen it and lived it—*What else can they do to me that they didn't do year one?* The monsters are still trying to take his head off, but now he hopefully has the composure not only to survive, but to lead. That's the difference one year can make.

Josh Allen—surprised me, in a good way

Josh Allen, the seventh overall pick by the Buffalo Bills, came out of Wyoming with eye-popping physical skills, but completions under 60 percent and a 1-to-1 TD-to-INT ratio—two worrisome omens. But second-year head coach Sean McDermott was totally on board with Allen. And the team was totally on board with McDermott. That would prove to be a critical plus.

As the season started, the Bills and McDermott showed un-NFL-like restraint and did not start Allen in the opener, instead going with fifth-round pick Nathan Peterman. It was probably one of the few examples of when the team should have started the rookie. Overmatched Peterman was blown out of the game by the Ravens, 47–3. Having shown restraint and failed miserably, the Bills put Allen into the game, way too late to do anything except show that he was now the starter.

Allen then started eleven games for the Bills where they went 5-6, completing only 52 percent of his passes and throwing 10 TDs to 12 INTs, a negative ratio—ouch, the omens came true! (In fairness, Allen's pickoffs were second in his draft class to Josh Rosen's, a case where finishing first is not an honor.) Allen did have one especially good game, beating the Vikings with good passing and thirty-nine yards on the ground. Allen was injured a few weeks later and missed part of the season. He came back as the starter—another team all in on their young hope—but the Bills' fate didn't change much and they finished at 6-10. What did we learn? The

Bills team is not good. But we knew that. Allen may be good if/ when the Bills get better. But we knew, or hoped, that too.

Allen comps—Flacco, Wentz, or someone else?

Still, Josh Allen had a more impressive season than I anticipated for him when the Bills drafted him as the seventh overall selection. While he was drawing comparisons to Joe Flacco in terms of frame and size, he hailed from the same system as Carson Wentz and was seen as a better raw athlete than Flacco. He certainly possessed the arm talent to drive the ball across the field and into tight windows with a quick and explosive release. A quick release is not to be underestimated. Think back to the pocket presence issue—the tsunami of rushers, the need to make swift, wise decisions—where the speed of release can be the difference between a completion and a busted play. Think of it the other way around. A fraction of a second extra, too elongated a release, and *boom*, you're on the ground looking up. In college, Josh Allen had the rare ability to throw the ball on the run, with the elite foot speed to be an impactful ball carrier when needed.

With all that said, Allen was still a "project" player from Wyoming; that is, a guy who comes into the NFL and needs to be rehabbed. I had real concerns about the higher level of competition he would face and whether his skills would translate into the NFL. Was this game going to be too big for him? It happens to some athletes who are very good but not good enough.

Problems: He wasn't the most efficient college passer and didn't possess the touch needed on some throws. "Touch" is another factor that we are, so far, unable to quantitatively measure, but we sure need to study it on the tapes. When you look at Allen's Wyoming game footage, there were times when he could have taken off some velocity and thrown a more catchable pass for his targets. That's touch. He could also have hit the open player on first read rather than force the ball down the field for the big play. That's decision-making. In other words, he didn't always just take what the defense gave him—which oftentimes can result in a high turnover rate: bad in college, disastrous in the NFL. What would happen to him at a higher level of competition? That was why I was cautious.

While the comparison to Flacco in terms of size, and the comparison to Wentz in coming from a small college program, were both reasonable, using what we learned from Josh Allen's rookie season, a more accurate player comp—and one to hold him to moving forward—would be Cam Newton.

Allen finished his rookie year with rookie-like numbers—low completion percentage, more picks than touchdowns, and a losing record. The low completion percentage was largely because he forced the ball downfield. That also elevated his interception numbers. The issue was decision-making: mentally going through the progressions and knowing when it's the right time to take a chance and when he can dump the football off to his first read and take an easy five-to-seven-yard completion…while being pursued in the pocket. What Allen did, which was unwise but somewhat predictable, was to attempt a lot of deep passes, more than any other QB in the NFL during the entire 2018 season—average air yards per attempt of 11.0 and total air distance per attempt of 23.9. Those numbers ranked him first in the NFL, but not in a good way. He was throwing long without a deep threat on the roster. Who was he throwing to? More desperation than smart field generaling.

But where Josh Allen was better than expected was with his legs. We expected him to be good—we knew he could run when he had to—we just didn't know how good. We didn't know that he could individually have an impact on the rushing attack. Allen was the first quarterback ever to rush for more than ninety-five yards in three consecutive games and was the first ever Bills quarterback to lead the team in passing yards *and* rushing yards. He broke the team record for most rushing yards by a quarterback in a single season with 631 and led the NFL in rushing touchdowns by a QB with eight. Who does this sound like? That's not Joe Flacco. That's not Carson Wentz. That's Cam Newton.

Head to head, Newton's rookie season was slightly more impressive than Allen's. Cam had a 60 percent completion rate, and he finished with four more touchdowns than picks, but he did throw seventeen interceptions. Over his career, his completion percentage is just under 60 percent, having dipped to 53 percent one year, but he's almost a perennial MVP candidate. Yeah, but everybody knows it's Newton's dual-threat ability that makes him so dominant, right? Take a look: Newton rushed for 44.6 yards per game over 16 games as a rookie. Allen rushed for 631 yards in 11 games for a per-game average of 57 yards. Allen had a better per-carry average at 7.1, compared to Newton's 5.6, so Josh is more efficient as well. Going strictly by the numbers, Allen was a more dominant rushing QB than Newton was as a rookie, and Newton was named Rookie of the Year in 2011. If this is the career trajectory for Allen, that's pretty promising.

What it shows is that when you look at numbers, you better look hard and deep. One metric, good or bad, isn't enough. Nothing should be looked at in a vacuum. Context is everything. Allen had a lousy completion percentage. No two ways about it. If you stop there, you throw in the towel. And you could be wrong, big-time. He showed us he has potential, maybe to win games differently. Maybe to use his arm and his legs. Maybe to work on his mental processes and decisions. And maybe he needs to have better weapons around him. That's for the scouts and GM to make happen next season.

Rehabbing—rebuilding the house on the existing foundation

What have the Bills done so far? A lot. They upgraded the center position with Mitch Morse in March 2019 and added a total of seven new offensive linemen in either free agency or the draft, and a lot of these new guys will be starters. The O-line is an unglamorous aspect of the game. We like to watch quarterbacks dazzle us, running backs evade tackles, and receivers juke past defenders. But the line is what makes it all possible. It's a wall…or a sieve. Ask any quarterback who's been sacked a lot. The Bills are building a better wall.

On the weapons front, they added a speedy receiver in John Brown from the Ravens, which will allow Allen to do something with that arm strength besides heaving and praying. In another comp with Newton (but this one not so good), Allen's deep throws often come out flat, lacking the velocity/loft/trajectory—that is, touch—for a receiver with elite speed to run under. That timing and chemistry are what Brown and Allen will be working on in the preseason, to develop a deep-threat combination. The Bills also added Cole Beasley, a supposedly too-small, undrafted free agent, who became a surprisingly effective third wide receiver for the

Cowboys (the guy defenses didn't pay enough attention to), racking up over 800 yards in 2016 and almost 700 in 2018. He brings Allen a target to work with underneath, and on intermediate routes, who can break down zone coverage and has run-after-catch ability. They also signed sure-handed tight end Tyler Kroft, a mid-round draft pick who became the Bengals' top receiver in 2016 but got injured and missed a good deal of '17. If Kroft is fully healed, he's an asset. And with Brown and Beasley—and an offensive line to protect him—Allen has different looks at wide receiver—speedy and elusive—instead of the bigger but clunkier style of Kelvin Benjamin. They improved their receiving corps a good deal but, candidly, not enough in my opinion.

The personnel changes could make for a significant second-year leap for Allen as a passer in terms of interceptions and passer rating. His twelve year-one interceptions could follow recent year-two jumps: Jared Goff—year one 5 TDs to 7 INTs in only seven games, year two 28 TDs to 7 INTs in a full season; Mitch Trubisky—year one 7 to 7 in twelve games, year two 24 TDs to 12 INTs in fourteen games; Carson Wentz—year one 16 TDs to 14 INTs in a full season, year two 33 TDs to 7 INTs in thirteen games. All of those guys, plus Andrew Luck, improved their passer rating by more than ten points from their first to second years, with Goff leading the way from 63.6 to 100.5. Wentz, the go-to Allen comp, having come out of a similar lower level of competition and similar offensive style, also saw a significant passer rating increase of 22.6 points, hitting 101.9 in his second year. Allen gave us glimpses of the potential to make that kind of jump in his final game of the 2018 season against the Dolphins, in which he went 17 of 26 for 224 yards, with 5 TDs—three passing and two rushing.

If the last game of 2018 is a harbinger of 2019, we could see a franchise quarterback emerge. Of the draft picks in his class, Baker Mayfield gets the limelight due to a good rookie year, but Josh Allen may have more upside. Expectations have risen beyond reason in Cleveland—playoffs and Super Bowl dreams—but in Buffalo, Allen can stay under the radar and just perform. A winning season in Buffalo would be a clear success. They're in a tough conference, dominated by the Patriots, but that means everybody is always looking at New England, so a where-did-they-come-from threat can arise and upset the balance. And the Bills have something else—the league's second-best total defense in 2018 and the best passing defense in total passing yards surrendered, at just 179.2 pass yards per game. With Tom Brady aging—yes, even he ages—and the Jets and Dolphins as much rebuilding projects as the Bills, or more so, the division is as open for the taking as it has been in recent memory. Next year, Allen could catapult himself into the conversation on young QBs who can carry a franchise for the next decade.

Consistency matters, especially to young quarterbacks

That's a long way from my early cautions on him during the draft. But it's more proof of some axioms of extrapolation: Look hard at what you can learn and project realistically, not hopefully, or hypefully. Sometimes we look at the wrong metrics. We try to measure the harder-to-quantify elements and don't study tape enough. But we should. Year one and year two are very different. Those worst teams who pick early have a chance to build into better teams. But coaching consistency makes a difference here. The Bills stuck with Sean McDermott. McDermott and GM Brandon Beane, who came in the same year as McDermott, together, in sync, have been building a team around Allen's talents. And it seems Buffalo may agree with my comparison to Cam Newton, because they brought in Ken Dorsey as quarterbacks coach, and Dorsey coached Newton at the Panthers.

Josh Rosen—I was right, but I wish I was wrong

Rosen, the Arizona Cardinals' number ten pick, had some spectacular and promising numbers at UCLA. But in college he went through multiple coordinators and systems, and there was always grumbling about his "maturity," which is a nice way of saying he could be volatile, egotistical, hard to coach…you name it. After Cardinals starter Sam Bradford (by the way, a number one overall pick himself) suffered two lopsided losses and was in the midst of a third, Rosen came into game three and was the starter from then on. Once again, so much for sitting behind the veteran. (*Kid, what did you learn from watching the veteran play all of 150 minutes?*) Under Rosen, the team went 3-10; he completed only 55 percent of his passes and had 11 TDs to 14 INTs, the worst record of the season. (Rosen didn't throw the most picks; that would be Roethlisberger, but the difference is, Ben threw thirty-four touchdowns.) Were those numbers a reflection of Rosen's immaturity, other team weaknesses, coaching problems and changes, or all of the above? Normally, I'd say year two will tell. But it turns out year two will be a whole different movie.

Fast-forward—you can't make this stuff up

The win-now lust, the demand for instant miracles, and everyone second-guessing everyone reached a new high (or low) with the story that played out in Arizona. Between weeks seven and eight, coming off another loss, Cardinals offensive coordinator Mike McCoy was fired and replaced by quarterbacks coach Byron Leftwich. After only one season as Arizona head coach, Steve Wilks was also fired. Not only were both coaches casualties of the win-or-else mentality, but for Rosen, who had a merry-go-round of coaches at UCLA, it meant getting used to yet another new offensive coordinator, another head coach, and another system. Or worse. And for Rosen, it turned out to be worse.

Shortly after the end of the regular season, the Cardinals hired former Texas Tech coach Kliff Kingsbury as their new head coach. It seems that while at Texas Tech, prior to any imminent prospect of becoming an NFL coach, Kingsbury responded to a reporter's "what if" question: *If*, by chance, he were an NFL coach, and *if* he had the top draft pick, who would he take? Kingsbury's answer was highly touted quarterback Kyler Murray coming out of Oklahoma. But "what if" turned into "what now?" A few days/hours into his new NFL job, reporters reminded Kingsbury of his wishful thinking on Murray. Now he *was* a head coach; now he *did* have a top pick. Did he still really mean what he'd said? He didn't say yes and he didn't say no. But on April 11, Murray visited the Cardinals camp and made quite an impression. And Rosen was worth plenty as trade bait. What might be good for Kingsbury could be bad for Rosen, or maybe good for Rosen, depending on where the wheel stopped spinning. Was Kingsbury's infatuation with Murray the real thing or just a passing fancy (pun intended)? In the 2019 draft, on April 25, the Cardinals took Murray with the number one pick. On April 26, they traded Rosen to the Dolphins, getting two good draft picks in return. The Dolphins had come off a not-so-bad/not-so-good season, finishing 7-9 behind the Patriots (but then everybody finished behind the Patriots). Blame for their season was put on (a) head coach Adam Gase, so they fired him and (b) starting quarterback Ryan Tannehill (himself a first-round pick out of Texas A&M), who struggled with injuries and a weak supporting cast...so in came Rosen. Will Rosen play for Miami or sit? Yes, he'll play, and soon. The question is really: Will Tannehill play? If so, for what team?

Number ten overall pick—what happened?

"It's way too early to call him a bust." That's a year-one postseason quote about Josh Rosen from Brett Anderson of CBSSports.com. What's scary about it isn't what he said about Rosen; after all, it's a defense, sorta. What's scary is that anyone would even be saying or thinking the word "bust" so soon after the guy was the tenth pick in the draft. When you have to say what someone isn't, at least not yet, all it does is raise the idea that he might be pretty soon. It means people, including Anderson, are thinking it. *Hey, Rosen isn't necessarily a washout. The jury is still out.* Anderson is kind of, in a backhanded way, sticking up for Rosen but raising all kinds of doubts and second-guessing in the process. Were the experts all wrong to rank him so high before? Did he fool us? Was his career at UCLA a sham? Or were the Arizona Cardinals so bad they made Rosen look as bad as they were?

Fact: We know that the Cardinals were a bust. Fact: We know that Rosen, who went through too many coordinators at UCLA, then in Arizona, went through head coach Steve Wilks and OC Mike McCoy—fired midseason. Fact: Now, in Miami,

Rosen will have to adjust to new head coach Brian Flores—former defensive coordinator with the Patriots—and offensive coordinator Chad O'Shea, also formerly with the Patriots (since Dolphins OC Dowell Loggains followed Adam Gase to the Jets to ignite Sam Darnold). So Rosen will go from one losing team with a weak supporting cast to another with, if this is possible, maybe a worse collection of talent. And now he'll be competing for starting quarterback with Ryan Fitzpatrick, who replaced Ryan Tannehill, who was sent off to the Texans to replace Marcus Mariota…

Unfortunately, Josh Rosen is a poster boy for the 50-50 Quarterback Success Rule. When he was taken midway through the first round, he looked like a promising prospect for the good side of 50. Now that one season has gone by, there's talk putting him in the bad 50. And the fact is, we don't know. It was 50-50 then; it's 50-50 now.

When he was drafted, the Cardinals, unlike some other teams with internal squabbles, were all in on Rosen. They traded their fifteenth pick and gave up third- and fifth-round picks to make sure they got him. He was their guy. He was going to turn the team around. But he didn't. Or rather, they didn't. The Cardinals started the 2018 season, started losing, and started making changes that didn't stop until their 3-13 season ended. Uh-oh, the bad 50?

Then the team jettisoned their head coach and hired Kingsbury, who could now make good or back off of his *if-you-were-a-head-coach-who-would-you-draft* sports reporter answer. Kliff convinced Arizona GM Steve Keim that the guy the team had fallen in love with only last year should be dumped in favor of Kingsbury's love, Kyler Murray. And Rosen was FedExed to Miami. That's a

THE Q FACTOR

lot of wooing and romancing and dumping and trading in a very short period of time. It shows you how fast you can fall in and out of love in the NFL.

Trying to be rational about all of this, maybe Steve Keim believes, as some people do, that the NFL is moving toward more of a college system; that is, signal callers who are more improvisers—passing outside the pocket or running when they have to—than traditional under-center drop-back passers. Maybe that's why he went for Murray, who is like Mahomes or Deshaun Watson, or so he hopes. Maybe that's why he hired Kingsbury. Maybe he's right. Maybe the NFL is changing. Or maybe not. Maybe some of these young quarterbacks can just play good football, in the pocket or out of it. In any case, Rosen didn't fit.

Now what for Rosen?

Will he fit in Miami? First he has to compete with Ryan Fitzpatrick. We all know what's going to happen. "Fitzmagic" will look good for a game or two, maybe three. Then things will fall apart, especially with the thin talent there, and Rosen will be sent in. The talent will still be thin, but now Rosen will really be tested. Remember, this is a guy whose biggest knock was his personal style, or immaturity, or egotism, or whatever you call it when people have to "explain" him. So much so that guys who like him sound like they're apologizing for him. Cardinals teammate Larry Fitzgerald said, "He's extremely confident and not in a bad way." What do you mean, "not in a bad way"? That means people assume he's cocky, not confident; self-important, not self-assured. Even the compliments he gets come with "buts." Before the draft, one GM said, "He's the

134

most talented passer I have seen. He's not the toughest..." Players respond to his "skill set, not his personality." Does that mean they can see he has ability but they just don't like him? Another described him as "extremely intelligent...but lacked the work ethic, will be the last one in, first to leave." With friends like that... Charley Casserly, former NFL GM, advised Rosen, "When you go to your new team, you find out what time the janitor comes in. Then you come in and open the place up."

I have to give the Dolphins credit for doing their homework and digging deep. They did their own checking on Rosen's character, style, and work ethic, way past the usual headlines and scuttlebutt. A year earlier, when Miami had been toying with drafting him, they sent a scout out to the West Coast to talk to tennis coach Steve Whitehead, who worked with Rosen when he was a twelve-year-old top-ranked tennis player. Whitehead not only liked his talent, he liked the person, even as a youngster, the combination of skills and drive and competitiveness. Whitehead says Josh pushed himself to learn shots that seemed to be beyond his adolescent abilities, and then mastered those shots. He practiced relentlessly. Whitehead said, "He's a fighter." And people, including his tennis teammates, liked him. All the characteristics you'd look for in a future leader. Even though Dolphins then-coach Gase didn't want Rosen in 2018, when the opportunity came up a year later to trade for him, the Miami brass felt confident they knew the real Josh Rosen and what he was made of.

So is Josh Rosen a lost cause? No. He's just off to an awful start. Does extrapolation apply when things go bad? Yes, it can. The talents that pushed him to the top of the draft chatter didn't disappear. He still has a great arm, excellent mechanics, the right body and stature for a quarterback. He still knows how to win. In his opening game, Cardinals vs. Seahawks, he coolly threw a fourth-quarter game-tying touchdown, only to lose by a field goal. In his second NFL game, he led his team to a big win over the 49ers, including a 75-yard pass for a touchdown to fellow rookie Christian Kirk. Then, down 15–3 in the fourth quarter, he led a late-game comeback to beat the 49ers again in week eight. And he took the Cardinals to an unlikely upset over the Packers, which may have been the last straw in Mike McCarthy's tenure in Green Bay.

You don't give up after one dismal season. You look at what went right and try to create more opportunities for that to happen. Josh Rosen needs time. Time to adjust to play at the pro level. Time to play for a team that believes in him. Time for that team to get better players around him. Time to get used to his coordinators and not see them whizzing past him in a revolving door. The NFL doesn't give you much time. But on those occasions when they do, it can work. Witness Jared Goff, who had a really awful first year with the Rams, 0-7 in games he started. That is zero wins. So was he suddenly *not* the guy they drafted number one overall in 2016? Was his talent a myth? Or . . . was he playing for a weak team, going through an initiation by fire in his first year in the National Football League? The Rams' front office believed in him, even if they did replace the head coach. The next year head coach Sean McVay also believed in Goff, worked with him, and built talent around him. The team went to the playoffs and Goff went to the Pro Bowl. The following year, 2018, without a change in coaching personnel, with more weapons added to the team, with continued time invested in the coach and the quarterback, the Rams went to the Super Bowl. Will Rosen get the time? Will the Miami Dolphins believe in him and see the leadership potential to stick with him? Will they give their coaches and quarterback time to get to know each other and learn to work together? Common sense says they should. History says no. Right now, I'd say it's 50-50.

Lamar Jackson—the biggest surprise of all

While the top four quarterbacks were taken pretty much as expected, there was some quiet maneuvering going on as the draft picks ticked off. The Ravens had kept their eye on Lamar Jackson from the beginning. They were undaunted by the he's-a-running-back-more-than-a-quarterback chatter. But they didn't tip their hand with their first pick, number twenty-five, which they used on South Carolina tight end Hayden Hurst. Then they watched other teams that had made quarterback noises, like the Steelers and the Jaguars, decide instead to fill other positions. So Ravens GM Ozzie Newsome and GM-in-the-wings Eric DeCosta did one of the things they do best, horse-trade for draft positions. Ozzie spoke to his counterparts at the Eagles and made an offer for their number thirty-two pick. Whatever he offered, the Eagles wanted more. Ozzie said, "Sorry, that's our best offer." The clock was ticking. More picks came off the board. The phone rang and DeCosta said, "That'll be Philly." Ozzie's poker playing paid off; the Eagles took his offer, and the Ravens grabbed the final pick of the first round.

Remember that in pre-draft conversations, head coach John Harbaugh vowed that if the team took Jackson, "...we'll build an offense around him." What that meant was, we won't force-fit him into a traditional scheme like we've run with Joe Flacco, a classic pocket-passer scheme. We'll make the most of Jackson's multiple talents. That was a green light to scrap and revamp all the entrenched thinking, all the routes, all the formations, and all the play calling for the talents—not yet proven in the NFL—of one guy. Translation: We'll stick with Joe Flacco and the old way of doing things...until it doesn't work. Then we're all in on Lamar Jackson and a new kind of football.

You should not underestimate what that decision signifies in the NFL. Coaches, especially coaches who have experienced a good deal of success like Super Bowl winner John Harbaugh, don't change their ways of doing things very often or very easily.

That reluctance to change goes a long way in explaining why every December there's a purge of NFL coaches. It's become as much a tradition as decorating the Christmas tree. By the end of 2017, five head coaches were sacked—Ben McAdoo/Giants, Jack Del Rio/Raiders, Chuck Pagano/Colts, Jim Caldwell/Lions, John Fox/Bears—and one retired (but threatened to come back), Bruce Arians/Cardinals. John Fox took the Carolina Panthers and the Denver Broncos to the Super Bowl and was fired by each team when their records went south. As offensive coordinator, Adam Gase helped John Fox take the Broncos to the Super Bowl, then went to Miami and took the Dolphins to the postseason for the first time in eight years. Two losing seasons later, Miami cut him loose, though the Jets then grabbed him. Chuck Pagano took the Colts to the playoffs for three consecutive seasons but was let go after a couple of losing seasons. Bruce Arians was a two-time coach of the year, led the Cardinals to their best records in years, made the playoffs for two years running, then hit a patch of losses and, though technically his choice, was out of a job by the end of 2017.

In the case of Harbaugh, fresh in his memory was that despite numerous trips to the postseason, after a dry spell team owner Steve Bisciotti had at least temporarily entertained letting his head coach go (NFL—Not For Long). At the last minute, Bisciotti decided to give Harbaugh another year. When owners get that itch, it's hard for them not to scratch it. Déjà vu to yours truly, who won a Super Bowl, then couldn't find a franchise quarterback, and became a December casualty. Maybe Harbaugh's near exit was the impetus for him to embrace a real change in the team's approach.

Instant adjustment

As it turns out, it was a good thing that John Harbaugh was open to a new approach. Joe Flacco hit trouble sooner than expected. After a pretty good start at 4-2, the team lost three in a row, and in the last of those, against Pittsburgh, Flacco sustained a hip injury.

Suddenly, in his rookie year, Lamar Jackson was the starting quarterback of a team with a 4-5 record and with an offense built for a classic pocket passer. In the seven days between games, the team did their best to adjust on the fly. Against the Bengals, who had beaten the Ravens earlier in the season, Jackson ran for 117 yards, the team record for a quarterback, completed 13 out of 19 passes, and Baltimore won 24–21. The next week, he led them over the Raiders 34–17. Then they beat the Falcons 26–16. The next game they lost to the red-hot Chiefs (led by scrambler-passer-runner Patrick Mahomes), but Lamar connected on two touchdown passes. The Ravens came back a week later and upset the Chargers 22–10, with Jackson passing for over 200 yards. Then they took on the Browns, against another 2018 first-round quarterback, Baker

Mayfield. Jackson passed for 179 yards, ran for 95 yards, including 2 touchdown runs of his own, and thanks to an incredible defensive effort, came away with a 26–24 win and iced the AFC North Championship. The Ravens were back in the postseason. At twenty-one, Lamar Jackson was the youngest quarterback ever to start in the postseason when they took on the Chargers in the wild card game. By then, the Chargers had studied Jackson and figured out how to better contain him, but his passing almost brought the team back from a twenty-point hole. The Ravens lost 23–17.

Still, a very impressive rookie record. Jackson went on a 6-1 run, and run is the right word. Relying heavily on his remarkable, elusive, defense-baffling rushing abilities, he took the team from 4-5 to 10-6 and the playoffs. Late in the season, when Flacco got healthy again, the team stuck with Jackson. He threw for 1,201 yards, 6 touchdowns, and outran all other quarterbacks—152 yards in one game—with 695 yards for the season, 5 TD runs of his own, and two games with over 200 yards passing and over 100 yards rushing. Yes, there were glitches and worries. His completions were under 60 percent, though his ratio was pretty good at 6 TDs to 3 INTs. But there were too many bad throws and near interceptions, too many fumbles, and maybe too much reliance on his legs. Lamar runs, which is great. But Lamar runs, which is scary. The conventional wisdom is that running quarterbacks tend to get hurt.

Lamar extrapolations

Can we build a mathematical model from Jackson's seven-game rookie year? If so, his rushing numbers for next season would be eye-popping: 336 carries for 1,589 yards. (By comparison, Ezekiel

Elliott, world-class running back, ran 304 times for 1,434 yards.) I can't buy the straight math projection, but factoring in some realities—more plays designed for his style, dialing down dangerous runs, improving pass accuracy, and assuming he stays healthy—my extrapolations are still staggering: pass completion rate of 60 percent or 240 of 400 passes, 2,800 yards, with 14 TDs to 7 INTs; rushing with 240 carries (15 per game average) for 1,135 yards.

For 2019, the questions will be: (1) Can Jackson really become a passing *and* running quarterback, not a running quarterback who passes when he has to? (2) Can GM DeCosta, John Harbaugh, and his coaches really construct a team around Jackson and his unique skill set? And (3) is he just a guy who had a very good (half) season, or is he a unicorn—a guy who is a true double threat every time he has the ball in his hands—a game-changer?

In case there was anyone who needed added reinforcement to be open to change, they got it in the annual December coach purge. By the end of the 2018 season, seven head coaches were shown the door—Todd Bowles/Jets, Vance Joseph/Broncos, Dirk Koetter/Buccaneers, Adam Gase/Dolphins, Steve Wilks/Cardinals, Marvin Lewis/Bengals, plus Mike McCarthy/Packers and Hue Jackson/Browns (and his OC Todd Haley), who were ushered out midseason. John Harbaugh was not on the list. He embraced the change. The final proof: The team traded a now-healthy Joe Flacco to the Broncos.

Building around that unicorn

If… if… if Lamar is what he could be—the one-of-a-kind talent, the unicorn—then there's a lot of work to be done. In the off-season, it would now be DeCosta's job to find wide receiver talent, add more running power to take the focus off of Jackson, and beef up the defense (having lost Eric Weddle and Terrell Suggs to free agency). Meanwhile, Harbaugh replaced offensive coordinator Marty Mornhinweg with Greg Roman, who had been at the Ravens in 2006–7 and had come back in 2017. Interesting note: Between his two Ravens stints, he worked as OC for John Harbaugh's brother Jim, first at Stanford and then at the 49ers. In San Francisco, Roman helped coach another mobile QB, Colin Kaepernick, to a Super Bowl, one that they lost to—small world—the Ravens. The point is, Greg knows how to develop the passer in a quarterback who has legs. And DeCosta knows how to draft and trade. In the 2019 draft, the Ravens used their number twenty-five pick for Marquise "Hollywood" Brown, a lightning-fast wide receiver from Oklahoma, now paired with last year's tight end picks, Hayden Hurst and Mark Andrews, and 2015's Nick Boyle. They then signed free-agent Pro Bowlers safety Earl Thomas III from the Seahawks and running back Mark Ingram from the Saints. The Ravens filled a critical hole at safety on defense, and on offense, they were doing as promised, assembling a team around their new quarterback. The addition of the offensive weapons at tight end and wide receiver, and a productive running back, take the focus off of Jackson's run threat. Now he's not the only guy in the backfield who might take off with the ball. Lamar might give the ball to a running back, or fake to the running back and keep it, or start to run and then throw, or fake the throw and then run...

There's a lot of talk that we are in a new era, a new style and prototype for NFL quarterbacks. The Ravens and Lamar Jackson could be the laboratory test of that hypothesis.

V

Year Two: The Real World

Rookie year is a glimpse of what your quarterback *could* be. Year two tells you what he *is*. Our 2018 rookies are no longer rookies. Now they're second-year NFL quarterbacks, which means we now expect them to play at the highest level of football there is, consistently, no excuses, week after week, and of course, bring their teams and fans and critics a playoff spot if not a Super Bowl. You don't get paid the big bucks for nothing.

In the off-season, each team had time, and as much money as they could muster under the salary cap rules, to tailor the team to fit their first-round quarterback—draft picks, free-agency players, new coaches for old, new schemes, new hopes.

So how did our top five do? Overall, Dennis Green's old observation, "They are who we thought they were," held true, but maybe not in the order we expected. Five first-rounders shook out to two to three promising quarterbacks and two to three who are struggling—one maybe on the exit bubble. Call it two and a half on each side of "promising QBs" and we're at the 50-50 rule. Statistically. But there is a major aberration in the projected outcome: The top pick of the five is performing at a questionable level, and the last pick set the league on fire. Why? How? Bad extrapolation? No extrapolation? We'll see.

Baker Mayfield—hot rookie, cold sophomore

In 2019, Baker Mayfield was all over television, on Fox Sports, on ESPN, on NFL RedZone, on Sunday afternoons, on Monday and Thursday nights...in commercials. In NFL highlight reels, not so much.

Mayfield had an impressive first year in which he hit a 63-plus percent completion mark, had 486 throws for 3,725 yards, and a 27–14 TD-to-INT ratio. He quarterbacked fourteen games, starting thirteen of them, so if you extrapolate that to a full sixteen-game season, it means 598 attempts with 382 completions for 4,585 yards and a 33–17 TD-to-INT ratio. Truly impressive numbers. In year one, the team record was 7-8-1 overall—7-7 with Baker under center—and 5-2 in his last seven games of the season. With some impressive performances even in losses, plus adding off-season talent, that would look to translate into a winning season in 2019. For a team that hasn't had a record in the plus column in years, that showed real promise. In fact, there was talk that the Cleveland Browns were the favorites to win the AFC North division. Not just sneak into the postseason as a wild card, but win it! Wow, that's a miracle in Cleveland akin to Lake Erie becoming the new Riviera. They haven't been in the playoffs since 2002, and haven't won a division title since 1989.

But the experts were gushing about the Browns and the future.

There is no doubt that the NFL's "it" team in 2019 is the Browns.
ESPN's NFL Insider Dan Graziano

Browns are headed to the playoffs and four more bold predictions for Cleveland's 2019 season.
CBS Sports online

Three writers for *Athlon Sports* had the Browns' season record at 11-5, 11-5, and 10-6.

SportsLine had them at 9.2 wins, enough to take the division. Bleacher Report had them at 10-6.

And the Las Vegas betting line had the Browns as +$140 favorites to win their division—that means a $100 bet gets you $140. By comparison, BetOnline had the Ravens' over/under at eight wins, finishing third in the AFC North, with the Browns on top at nine wins and the Steelers in between at 8.5. Spoiler alert: The oddsmakers were wrong. Real wrong.

How did Mayfield's real numbers stack up against the preseason extrapolations? In spite of a major import of receiving talent, his completion percentage was 59.4 on 534 throws for 3,827 yards (only a handful more than he threw in a fourteen-game rookie year), and worst of all, he had a 22–21 TD-to-INT ratio. And it's not as if he made up for it on the ground. Mayfield is not a runner and he showed it, gaining only 141 rushing yards for the season. (By contrast—unfair contrast, admittedly—Lamar Jackson ran for more than that in one game.) To make matters a little worse, Baker Mayfield had six fumbles, though he lost only two of them.

Okay, we know what happened. But more importantly, why? High expectations. Very high. In his first year, Mayfield could, in his own words, "just be me." He was walking into a team that had nothing to lose. You might say they'd already lost all they could. He could throw the ball up and see what happened, no consequences. If your team is expected to lose and you win, it's not just a W, it's a celebration. Seven W's and the whole world opens up. But it opens up with pressure, only increased by the sports headlines and predictions that were made. How would the number one overall draft pick handle that pressure? Would he show the maturity needed to steer through a heady atmosphere? Would he click with his new coach? Would he connect with his new receivers? Would he lead when the heat was on?

Game one, unfortunately, was a preview of coming attractions, or rather, distractions. It began with a 1 TD to 3 INTs performance, at home against Tennessee in a 43–13 loss. After the Titans game, Mayfield told the media, "Everybody's going to throw us in the trash, and I think that's good…We don't really give a damn what's going on on the outside." Brash? Maybe. Angry and petulant? Yeah, that too. Not exactly mature, but that's to be expected now and then, especially when you start with disappointment. No big deal. It all depends on how the rest of the season goes.

First there was déjà disappointment against the Seahawks. Mayfield had a virtual rerun of the opening game, this time with a 1–3 TD-to-INT ratio, completions below 60 percent, and a 32–28 loss. Fast-forward to the last game of the season, against Cincinnati. Baker threw for three touchdowns but also had three picks.

He completed a paltry 44 percent and, needless to say, lost the game, 33–23. This, let me repeat, was against the Bengals, a team that had a 2 and 14 record. You shouldn't lose to the Bengals.

Did he have a good game during the 2019 season? For sure. And it was early in the season—game four—when it could have, should have, made a big difference. Mayfield and the Browns went into Baltimore and on the Ravens' home field came away with a 40–25 win. He threw the ball only thirty times, but for 342 yards, with one touchdown and one interception. The Browns ran for 193 yards—Nick Chubb racked up 165 yards—and the offense edged out the Ravens in time of possession, which turned out to be a rarity against Baltimore. The win took Cleveland to 2-2, which turned out to be their best standing of the year.

From there on, things seemed to unravel. And the more they unraveled, the more we saw of the Baker Mayfield we were afraid we'd see, way back in the pre-draft days. His immaturity exhibited itself several times, the worst of them being when he blasted the Browns medical staff over wide receiver Odell Beckham Jr.'s sports hernia injury. Mayfield told reporters, "It wasn't handled the right way in our training room" and said that the injury "wasn't addressed early enough." Suddenly, Baker Mayfield was a sports medicine expert. Didn't anybody tell him he needs the medical people on his side? He at least tried some damage control afterward, tweeting, "My intentions were not to throw our medical staff under the bus. No I don't know all the facts about Odell's injury. It was emotionally answered because I can sense his [Odell's] frustration and I care about my team and putting us in the best position to win."

That incident wasn't isolated though. After the Browns' loss to the Patriots, when Cleveland reporter Tony Grossi asked Mayfield about a drive that fell short, Baker started to answer, and Grossi added a follow-up: "But…" he began. And Baker snapped. "Stop saying 'but.' I just told you the clock was running and we had a penalty. You want to give them the ball back? No. You don't play, you don't know. That's just plain and simple." Grossi said, "Were you happy with that drive?" And Baker really blew. "Was I happy with the drive? No, we didn't score points. That's the dumbest question you could ask. What? Jesus, Tony." Reporters can get on any player's nerves. They ask difficult, sometimes aggravating questions. But that's what they do. And without them, fewer fans watch and cheer and buy tickets. So you have to face reality and answer aggravating questions. Paste a smile on your face and offer sports cliché answers. *It was a tough loss… We'll just have to work on execution… We know what we have to do… No excuses, it's a team game… Blah-blah-blah.* Talking to the media is part of your job. Unless you're Bill Belichick and you can grunt, nod your head, and let people remember all the rings you've won.

I like to say, "Go back to the film when evaluating a player." Well, players might do well to go to the film to watch Tom Brady, Aaron Rodgers, Drew Brees, Peyton Manning facing the media, not after wins but after losses. Imagine how many times they've been asked dopey questions. *Tom, how does it feel to lose to a team with such a poor record?… Peyton, what went wrong today?… Drew, when the final drive fell short, what happened?* Watch the responses. You can almost see the thought process: *Hmm, that was a stupid question.* Pause. Bite your bottom lip. And then break the play down, the play the reporter already knows, the play the world can watch on TV tonight or on video over and over for the next week. Walk through the play, step by step, from drop back to blitz to scramble to throw to interception, what the reporter already knows, but showing that you, the quarterback, knew exactly what was happening even as the world was caving in. Or if you don't want to relive the pain, second by second, just shake your head. Look down. Breathe hard. Get very serious. Look up and say, "Guys, I have no excuse. It falls on me…" But don't, don't, don't blame the reporter for your shitty game.

One other thing: officiating. You're not the first or only guy to feel like some bad calls hurt your team on a given day. The truth is, a bad call can mean the difference between winning and losing. But here are some realities. Yes, the refs sometimes call penalties on your team or miss penalty calls on the other team that they shouldn't and that really really hurt your team—defensive holding or pass interference. But they also sometimes miss penalties on your team that help you—holding, offsides, offensive pass interference, pushing off. They're human. Sometimes they're good and sometimes they're bad. And sometimes they need to be criticized and sent back for more training…by the league, not by a losing quarterback. Don't, don't, don't ever blame a game on the refs.

But after a four-point loss to the Seahawks, that's what Baker Mayfield did. He put the onus on the officials and it was—there's no other word for it—dumb. It was not worthy of an NFL quarterback. It's not leadership. It's whining. You have to take the heat and accountability yourself. Even if and when the refs are dead wrong. It should come as no surprise that Mayfield was fined $12,500 for his rant. And an expert on not living up to NFL expectations, Ryan Leaf, called Mayfield out on the bad behavior in a radio interview.

In fairness, Mayfield did show the right response to one incident.

His teammate Myles Garrett got in a fight with Pittsburgh quarterback Mason Rudolph at the end of the Browns-Steelers game. Garrett had tackled Rudolph; Rudolph got hot and pulled at Garrett's helmet; Garrett retaliated by ripping Rudolph's helmet off and using it to bang the quarterback in the head. By the way, the clock had run out and the Browns had won the game. So no, there was nothing on the line, no emotional explanation, nothing. After the game, Mayfield was blunt: "It's inexcusable. I don't care, rivalry or not, we can't do that...The reality is he is going to get suspended. We don't know how long and that hurts our team. It's inexcusable." The league agreed. Myles Garrett was suspended for the rest of the season, the longest suspension for on-field behavior ever. If only Mayfield showed that kind of leadership and wisdom consistently. If only that was his pattern.

There was one other vulnerable spot for Mayfield. He had capitalized on his rookie-year promise by doing a lot of big-time network television commercials. Six ads for Progressive Insurance. Another for Hulu. Another for Nissan. He was all over TV with his spots. Meantime, he was having a disappointing year. So he was an easy target for the critics. At one point in the season, he was called out for having more ads than touchdown passes. It was the combination of being a pitchman and not pitching the ball very well. If you can do both, you won't find many critics. Peyton Manning, Tom Brady, and Aaron Rodgers have had equal if not greater off-field activities.

But there's a good lesson in Tom Brady's very wise decision when offered one of his first commercials, an offer that came well *after* he was named Super Bowl MVP in 2003. He was an established star, not a guy who might become a star. Visa, the credit card company, approached Tom and his agent with an opportunity for a national commercial, with high exposure and no doubt a lucrative payday, an ad about the security and protection that Visa provides its cardholders. Brady said yes, but with a condition that the ad include his offensive linemen. As the ad agency shaped the final spot, the linemen would be the "metaphors" for security and protection, just like they are for their star quarterback. The ad was a hit. It was clever and fun—good marketing. But the best marketing was Tom's approach. *I want to share the spotlight*—the sign of a brilliant leader. He needed those guys around him more than he needed his face on TV or another paycheck. It's no surprise that Tom also became known for not demanding the biggest contracts in the game so that the team's salary cap had room for the guys he needed on the team. Some people have calculated he left as much as $60 million on the table in order to have the talent that would keep the team winning. You could say it's selfless. Or you could say it's the ultimate form of selfish, increasing your chances of long-term success instead of going for a short-term score.

It's worth noting that Patrick Mahomes held back until after a great season—an MVP season, not just a promising one—to join Rodgers in those State Farm ads. Somebody gave him good advice. Or he has good instincts. All of these guys have cashed in on their fame, but they all produced on the field on a consistent basis. Mayfield may have found his teammates and fans and the sports media less understanding of his high profile, given the scores at the end of each game.

After the season, after another losing record—this one worse than the season before—first-year and first-time head coach

Freddie Kitchens was, not surprisingly, fired, and GM Dorsey, surprisingly, departed too. The Browns hired Kevin Stefanski, offensive coordinator of the Vikings, as their new head coach. It's interesting to note that Stefanski had only one year as play caller in the NFL, and he had a lot of help from Gary Kubiak, whose résumé reads like a professor of offense (backup to John Elway, quarterback coach, offensive coordinator, and Super Bowl–winning head coach), brought in to work with Vikings quarterback Kirk Cousins. Did the Browns spot head-coaching talent early? Was there enough evidence to extrapolate? Can Stefanski do what Kitchens couldn't? Can new GM Andrew Berry do better than John Dorsey? Well, the first thing Berry did after getting the job was to give a full-throated endorsement to Baker Mayfield. No qualifiers. No ifs. No we'll-sees. ESPN talking head Stephen A. Smith, among others, went ballistic. He addressed Mayfield directly: "You don't deserve support. You deserve scrutiny. You threw twenty-two touchdowns, twenty-one interceptions." And his earlier quip that Mayfield had more commercials than wins was only a slight exaggeration.

So, what went wrong with Baker Mayfield? Should he not have been the number one overall pick? Were the experts all fooled? Were we blinded by his stats, and did we miss the bigger picture? Or is he a work in progress? Did we extrapolate or did we exaggerate and fabricate what we wanted to see? Yes and no. Yes, his stats were that good and they cannot be ignored. But there were two metrics that did not get studied enough, the hardest ones to evaluate but perhaps the most important: maturity and the leadership (or lack thereof) that results from it. Remember, everything should take you back to the footage—film, tapes, records, previous patterns of behavior. Frame by frame. Incident by incident. You can extrapolate from that behavior and see if the trend is going the right way, stalling where it is, or even trending down.

Temperamental/stupid/egotistical responses alone are not eliminators. Consistent temperamental/stupid/egotistical responses are, especially when coupled with bad performance. What is worrisome is that Baker Mayfield doesn't seem to be learning from experience, from repeated moments and challenges. Instead, we're seeing behavior Mayfield showed in college, maybe even as a high schooler. Back then, a lot of it was written off as immaturity or cockiness or blowing off steam, having fun. Maybe. Maybe if he did a crotch-grab at the Kansas game; *or* if he planted the Oklahoma flag on the Ohio Stadium turf; *or* if he taunted Baylor, "You forgot who Daddy is. I'm going to have to spank you today"; *or* if he got drunk in Fayetteville, Arkansas, got tackled and arrested by a police officer…If he'd done just one of those things or even two, if he'd done them as a freshman or sophomore, or if he didn't seem to brag about what he'd done, then maybe we could chalk it up to his brash nature and say he's got spunk. But when it keeps happening, it's not spunk. When, two years into his pro career, he's still doing battle with the media—a battle he's not going to win—it's not a fluke. It's a pattern, a bad pattern. It's why, before the 2018 draft, scouts were divided between fawning over Mayfield's skills and worrying about his character: At the Senior Bowl, one unnamed scout said, "Baker has a pattern of disrespect." A pattern again. Uh-oh. Wait, it gets worse. The scout added, "Off the field, he's Johnny Manziel." If that isn't a neon warning sign, nothing is. Manziel also won the Heisman, also got drafted by Cleveland, but he lasted two seasons and disappeared from football. We didn't extrapolate on Manziel, and though I'm not saying he's Manziel, it appears we didn't on

Mayfield either. Some saw it, the mixed signals of petulance and performance, but the rest didn't want to see it.

But we can't put all of the blame on Baker. We can put a lot of it on first-year head coach Freddie Kitchens, the former offensive coordinator and former Alabama quarterback, who took over the season after Hue Jackson. Being as charitable as I can be, and empathizing as a head coach and play caller myself, I just haven't seen a worse run of plays called in the NFL in a long time. Not one or two or three, but a string of them. It's hard to pick the highlights, or lowlights. But in game three, in late September, well before the Browns imploded, Freddie gave us a preview of calls to come. The Browns had the ball on the Rams' twenty-eight-yard line on fourth and nine. Freddie called a draw play. True, they were not in automatic field goal range for their young kicker. True, they were too close to punt. But a draw play? With a quarterback with a good arm and receivers like Odell Beckham and Jarvis Landry? Mayfield gave the ball to Nick Chubb and got clobbered. It was a gift to the Rams defense. Mayfield didn't point to Kitchens. But Kitchens owned up to it. Rightly so. But worse, he didn't seem to learn from it. After a number of bad goal-line calls, some unexplainable timeouts and challenges, and flatly refusing to turn the play calling over to his offensive coordinator, he made a call that was a classic example of snatching defeat from the jaws of victory. The Browns were at home, their record was 6 and 8, but they still had their pride on the line and they were playing their hated rivals, the Ravens. The Browns were leading on two field goals, and through almost the entire first half, the Browns defense had shut Baltimore down. With a little over two minutes to go in the half, Cleveland had the ball, third and one on their own twenty-two. Get a first down, then another, and they go into the locker room with a six-point lead and great momentum. All they had to do was pick up one yard. They had Nick Chubb and Kareem Hunt, two good running backs, on the field. And Baker had his Pro Bowl wideouts. A short run or a short pass and you've got one of your two first downs... Or you could call a trick play: Instead of having your solid running back run, you have your quarterback pitch him the ball and have him throw a pass—or try to throw a pass while being smothered by the Ravens defense, which smelled the play. Rather than running the clock out, now the Browns had to punt with a lot of time left. Baltimore took two plays and scored a touchdown. That's what the Ravens were doing all year. You can't give them extra chances. Down 7–6, the Browns get the ball back. Maybe they can make a few yards, run the clock down, and get in field goal range. Or they can give the ball back after eleven seconds. Now you've given the Ravens another extra chance. Seven plays and they're in your end zone again. Half-time score: Ravens 14, Browns 6. Final score: Ravens 31, Browns 15, Kitchens done. And Baker Mayfield's promising second year was a disappointment.

So is Baker Mayfield finished? No. Is he a lost cause? Hardly. He's still an enormously talented guy. Which side of the 50-50 rule is he? I'd say slightly on the good side. Maybe a new coach... Maybe a new GM... Maybe another year under his belt...

Sam Darnold—so far, not Joe

It's 1968. A kid with a busted nose and a cocky attitude from a Pennsylvania steel town and Alabama football has somehow led the New York Jets to Super Bowl III (the first AFC-NFC Championship Game to even be called the "Super Bowl"). The Jets are taking on the daunting

Baltimore Colts. The Colts are favored by eighteen points. The Jets shouldn't even show up. But the kid goes on national television and guarantees a win. Just publicity? Just trash talk? No, they win. The New York Jets beat the mighty Colts 16–7. The world changed that day. The AFC was real. The Jets were a force. Joe Namath was a god.

That was fifty-two years ago. New York Jets fans have been waiting for a brash, bold, winning successor to Joe Willie Namath ever since. They've had thirty-one starting quarterbacks since Namath. The Jets used the number three draft pick to take Sam Darnold. He is talented, athletic, and had a stellar college career. He is not brash, or bold, and so far, he is not winning. The wait goes on.

In the pre-2018 draft days, the debates raged over who should be number one: Mayfield, Darnold, or maybe Josh Allen. The experts were divided; plenty had Darnold at the top. He had good numbers at USC in year one, beating Penn State in the Rose Bowl, and in his second starting year he led the Trojans to the Pac-12 Championship and the Cotton Bowl, and was a Heisman candidate. At six three and 225 pounds, a star athlete from the time he was a kid, Sam had the "look" of a quarterback. The only question mark was his less-than-fiery personality and drive. Sam was calm—that word came up over and over—but the issue was, calm as in steady or calm as in subdued? It can be the difference between winning and losing. Here's what he said about himself in an interview: "It's who I am and I'm not trying extra hard. I just try to be calm." Even his own father, Mike, said, "It's always been a joke in our family that he was the flatliner." So is it poise and cool under fire or is it placid and lacking fire? GMs evaluating Darnold before the draft were divided. Eric DeCosta of the Ravens said, "We liked what you saw in the tape at USC, but no one was really shot in the ass [Eric's expression for 'over the top'] with this guy. No one would stand on the table and fight for him. Everyone liked him. No one loved him." The Jets did. They bet their future on him.

So far? So flat. Almost literally. After a rookie season to get his feet on the ground, Darnold and the Jets finished 2019 at 7-9. In the thirteen games he played in each of the last two seasons, his numbers remained very consistent…and average. In 2018, he had just over 400 pass attempts, completing under 60 percent, for 2,865 yards, averaging 6.9 yards per attempt (which is low), with 17 TDs to 15 INTs. The 2019 season showed very similar results: a little better completion percentage at 62 percent, but still only 6.9 yards per attempt, and a slight improvement to 19 TDs to 13 INTs. After an 0-4 start, and after Darnold missed three games with mono-nucleosis, all losses led by another 2018 draft QB, Luke Falk, the Jets and Sam came back in week six to upset the Cowboys 24–22. Darnold threw for 330-plus yards and two TDs. But the good news didn't last. The Patriots came into New York and shut out the Jets 33–0 in week seven, when Darnold threw four picks and had 34 percent completions. And that loss was followed by two more, even one against the lowly Dolphins, who got their first win of the year. But, at week ten, the Jets had something of a turnaround, finishing the season with a 6-2 run. Darnold did have some good games. Against the Redskins, he was 63 percent on 30 throws for 293 yards and 4 TDs. For his starts, he went 7-6, technically a winning record…if only a football season were thirteen games instead of sixteen.

What was Sam's leadership style in the face of setbacks? Pretty much as expected, the usual sports clichés. After dropping the week-one game to the Bills, Darnold said, "We just need to bounce back... We'll come to work and get ready for Cleveland." He was ruled out for the Cleveland game, the first of his mono misses. Later, after they fell to Miami, Darnold offered textbook support for his coach and more standard media yak: "Coach Gase is one of the best coaches I've ever been around... It's just about staying consistent and executing and putting really good drives together." The only time he showed signs of emotion, unfortunately, was during the Patriots debacle, when he was miked up, and after a turnover, he said, "I'm seeing ghosts," not exactly the kind of inspiration you want for your team. At least it wasn't flat. It was real. Probably every NFL quarterback has felt that way at some time in his career. It's like the world is crashing in on you, because it is— rhino-sized linemen and circling vulture cornerbacks seem too big, too fast, too many.

Bottom line: It's hard to see where the upside is for this guy. Although he's been on a weak team, he just doesn't seem to do anything special. The fact that the Jets brought in a quarterback whisperer in Adam Gase to tap into and bring out Darnold's potential, and he comes up with virtually the same results and level of play... well, that is concerning. More than concerning. In fairness, Darnold was out for part of the season. But the NFL doesn't allow you much time to heal. With the production of young quarterbacks like Patrick Mahomes, or the promise of the Giants' Daniel Jones, or the growth of Josh Allen, or the phenomenon of Lamar Jackson, there's plenty of pressure on Sam Darnold. His third season may be his verdict season. The personality/character/leadership factor of "calm" will either be his hallmark or his stain. (He's almost the opposite of Baker Mayfield, both extremes of emotion, or lack thereof.) I used to say I like my young QBs to show a little panic—not exactly like he did against the Patriots, but to show emotion, to show what he can do under intense heat, how he can fight back. Seeing ghosts translates to, "I'm not seeing the field any better in year two than year one."

So where does that leave Sam? What do the Jets do next? Build around him through the draft? Look for free agents? Make some sharp trades? Or go for knee-jerk reactions? Right after supposedly giving GM Mike Maccagnan free rein over upcoming draft picks, they "un-gave" it to him by thanking him for his service and replacing him with Joe Douglas. Joe is a smart guy; he was a scout for me at the Ravens and he really knows his stuff on player personnel. But, unfortunately, this is another knee-jerk management move from a team with a history of knee-jerk management moves. They say the definition of insanity is doing the same thing over and over and expecting different results. New GM. Second-year coach—now on the hot seat. Third-year quarterback. Here's the good news for Sam. The new GM is the same Joe Douglas who, when he was head of player personnel for Philadelphia during the 2018 draft, had Darnold at the top of the Eagles' draft board. The Eagles didn't need a quarterback (or so they thought at the time), and they didn't have a high enough pick to get him anyway. Joe liked Sam then and he likes him now…though, having not picked him at the Jets, he isn't personally invested in him. It's now or never for Sam Darnold.

Josh Allen—tipping point

On Friday and Saturday in late November, the temperature was in the mid-forties in Miami, cold for Florida, toasty for visitors from Buffalo. By game time on Sunday it was 72 degrees—no excuses for anybody. The Bills take the opening kickoff. Devin Singletary runs for twenty-two. No huddle. Allen throws to McKenzie for six. Allen throws to Knox for nine. First down. Singletary up the middle for one. Third and nine. No huddle. Allen throws to Beasley for four. Bills field goal. Defense stops Miami. Punt. Bills repeat the opening drive for three more. Defense stops Miami. Allen passes to Brown for twenty-four. No huddle. Allen passes to Beasley for seven. Allen drops back, looks, moves, finds Brown for a forty-yard TD. From then on it was Allen, Allen, Allen, with a healthy dose of defense, defense, defense. He threw for 256 yards, ran for 57, did not fumble, did not throw a pick, did not even take a sack. Josh Allen was named AFC Offensive Player of the Week.

If most weeks had gone like that, we'd have a real handle on Josh Allen. Instead, he's still the biggest unknown among the QBs of the 2018 draft class. Going into 2020, he is the most difficult to evaluate, with mostly positive reviews, some looming question marks, but he's definitely the one who could tip the balance to the positive or negative side of the 50-50 scale. Allen has been playing on a solid team, the Bills, that runs the ball well and plays what has been a powerful defense. The other side of the ball—a good defense—is never a small thing for an up-and-coming quarterback. Or any quarterback. Take it from a head coach—me—who was hired by the Ravens for my record in steering the offense for the Vikings, came to Baltimore, and won a Super Bowl, not with offense but with one of the all-time great defenses in the NFL, plus special teams standouts and a can't-miss kicker. Our greatest offensive weapon was our defense. The 2000 Ravens defense held opponents to a record-setting low of 10.3 points per game. All we had to do was score one touchdown and two field goals to win. There's no overestimating the value of a great defense to an offense, and to a quarterback.

That's not to take anything away from Josh Allen. He has shown signs of his own that are hopeful. But he's sent up some worry flares too. On the plus side, the run strength of the Bills—including Allen, who was third on the team with 510 yards behind his two running backs—racked up over 2,000 yards on the ground. All that running meant Allen only had to launch the ball 461 times. (Compare that with Tom Brady at 613 or Russell Wilson at 516.) Josh's completions were still under 60 percent, but he did come up with 20 TDs to 9 INTs, a good ratio.

The team turned in a 10-6 season and made the playoffs. A good part of that success goes back to Josh Allen's athleticism, which showed itself back in the draft. (Remember back then: The plus was his athleticism and improvisation; the minus was passing accuracy. Same plus and minus in the NFL.) When he had to, he ran and ran well. He's not in Lamar Jackson's category, but no one is. Allen did rank third in the NFL among quarterbacks on the ground, behind Jackson and Kyler Murray. A lot of his yards were on third downs to keep drives alive—good under pressure—and he also took the ball into the end zone nine times, ahead of both Murray and Jackson at seven each.

But when he had to throw a lot—thirty-nine or more times twice—the Bills lost the games, one to Baltimore, the other to Cleveland. Both times he was well under 60 percent, indicating he was throwing more desperately, and when passes are desperate, they miss the mark. He is good with play-action passes where he comes out of the fake and has a clear view of his receivers. Again, that agility and athletic ability to adapt. He has a powerful arm that can hit tight areas, but throwing into a zone defense is not his strength.

There's one other thing, not a good thing: turnovers. Josh Allen had too many, and too many clustered in the same games, meaning, when things went bad, they went worse. He fumbled sixteen times in seventeen games, though he only lost the ball four times. Add that to his nine picks and you've got a troublesome statistic.

His promising moments: Allen and the Bills had their best game against the Dolphins (though Miami provided the highlight reels for a lot of teams this season), hitting on 63 percent of his throws for 256 yards and three touchdowns. No surprise, his worst game was against the Patriots and Belichick, who likes to chew up young quarterbacks. Allen got picked off three times and completed a dismal 46 percent of his passes. Still, with all those troubles, he and the team showed poise, hanging in on a tight 16–10 loss. Their wild card game, only their second playoff spot since 1999, was against Houston, and it was a tough game from start to finish. Thanks to their stingy defense, an early TD pass, and two field goals, the Bills scored the only points in the first half, leading 13–0 at the break. A typical, good Bills game plan. Buffalo added three points on another field goal and led 16–0. But Deshaun Watson, another quarterback improviser, was not to be counted out, running for a twenty-yard touchdown and converting for two to make it 16–8. Houston began to control the game from then on, with Watson taking the team down the field, first for a field goal and then for another TD and another two-point conversion, and a 19–16 lead. The Bills never quit, coming back with ten seconds on the clock for a forty-seven-yard game-tying field goal, which took the game into overtime. That's as far as the Bills' playoffs hopes went, as the Texans kicked a game-winning field goal to win 22–19.

But let's look at Allen in that game, the good, the bad, and the déjà vu. The good—he rushed for almost 100 yards on 9 carries. The bad—he had to throw the ball 46 times (too many for him) and completed only 52 percent. The déjà vu—Allen fumbled, and that turnover led to the Texans owning the momentum in the second half. In overtime, on the Bills' final drive, Allen did convert two third downs, carrying the ball himself, but it wasn't enough and they had to punt. Watson took his team down the field again, and they sealed the win with a twenty-eight-yard field goal.

Conclusions: A good defense can keep you alive. Fumbles and turnovers can kill you. Completion percentage is the litmus test. Above 60 percent, you can survive. Below 60 percent, you can't. And unless you're Lamar Jackson or Patrick Mahomes or Cam Newton when he's healthy, don't rely on your legs to save the day.

So who is Josh Allen going to be? What's his fate? We often equate him to Ben Roethlisberger—same-size guys with similar styles—but Josh is a far better runner than Ben. In fact, most people you know are far better runners than Ben. He averages under a hundred yards a season, and for good reason. He's big and slow, with exactly no deceptive moves. But he can throw the ball. His completions have been well above 60 percent almost every year. He has six seasons of throwing for more than 4,000 yards. And it's hard to take him down. So the comparison of Josh to Ben goes only so far. Roethlisberger took the Steelers to the playoffs his rookie year and almost every year since, plus the Super Bowl in years two, five, and seven, winning two of those. Can Josh Allen become Ben Roethlisberger? He has good coaching like Ben. He has a good defense like Ben. He's big and strong, like Ben. He can take a hit, like Ben. He plays for a tough, no-frills team in a tough, no-frills market, like Ben. But he remains a question mark. At the moment, of our five QBs, we've got two on the good side—one slightly, one clearly—two on the not-so-good side—one slightly, one clearly—and Josh Allen in the middle. He may be the tiebreaker, one way or the other, in our 50-50 rule.

But here's what may tilt him to the good side: consistency of coaching, good coaching. He's one of only two of the 2018 first-round quarterbacks to have had the same head coach through his first two, and now third, years. Sean McDermott is working with Josh Allen and arguably making progress.

GM Brandon Beane was brought in to the Bills in 2017, reuniting him with former Panthers defensive coordinator, now Bills head coach, Sean McDermott. In their initial year together, they returned to the postseason for the first time in a long time. Together, and I emphasize that word, they picked Josh Allen. No internal squabbles. In sync. And they made all of their draft picks, trades, and re-signings that way. And most importantly, they're two smart guys. With Allen at quarterback, they returned to the playoffs. Progress. Ownership placed faith in them and stuck with them. So far. (After all, this is the NFL.)

Josh Rosen—two and out?

Unfortunately, the high point of Josh Rosen's NFL career so far has been the 2018 draft. Even though he was picked at number ten by the Cardinals, he was disappointed and showed it. His post-draft tweet was, "There were nine mistakes ahead of me." Not humble, but he did have plenty of believers. Now he has fewer.

Are we being fair to Josh Rosen? Might we be giving him better reviews and seeing a brighter future if he had been picked by another team—the Browns or Jets or Bills? He'd have had plenty to complain about in Cleveland, with friction in the coaching-management-ownership ranks and weak talent around him even in year two, and then another coaching change. In New York, he'd have had a new coach, a lackluster team, impatient ownership, but fans who would have liked his cockiness…as long as he won. In Buffalo things might have been better, with consistent coaching and a strong defense and a playbook that calls for conservative schemes, not a spotlight for a big-arm quarterback. He may well have fared better in Baltimore, but that was never going to happen: a chemistry mismatch even before the draft, and his ego would have been even more battered to be taken last in the round. Before he was drafted, the concern with Rosen was his attitude, cockiness, coachability, petulance, ego, etc. Two years later, he's been humbled by a bad first year, by getting traded, by losing the starting job to a journeyman. Now the concern with him isn't attitude and ego; it's talent at the NFL level.

There's no two ways about it. Short of a miracle, Josh Rosen is clearly on the negative side of the quarterback pick equation. He went into a bad situation in Arizona; it's hard to imagine a worse one, but he got it when he was traded to Miami. In Arizona, the team had gone 3-13 overall and 3-10 when Rosen was on the field. In came Kliff Kingsbury who, as promised, drafted Kyler Murray, and Josh was shipped off to the Dolphins, the only team that could make the Cardinals look good. (By the way, things didn't get much better for Arizona, finishing at 5-10-1 but with Murray showing potential.) In Miami, things went from bad to worse for Rosen. The team had fired head coach Adam Gase, hired Brian Flores from the Patriots, and sent veteran quarterback Ryan Tannehill to Tennessee. They figured Tannehill was, to coin a phrase, over the hill, but with the Titans, he caught fire and, along with amazing running back Derrick Henry, took them to the playoffs.

Rosen played in only a handful of games for Miami, and started even fewer. He came into the week-one game, a 59–10 disaster against the Ravens, too late to do anything and did exactly nothing. Game three against the Cowboys, Rosen started, and presided over another lopsided loss, 31–6. After a further loss and then a bad performance in the first three quarters—eighty-five yards and two interceptions—against the Redskins, he was benched for Ryan Fitzpatrick, aka Fitzmagic, the thirty-seven-year-old playing for his eighth NFL team. The Dolphins still lost 17–16 and were accused of losing on purpose to gain a higher draft pick. Meantime, Josh Rosen was relegated to the bench while Fitz finally turned in wins against the Jets and then the Colts. So much for losing on purpose. They even upset the Eagles late in the season and the Patriots in the final week, all games that Rosen just watched. When your coach chooses to bet on a guy who is the definition of a backup—solid, reliable, unexciting—then you know your future is in trouble.

Preview: It may get worse. The scuttlebutt, conjecture, and mock drafts leading into the 2020 draft had the Dolphins using their number five pick, or even giving away a boatload of other picks for the Redskins' number two slot (the Bengals have number one and aren't going to part with it)…all in order to take quarterback Tua Tagovailoa out of Alabama. Tua began his college career on fire but ended it on crutches. Midway through his junior season, against Tennessee, he incurred a high ankle sprain requiring surgery, and after recovering, again went down, this time against Mississippi State, with a dislocated hip, posterior wall fracture, broken nose, and concussion. Despite some impressive games and even more impressive numbers, that was the end of Tua's season, and his college days. Fast-forward: In January 2020, he declared for the 2020 draft. The scuttlebutt was right. The Dolphins used their number five pick to take him. For Rosen, it's a pretty clear vote of no-confidence when your team is willing to give away the store to get a guy who is either a bionic man or poster boy for the injured reserve list.

Josh Rosen is undeniably a man of many individual skills and abilities. So far, they haven't added up. The whole does not equal the sum of the parts.

Lamar Jackson—unicorn?

It's late in the third quarter and the Ravens and Seahawks are tied at 13. Two Mark Ingram runs. Pass from Jackson to tight end Hayden Hurst for ten. Runs from Gus Edwards and Ingram. The Ravens are deep in Seahawks territory, third and fifteen; Jackson scrambles and picks up thirteen, short of the first down. Fourth and two, ball on the eight-yard line. Justin Tucker, Baltimore's virtually automatic field goal kicker, trots onto the field for a chip shot. Lamar Jackson heads to the sideline, disgruntled, not content to settle for three points. John Harbaugh asks him, "Do you want to go for that?" Jackson doesn't take a breath. "Hell, yeah, Coach. Let's go for it." Lamar turns to his teammates on the sideline. "Do you want to go for it?" He doesn't even give them a chance to answer. He says, "Let's go for it!"...Baltimore called time-out, came up with a play call—three-tight-end formation. Jackson took the snap, saw daylight, and didn't just pick up the first down. He took it to the end zone. Ravens led 20–13. And they never lost the lead.

That story was the story of Lamar Jackson and the Ravens' season. Going for it in every sense—using his arm, his legs, his field vision, dodging tackles, making defenders miss, being—as his teammates and opponents put it—"a freak." Or as I and other commentators put it, a unicorn—the once-in-a-generation athlete who can do what he isn't supposed to be able to do. Other teams took Baker Mayfield, Sam Darnold, Josh Allen, and Josh Rosen ahead of Lamar Jackson, and none of those quarterbacks had a rookie season or second season as good as Lamar. In fact, most quarterbacks in the NFL didn't come close. That's a unicorn. The dictionary defines it as: "1. a mythical animal typically represented as a horse with a single straight horn projecting from its forehead," and "2. something that is highly desirable but difficult to find…" Lamar Jackson is not mythical but he sure is "something that is highly desirable but difficult to find."

He is the Cinderella story of the 2018 draft—the overlooked beauty who rises from obscurity to the spotlight. But maybe we should have seen him coming. Maybe some people did. Lamar was the thirty-second pick, the last of the first round. But we should all remind ourselves that the last pick of the first round is still the first round. It's like the old joke: What do you call the person who graduates last in med school? Doctor. It wasn't lack of talent that kept Lamar from being an earlier pick; it was the debate over how his talents would work best in the NFL. Could he put his running ability to work at the pro level? Could he throw at the pro level? Could he up his completion percentages with better receivers? Could he run and pass and scramble and stay healthy? Or should he be a wide receiver instead? It turns out the answers are yes, yes, yes, yes, and no.

If there were any doubters, they disappeared in the Ravens' first game of 2019, where the Ravens pummeled the Dolphins 59–10; where Jackson threw for 324 yards and 5 touchdowns—23 completions on 26 passes; where he connected on an 83-yard pass play to Marquise Brown; where the team gained 265 yards on the ground, led by Mark Ingram's 107 yards; where the team went 2 for 2 on fourth-down conversions; where they ran up a time of possession of 40 minutes versus just under 20 minutes; where even backup quarterback Robert Griffin III picked up a touchdown; where Lamar Jackson, accused of relying on his feet too much, ran for… six yards all day. He did it all without his feet. Okay, the Dolphins are weak. But any team in the NFL should be able to keep the score under 40; any team should be able to put more than one touchdown on the board. Unless you're taking on a unicorn. After the game, Jackson faced the press. His opening comment, made with a big happy grin on his face, was "Not bad for a running back." Not bad indeed.

Of course, that didn't mean Lamar wouldn't run. It just meant he didn't have to. But he could. And he did. Unless he used his other running backs. Or unless he threw. Or unless he dropped back to throw, couldn't find a receiver, and ran and ran and ran. Or unless he rolled out to throw, ducked a tackle, started to run, and then threw. Or…All of the "unlesses" meant the Ravens were a bigger threat than defenses could prepare for. Defenses had to stop eleven players on the offense instead of the usual ten. The quarterback's threat is most often his arm. Not so with Lamar.

Between the 2018 and '19 seasons, as promised, the Ravens constructed a team around Lamar Jackson. Besides signing running back Mark Ingram from the Saints and drafting Justice Hill, they added wide receivers "Hollywood" Brown and Miles Boykin, to join their tight ends Hurst, Andrews, and Boyle.

According to sources inside the camp, John Harbaugh said something to the effect of "We can't run a West Coast offense [Joe Montana's offense with Bill Walsh], so let's tailor this thing to what this kid can do." They were all in. (They even rebuilt a defense for him, filling free-agency losses with future Hall of Famers Earl Thomas from the Seahawks and Marcus Peters from the Rams.) The promotion of Greg Roman to offensive coordinator and putting James Urban in as quarterbacks coach were further commitments to the new game.

I asked Roman to reconstruct what unfolded. First he was candid about the early assessments of Jackson. "We saw and were intrigued by the special abilities Lamar had, but honestly, I could not say we took him knowing he was going to be the MVP in his second year." The Ravens were counting on Joe Flacco, with Jackson as a "just in case." But events intervened, as they always do. Inside the cloud of Joe Flacco's injury was the silver lining that allowed the Ravens to see what Jackson could do. As Greg tells it, "What happened with Lamar was the perfect sequence of events that got us to this point. Came in as the backup, had a chance to refine his skills, then got put into the game, and with his special skills got us to the playoffs. It is hard to imagine we would have been able to totally commit to Lamar's style of play without seeing what we did at the end of 2018. What did leap out early is that he had rare vision. He sees everything quickly at the snap of the ball."

In the 2019 season, Lamar Jackson put up numbers that are mind-boggling. And he did it over and over, all season, not in a game or two, not against one team or two, not playing a certain type of defense, but against everyone and everything. His college completions averaged 57 percent. His second year with the Ravens, he was at 66 percent, throwing 401 passes for over 3,000 yards, with a staggering 36 TD to 6 INT ratio. And he hardly abandoned the run, chalking up 1,206 yards and 7 touchdowns of his own. Lamar Jackson, quarterback, ranked sixth in the NFL among running backs. His remark "not bad for a running back" turned out to be more than a punch line; he *was* more than not bad for a running back.

But of all the stats, one of the most telling is what he does under pressure. Defenses like to blitz young quarterbacks, even if it's not the best way to contain them. They like to shake up the kid. They want to break his concentration so he misses his reads, or has to scramble in the backfield. Too bad for those defenses, because Jackson loves to scramble. It's one of his best plays—finding a way to keep the play alive instead of taking a sack or throwing the ball away. Remember what Eric DeCosta saw in Lamar's college performance? Well, it turned out to be dead-on. Pressure was no pressure. Opponents threw their best blitz packages at Lamar Jackson so he had to scramble thirty-nine times—that's a lot—but he still picked up eleven yards per scramble. *He averaged a first down on every scramble.* Here are some comps from ProFootballReference. com: Jimmy Garoppolo faced 12 scrambles all year, for 4.7 yards per. The GOAT, Tom Brady, had 3 scrambles but he did pick up 11 yards on each. Baker Mayfield had 17 for 7.9 yards each. And Super Bowl winner Patrick Mahomes, no slouch at keeping plays alive, had 23 scrambles for 9.3 yards each.

What's next after an incredible sophomore season? At heart, despite his experience with Kaepernick and now Jackson, Roman is a believer in the pocket quarterback. "We will evolve the offense to more pocket passes as Lamar evolves, and we think he will. Running outside the pocket is still what he does best, and it is where he is the safest." Is Lamar one of a kind or has Roman seen anyone else like him? Greg put it this way: "Kaepernick had this type of potential, but he could not sustain it. Lamar loves the game and loves the competition, every day." The "could not sustain it" comment wasn't referring to Colin's political or social stances but to his lack of dedication to the game. The word around the 49ers was that some days he was intent on becoming the next Joe Montana, and some days to becoming a hip-hop music star. Greg says Lamar Jackson is a unicorn. If not a unicorn, a plenty rare species. And laser focused on football.

Game ten of the season, Ravens vs. Bengals. Midway through the third quarter, Baltimore is up 28–10. Second down and three. Perfect time to call Mark Ingram's number. Jackson fakes to Ingram, keeps, but defensive end Carlos Dunlap has him. Had him. Jackson is too fast. But safety Jessie Bates is there. Was there. Feint to the left and Bates is in the rearview mirror. Jackson is into the secondary. Trapped again. For sure. They close in. Lamar…spins…360 degrees. In midrun. Safety Shawn Williams grabs air instead of jersey. Linebacker Nick Vigil has him. No. He reaches, loses his balance, and falls, taking another Bengal with him. Clear sailing now. Touchdown Jackson! Forty-seven yards. Instead of a sack. Instead of a short gain. Instead of a first down. He gains half a buck and six points.

That's what they call an ankle-breaker play. The defenders trying to stop on a dime wrap their arms around a hologram and trip over themselves. Commentator Kevin Harlan said, "He is Houdini!" Lamar Jackson was proving to be an escape artist.

The Ravens went on to a 14-2 season, the best record in the NFL. The Lamar accolades were constant, nonstop adoration and fawning—but well-earned fawning, and from every corner of the league and even outside of football. Michael Vick, to whom Jackson is often compared, tweeted: "Lamar Jackson 5x better than what I was at V-Tech…Enough said!!" The Seahawks' Jadeveon Clowney: "I always wanted to play against Michael Vick, I guess I'm getting the new era with Lamar Jackson right there." Richard Sherman, San Francisco cornerback, after their loss to the Ravens: "He knows angles, he knows leverage, he knows when to get down, he knows when to stay up, he knows when to cut back, he knows when to keep it, he knows when to bounce outside." Bill Belichick, not known for gushy compliments, gave Jackson his highest grade—problem: "…a hard guy to handle…definitely a problem." Sean McDermott of the Buffalo Bills: "I don't think there's been a defense that's cracked the code." Pete Carroll, Seahawks coach: "When you saw him in person, he's faster than we saw him on film." Sean McVay, Rams coach: "There is a reason why people are talking about him as an MVP." Kliff Kingsbury, Arizona Cardinals: "He can stand there and throw it and beat you that way, and he can beat you with his legs." Tom Brady, New England Patriots: "You're never really quite sure who's got it…" Bill Polian, Hall of Fame GM, who had originally said Jackson should be a wide receiver, felt the need to issue an official retraction: "I was wrong." Jackson and head coach John Harbaugh developed a bond uncommon even among coaches and quarterbacks. "I love the way you play," Harbaugh told Jackson. "You just don't flinch. You just attack. All you do is attack…You changed the game, man." This is a fifty-seven-year-old man professing his admiration for a twenty-three-year-old kid/magician.

Then there's the "freak" factor. James Burgess, New York Jets: "The guy is a freak of nature. One of a kind." Clemson linebacker Ben Boulware: "He's a freak athlete and he can fly." During the draft, 49ers head coach Kyle Shanahan looked at Jackson's game films: "He's a freak of nature." And Ravens teammate, receiver Seth Roberts, nicknamed Lamar " 'Freaky-L'...he can do anything out there. He's just freaky." Mark Ingram became Jackson's self-appointed publicity agent, promoting him for MVP every time he found a microphone: "I would like to introduce y'all to the man, the myth, the legend. The MVP frontrunner. If anybody else has gotta say something different about that, then come see me. I'm right here in B-More outside the bank [M&T Bank Stadium]. If you got an issue with that, come see me. I'm 'bout that! Big Truss, Lamar Jackson. In the flesh."

"Big Truss" was a term that no one could quite explain, that Lamar brought with him from his childhood in Florida. Roughly translated, it means we are all with you all the way, no matter what, no matter where...trust, faith, belief, solid.

Jackson's fans came from far beyond Baltimore or the NFL. Rapper Quavo, a member of the trio Migos, is a follower. Gucci Mane, another rapper, echoed the team's slogan: "Nobody cares. Work harder." Al Pacino said Jackson's style was "an inspiration to actors." The Archbishop of Baltimore brought a Jackson number 8 jersey to the pope! Even the *Wall Street Journal* ran a story headlined, "Stop What You're Doing. Watch Lamar Jackson Change Football," which opened with these words: "There needs to be a Lamar Jackson channel. I'm serious. Nothing but Lamar, Lamar, Lamar, all Jackson, all the time, 24/7." The *Wall Street Journal*!

It was a dream season...almost. The Ravens went into the

playoffs with the best record in football, drawing a bye in week one and home field advantage in the playoffs. As the top seed, they would play the Tennessee Titans, a resuscitated team led by comeback QB Ryan Tannehill (discarded by the Dolphins) and anchored by the relentless, unstoppable running of Derrick Henry. A good and surprising team, but nine-and-a-half-point underdogs to the amazing Ravens and Lamar Jackson. But it's any given Sunday in the NFL, and the Titans upset the Ravens 28–12. Dream over. Abruptly. It was a crushing disappointment for Lamar, for Baltimore, for football fans in general, in fact, who had been counting on the Ravens vs. Somebody in the Super Bowl. Lamar skulked to the sidelines. He shook his head. He was mad. He was lost. He later admitted he couldn't even come out of his room for days. He was disappointed in himself. Understandable. But, as a leader, he'll have to keep his head up. He'll learn.

The reality is, Lamar Jackson was still the best quarterback in the NFL in 2019, All-Pro, unanimous pick for MVP, record setter, maybe game-changer. His head coach, John Harbaugh, was rightly declared Coach of the Year for the foresight, guts, and creativity to build a new team and new strategy around the unique skills of his quarterback instead of following the NFL tradition of trying to turn every college quarterback into a drop-back passer. How did it all happen? Why did it happen? Eric Mangini, who has been a defensive coordinator and head coach and commentator, who has been up and down and learned a lot along the way, says the situation with John Harbaugh and Lamar Jackson was "the perfect storm"—the right quarterback, the right coach, the right offensive coordinator, at the right time, on the right team. Mangini raised and in essence answered the questions that account for that perfect storm: Did John Harbaugh learn from watching brother Jim coach the 49ers with perhaps the only other double-threat QB in recent time, Colin Kaepernick? Did he learn from seeing 49ers quarterback coach Greg Roman create designed runs, not just scrambles, for Kaepernick? Did he learn from the second-half performance Kaepernick put on to nearly bring his team back from a 28–6 deficit in the Ravens-49ers Super Bowl? Did John go out and get Greg Roman to work the same way with Lamar Jackson? Did John and GM Eric DeCosta and Greg and quarterback coach James Urban build an entirely new offense around Jackson's talents? Yes to all. Above all, John Harbaugh had what head coaches are not known for having—an open mind. Work with what you have; don't try to turn what you have into something else. A simple lesson, not often learned.

Despite the postseason disappointment, the Ravens and Lamar Jackson were, and likely are, a remarkable force. If losing in the postseason early in a quarterback's career is indicative of anything, it may be of long-term success. Peyton Manning holds the record for most postseason losses at thirteen, and nine of those were first-round losses. But he also went to the Super Bowl four times and won twice. Besides Peyton, John Elway, Dan Marino, Drew Brees, and Aaron Rodgers all started their postseason careers with losses, and it's safe to say their NFL legacies are in good shape.

So yes, the Ravens are for real. Lamar Jackson is very much for real. He is, without question, the standout of the 2018 draft class. Most of all, he's a one-man case study in how we evaluate quarterbacks…and what we do or don't extrapolate correctly. We *didn't* extrapolate from the data on Lamar's cool and competency in pressure throws, a good indicator of field vision, decision-making, and leadership in the most adverse circumstances. We *didn't* extrapolate on the wisdom and maturity of Lamar's resolve to stick with his quarterback ambitions and not give in to conventional/old thinking on switching to a running or receiving position. And we *didn't* extrapolate from his confident humility—not a contradiction in terms, but rather an ideal character trait—the ability to lead others, even those older and more established. (It's Lamar's version of my "athletic arrogance"—the ability plus the self-assuredness.) The data, trends, anecdotes were there if we had looked harder and "checked the film" of Lamar's career and life, on and off the field. He was always this good. But a lot of people missed it.

Now comes the revisionist thinking. Just as experts said Russell Wilson wasn't tall enough to make it in the NFL, and Patrick Mahomes was undisciplined and "freelanced" too much, they said Lamar Jackson couldn't run *and* pass...until he did. (Maybe they should have looked at Jackson's passing yards in college—years two and three, over 3,500 yards in each—added to his run yards—beyond almost any comp—and extrapolated from those numbers.) Now, suddenly, those skeptical experts are converts. Witness the scouts checking out previously "short" quarterbacks. Witness the worship of "genius" Andy Reid at the Chiefs, who was shown the door in Philadelphia. Witness not only John Harbaugh's anointment as a coaching wizard, but the high demand to interview his OC, Greg Roman, for a head coaching job. Witness the accolades for Ravens quarterback coach James Urban. Witness the PSL stampede in Baltimore, where seats were vacant not long ago. And most of all, watch the other teams in the NFL saying to their GMs, "Find me the next Lamar Jackson," or "the next Patrick Mahomes"...which, as this book shows, is not an easy feat.

VI

Is the Game Changing?

Is the game changing? Yes, next question.

Is the college style of play usurping the old pro style? Is the wide-open game the game of the future? Is this a new day? *Is the game changing?* This question, in one form or another, has been the barstool issue of sports fans and experts for the last few years. *Yes, it is changing; just look at Russell Wilson, Patrick Mahomes, and Lamar Jackson...No, it isn't changing; just look at Tom Brady, Aaron Rodgers, Carson Wentz, and maybe young Daniel Jones.* Plenty of people, me included, were hesitant to say there was a real and meaningful change in the game. Yes, passing is on the rise. Yes, scores are going up. Yes, there's more improvising in midplay. Yes, quarterbacks are increasingly dual threats, or at least a threat and a half, running better when they have to. Yes, college-style offenses are making their way into the NFL. Yes, college coaches are here too. But the question is...

Are we witnessing unicorns—once-in-a-generation talents—or a sea-change trend in the game?

We've had scrambling run-pass quarterbacks for a long, long time. Randall Cunningham, drafted in 1985, played for ten years with the Eagles and put up almost 30,000 passing yards and nearly 5,000 rushing. Going way back to a QB drafted in 1961, the Vikings' Fran Tarkenton had over 47,000 passing yards and 3,600-plus running yards, and he's the guy who popularized the term "scrambling quarterback." Michael Vick, with the Falcons and the Eagles, threw for over 22,000 yards and ran for over 6,000, with a 1,000-yard single season. Did we say these guys were changing the game? No, we just said they're outstanding talents at quarterback. Just like Joe Montana, Terry Bradshaw, Dan Marino, Peyton Manning, Drew Brees, and Tom Brady.

So what makes people say the game is really changing this time? It's not just the numbers, it's the style of play. What we're seeing is an updated Tarkenton style—quarterbacks reading the defense and modifying in real time, with last-second audibles or play-action improv, literally changing the call in midplay. But now it's being executed with even more innovation, more options, more sophisticated plays, more data, and a whole lot more preparation from playing that way in college.

For a long time the popular wisdom was that the college approach wouldn't translate to the NFL, where the linemen are bigger, the safeties stronger and more agile, and the secondary is faster. No matter who that quarterback faced in college, now he's facing the elite defensive players from every conference, from every top college team, from every bowl game. These guys can adjust on a dime and they're not easily fooled. But, it turns out, this new breed of quarterback can also adjust on a dime, and they're not easily fooled either. And most importantly, the quarterback and the offense initiate the play; the defense reacts.

When Cam Newton joined the Panthers, he didn't adjust to the NFL; it adjusted to him. He put up almost 30,000 yards in the air plus 4,800 with his legs... by age thirty. Russell Wilson, also only thirty, has piled up nearly the same numbers. Now the defenses are the ones scrambling. Then along comes Patrick Mahomes and the game is thrown even more wide open. We simply don't know what he's going to do on any given play—drop back and throw deep, roll out and throw short, or cut back and run, or start to run and throw sidearm to a running back, or change his mind twice during the play and drop back and throw deep. He's only twenty-four and he's already thrown for over 9,000 yards. He hit 5,000 in one season! Now there's Lamar Jackson, who is a whole lot more than a scrambling quarterback. He uses run-pass options with designed runs— runs designed for him, not his running backs. He's connecting on well over 60 percent of his passes, while he's gaining enough yards on the ground to be ranked with the top running backs. He is, as the opposing coaches say, that eleventh man to worry about.

And in case you still doubt the game has changed, ask coaches, players, and talking heads about defending against this new breed. Von Miller, Broncos linebacker, on Patrick Mahomes: "It was a whole other level." Bill Belichick: "If the ball is on their twenty-yard line, you've still got to defend the goal line against him." Titans offensive lineman Taylor Lewan: "Yeah, he's like really good at football." Pat McAfee, former punter and now analyst: "Patrick Mahomes is just an alien." Belichick on Lamar Jackson: "There's not another quarterback in the league like this." Patriots cornerback Stephon Gilmore: "He can outrun anybody on the front seven probably, and probably in the secondary too." Ex-Ravens, now Rams safety Eric Weddle: "Russell Wilson's playing out of his mind right now." Hall of Famer Troy Polamalu on Jackson and the new breed of QB: "I don't think we've seen anything like him...But [now]...there's a lot of quarterbacks that really are true dual threats that can throw the ball [and] that can run the ball."

The accolades and admiration go on and on. From teammates and from opponents, especially the ones who've just been beaten by this new style of play.

That's a pretty solid case that the game is changing. Or is it?

Is it the individual talents of great athletes, something we've always had—guys with big arms, or guys who use brute force, or guys who read defenses, or guys who have pinpoint accuracy, or guys who inspire their teams, even guys who can run or pass or both and make defenses crazy? Or is it a trend line toward a new era in the game of professional football? *Here's an irreverent answer: What difference does it make?*

Whether the game itself is changing may not matter. The guys we're seeing are *game-changers*. They can change individual games with their unique skills. But for that to result in a transformational change in the pro game, the coaches have to embrace the change. Do they? Will they? Why? Why not?

When old style meets new style, something has to give

If college-style offensive schemes, mobile quarterbacks, and a wide-open game work, why don't we change even faster? Because, as ironic as it seems, success often leads to complacency. *I know what works.* Until it doesn't. No matter how different, exciting, bold, game-changing players who come out of college may be, change isn't up to them. Change on an NFL team doesn't start with players; it starts with the coaches. If coaches, or any leaders in any endeavor, have had success with one way of doing things, they tend to stick with it. Often way too long.

Change is hard. Especially if you've had success.

If, as we've seen, coaches lose their jobs when their old ways of coaching sputter, why don't they change, or try to change, before they get the pink slip? Some are stubborn. *I'm smart. I know what I'm doing. Look at my record.* Some are too old. *I've always done it this way. I'm not chasing some fad.* And some just don't know how. *Huh?* That's not just me saying it. It's gurus with much fancier degrees than I have.

Trying to explain that phenomenon is the basis of a research project and paper published by, of all places, the Harvard Business School (in their *Working Knowledge* publication). Three academic scholars (armchair quarterbacks, it's safe to say) explored the parallels between business leaders who are reluctant to change in the face of business reversals and NFL coaches who have the same it-can't-be-me affliction. Their work delves into why business bosses get replaced after weak earnings reports and the NFL seems to get rid of coaches every December. Hint: It is not just to send them home to spend the holidays with their families.

We spoke with Harvard Business School professor Boris Groysberg, who along with two researchers, Evan Hecht and Abhijit Naik, wrote the article "What Football Firings Teach Managers About Staying Relevant." In it they refer to "Black Monday," the day after the NFL regular season ends, the day the coaches are given their pink slips. The authors point to the six casualties of 2018 and draw parallels to the fate of executives in various industries. Not only are the business world and sports world equally impatient for results, but the time each allows for success keeps getting shorter. In sports it can be one losing season. In business it can be a quarter or two with no dividends. In an age of increased reliance on metrics—we can measure everything—coaches and business execs are sitting on hot seats. Granted they're plush, leather, gold-trimmed hot seats, but they're getting hotter every year. As the article authors say, "It is more important than ever for managers to make increased efforts to stay relevant and protect against skill obsolescence." They suggest that business managers study what they call the "NFL coaching carousel."

I agree with everything Groysberg and his colleagues conclude. And I've added some color and evidence from my own observations—Harvard with a dash of Billick (Brigham Young University, '77).

Groysberg and Billick agree that certain managers/coaches/leaders do keep up impressive results by "adapting and staying relevant, while others do not." The Harvard prof and his colleagues created a model to analyze the connection between a coach's time on the job and effectiveness in the NFL, from 2000 to 2015, using winning percentage as the key measure. They factored in many variables, including the following: (1) coach tenure, (2) player quality (somewhat subjective but, due to data, pretty quantifiable), (3) team salary (not an absolute, but a good indicator), and (4) injuries vs. active players. The bottom line: The peak for a head coach is six years. Well, guess what? Check out the actual tenures of coaches. Either they get the boot after about six years or their performance drops and they ride on past glory for a while longer... but arguably should've gotten the boot. Up to year six, it's the opposite. As the coach notches more seasons, team records tend to improve... until they hit a ceiling (postseason appearances, division titles, and sometimes Super Bowls). After that, on average, most coaches— not all—tend to head south on the data curve. At that point, fans, sportswriters, and most importantly team owners get impatient.

Statistically, they all have pretty good reasons for that impatience. On average, winning percentages for all coaches combined for the first half of their tenures were 15 percent higher than in the second half of their tenure. The authors called this, appropriately, "the second-half tenure penalty." A drop of 15 percent is kind of the equivalent of a 15-yard penalty on the field, a big setback.

What about coaches who stay longer vs. those who don't? Again, no surprises. Super Bowl winners get to stay longer—an average of ten-plus seasons—as do coaches who make the postseason, even if they don't get to the big game. And neither group incurs as drastic a second-half decline. Conversely, non–Super Bowl coaches, short-tenured coaches, and first-timers get hit with the biggest penalties—losing seems to lead to more losing.

Then there are those coaches who hardly suffer from the penalty at all and have long tenures, ten or more seasons with one team, and seem to keep winning. The best ones "stay consistent and win over long periods of time due to exceptional management skills." It looks like the same skills that coaches need to stay current are the ones that business managers need. Otherwise, both become casualties, clinging to past methods long after they stop working.

So when we look at Andy Reid, we see a guy who won with Donovan McNabb at the Eagles but not with his next few quarterbacks. He could have concluded, *Hey, my way works, I just haven't found the next right guy.* But the team got impatient and he got fired, which may have been a good thing. Nothing clears your mind like sitting on the couch wondering where your next job will come from. Andy landed the head coaching job with the Chiefs and got paired up with a young quarterback who didn't fit the old pocket-passer mold. Did he try to reshape Patrick Mahomes, or did he adapt, taking what he had in Mahomes and building around him? The 2020 Super Bowl trophy answers that question. Same goes for Pete Carroll, who took a too-short but mobile QB and remade the Seahawks and maybe the entire definition of a franchise quarterback.

The best case study of all may be John Harbaugh, who had won a Super Bowl with a classic drop-back QB in Joe Flacco, then stalled when Flacco stalled. But thanks to Ozzie Newsome, Eric DeCosta, and the good fortune of the final pick of the first round of the '18 draft, he had the exciting but unknown quantity of Lamar Jackson to come in from the bench. Did he jam Lamar into a Joe scheme? No. He modified on the fly, halfway through the season, and Jackson led the team back to the playoffs for the first time since 2014. Then Harbaugh and DeCosta did a total offensive rehab in the off-season. And the team went 14-2. John didn't let previous success stand in the way of change.

You'd think the annual December purge, combined with the turnaround success of those who are willing to embrace open-mindedness, would lead more coaches to pry their minds open. You'd think...

But more is undergoing change than coaches, offensive schemes, and designed runs. A lot more. Our whole definition of what constitutes a promising quarterback is changing. What we thought we knew we are now rethinking. To put a twist on former secretary of defense Donald Rumsfeld's "known knowns"—facts—"known unknowns"—what to look for—and "unknown unknowns"—where the surprises lie—we're finally taking a hard look at the latter category. That's where we will redefine who to draft, when, and why.

Mobility—weapon or vulnerability?

You can't have a running quarterback, at least not for long, because he's going to get hurt. He's running in the open field, being chased by guys who are bigger than he is, who are going to hit him from someplace he can't see—behind him, next to him, and maybe two or three of those big guys at once—and they're going to fall on top of him. And they're going to break him into pieces. Proof: Robert Griffin III, Heisman Trophy winner from Baylor, came into the NFL and the Washington Redskins and set them on fire in his rookie year with breathtaking scrambles and runs—815 total yards on the ground, including one run for 76 yards—while completing his passes at over 65 percent, for 3,200 yards and 20 TDs. But he got hit in game thirteen against the Ravens, by Haloti

Ngata, six foot four and 338 pounds, and suffered an LCL sprain. RG3 returned two games later (maybe he shouldn't have) and then went into the wild card game. He got hit again, came out again, went back in again (definitely shouldn't have), and limped off the field with a torn LCL, ACL, and meniscus that had to be reconstructed altogether. He has not been the same since. Ironically, he's now the backup to Lamar Jackson at the Ravens. Hot career as an open-field runner. Done after a season or two at most. Other run-prone QBs like Michael Vick, Randall Cunningham, and Donovan McNabb each lost a season to injury. Running is dangerous. Case closed.

Not so fast. Classic drop-back quarterbacks Tom Brady, Ben Roethlisberger, Peyton Manning, and Aaron Rodgers each lost at least a season due to injury. Nobody likes to run less than Brady (he throws the ball twenty times more than he runs!). Okay, maybe Big Ben likes to run less and is even slower on his feet. All of these guys are pocket quarterbacks. And none of us can forget the hit to Redskins star Joe Theismann when he got clobbered by Giants Lawrence Taylor and Harry Carson on *Monday Night Football*. We all watched on national television when Joe's right leg almost literally crumbled, a compound fracture of the tibia and fibula. It was ugly and career-ending. And he had been standing in the pocket.

Here's what Joe Flacco said about his opponent, run-threat Colin Kaepernick, before the 2013 Super Bowl: "Quarterbacks like [Kaepernick] are eventually going to have to become mostly pocket passers to survive in this league." The Ravens won the Super Bowl so maybe Flacco was right. But Kaepernick almost single-handedly led a second-half comeback that nearly took the win away, so maybe Flacco was witnessing the league's and his own future being written.

Is the Game Changing?

Which is it? Mobile is dangerous or mobile escapes injury? The pocket is protection or the pocket is an easy target? Up to this point we've been going by so-called data that was largely anecdotal. A smaller guy gets hit by a bigger guy or guys while he's in motion and vulnerable. What looks dangerous must be dangerous. Too much risk to a franchise quarterback and his team. The data hasn't been data because conventional wisdom was that an NFL quarterback should be a pocket passer. From Bart Starr to Joe Montana to John Elway to Tom Brady. Finally, we're looking at the real numbers harder, more closely, and without the historical prejudice.

Here is some real data from John Verros of Sports Info Solutions, which gathers and analyzes numerical data in multiple sports and, by the way, is co-owned by the wonk of all sports wonks, baseball stats guru Bill James. Now Verros, a young wonk himself, has actually studied the issue of running quarterback risk like a mathematician or statistician instead of a craggy, cranky veteran scout sharing years of sage assessments. *Running QBs run into trouble.... Long runs make short careers.* Verros determined that the actual, documented risk of injury on a designed run is 1 in 236 plays. What about a scramble? Admittedly, it's a higher risk; the QB gets injured once in every 91.7 "events"—that is, knockdown, sack, designed run, or scramble. For comparison, that supposedly much safer pocket passer gets injured once in...92.5 such events. That's a 0.8 difference. In a game that is physical and therefore carries danger, no matter what position you play or how you play it. Even placekickers get hurt. But some plays must be more dangerous than others, right? For sure. And Verros determined that a "knockdown"—when a quarterback is taken to the ground while passing, in the middle of the throw—is "the most dangerous play type, because the quarterback is unprepared for getting hit while focusing down the field to attempt a pass." That means he could be hit while in the pocket or rolling out or mid-scramble, still looking for a receiver. In contrast, Verros says, "In a designed run, the QB can prepare his mindset of being the ball carrier, such as planning ahead for where he plans on going and what he may encounter during a play." In a knockdown, Verros's stats show the quarterback can get hurt once in a little more than 57 events. Of course, to be true to the stats, you have to factor in that the quarterback who likes to run will run more often, so he exposes himself more times during a game. It would seem so. But…

Russell Wilson has been playing for the Seahawks for eight seasons and 143 games—128 regular-season games plus 15 playoff games. And Russell Wilson, who likes to run, either as a called play or a scramble, has played in what percentage of those games? One hundred percent. In two full seasons, Patrick Mahomes has played in thirty regular-season games and five playoff games. He missed two games in 2019 with a dislocated kneecap…but he never missed a practice during those two weeks. In a half season and one full season, Lamar Jackson has started twenty-two regular-season games and two playoff games, missing one game in 2019 because the Ravens had wrapped up the division and rested him. And nobody, nobody in the NFL, ever ran more than Lamar. Okay, on the other side of the ledger, Cam Newton suffered shoulder and foot injuries, the latter of which came on a sack, not a run, and now Cam seems to have his future in question. Permanently? We don't know. After nine years, he could be as beat up as, say…Andrew Luck, the number one pick from the year after Cam, called the best pocket passer since Peyton Manning, who just retired from football because he didn't want to get beat up anymore. As a former college QB, NFL backup, Super Bowl head coach, and now offensive coach at the Vikings, Gary Kubiak, who has seen every kind of quarterback, says in his veteran wisdom, "There's an old saying: If your guy sits in the same spot seven and a half yards behind center, the guy will get hit and get hurt."

How do these running quarterbacks survive relatively unscathed? Partly by being in motion. It's easier to hit a statue standing still in one place, or even in a six-yard box, than a moving target. That's how Ben Roethlisberger got hit in a season-ending elbow injury. And how Drew Brees had his thumb dislocated. A lot of running quarterbacks played baseball in high school and even later. Russell Wilson played Minor League Baseball. Patrick Mahomes didn't decide which sport to pick until after his sophomore year of college. Baseball players have to learn to slide. They turn short hits into singles, singles into doubles, and they steal bases. Sliding helps quarterbacks. So does running out of bounds. It may be counterintuitive to a guy on the run who sees more daylight, but it can be taught. Just look at the difference between Lamar Jackson in 2018 versus 2019. In 2018, he ran for any opening. In 2019 he ran, and then often ran out of bounds. In 2019 he gained 1,206 yards, more yards per carry than in the previous year.

Verros looked at the 2018 Ravens as a perfect case study because in one season they used a pocket passer, Joe Flacco, *and* a mobile quarterback, Lamar Jackson. When Jackson was on the field, the Ravens, as a team—not just Lamar vs. Joe—averaged two more yards per carry than when Flacco was on the field. Why? Because defenses relied heavily on six defensive back personnel (dime package) to try to contain the speed of Lamar. And that created an opportunity for other runners. Ravens running back Gus Edwards had a great year, thanks to Lamar Jackson just being on the field. Opposing defenses also played less man coverage with Lamar at QB (31 percent to 43 percent), and blitzed slightly less often, leaving him more time to find receivers in a pass play. Advantage: mobile quarterback.

Still, the skepticism of the mobile quarterback persists. Still, conventional wisdom rules. It's almost as if being a successful runner makes you a target for criticism, while being a lousy or at least reluctant runner makes you a better NFL quarterback. Now, that's illogical. That's what's wrong with conventional wisdom. It's old instead of open-minded.

The data, the real data, is the compilation of play-by-play, game-by-game results, comps of run-pass-option quarterbacks versus pocket passers, actual hits, actual injuries, actual games played and games missed, then extrapolated into conclusions. And the conclusion is…drum roll…running quarterbacks are successful. So are pocket quarterbacks. It's not significantly statistically better to be one or the other. It's statistically better to be a better runner than other running quarterbacks. It's statistically better to be a better pocket passer than other pocket passers. And it's statistically better to combine the two skills when you need to. In other words, the game is wide open to talent, pure superior talent. And that is a change. The prejudice of the pocket passer over the runner is subsiding—maybe slowly, but it is on its way out of town. That doesn't mean mobile quarterbacks are the only way to go for the future. It's that now we finally recognize how effective they can be, for an entire career, not for a fleeting moment. Good is good. It's a meritocracy…almost.

The B-word

There's another element that is changing in the game; this one more delicate to deal with. The color—that is, ethnicity—of quarterbacks. And what color has meant over the years. Black quarterbacks have been around the college and professional game for decades. Marlin Briscoe was the first to start for a pro team, the Denver Broncos. James "Shack" Harris was early in the game and one of the first to go on to become a team executive. Warren Moon, of the Houston Oilers, was the first Black Hall of Fame QB. And Doug Williams of the Redskins was the first to win a Super Bowl. But quarterbacks of color have been few and far between. Until recently.

There has been a stigma, unstated, or stated in euphemisms, that relegated those quarterbacks to a different status than their white counterparts.

For years, Black quarterbacks were characterized as runners more than passers. Another preconceived notion, accurate or not, about the notable speed and agility of Black athletes overall, tended to be applied to quarterbacks too. Sometimes the compliments were veiled criticisms. Terms like "dual-threat," instead of suggesting the guy could do two things, not just one, meant he was really a run-first guy who maybe wasn't quite good enough as a pocket passer to be an NFL-level quarterback. Before he came out of Clemson to enter the 2017 draft, Deshaun Watson said in an interview with Bleacher Report, "People think, 'Oh, he's a Black quarterback, he must be dual-threat.' People throw around that word all the time. It's lazy... People have their opinions, and I can't change them. But I can show them what they're missing." And he has done just that.

Even the word "athletic" has sometimes been code to suggest a player was more physically adept and perhaps less of a thinker. And quarterback is the ultimate thinking position on the field.

The progress of Black quarterbacks has been historically too slow, from high school to college, and then from college to the pros. But eventually, every coach, every team, every fan simply wants to win. So the best players emerge, regardless of height, weight, ethnicity, style of play, or style of hair. It's happening. The best are just the best.

James "Shack" Harris has had not only personal experience as a quarterback of color, but also a perspective from the front offices of NFL teams. After his playing days, he went on to become an executive, first at the Ravens—where I worked with him—as director of pro personnel, then in Jacksonville as VP of player personnel, and later with the Lions as senior personnel executive. Harris also was on the NFL committee on college relations. I asked him for his take on current quarterbacks and the issue overall today. Looking back, he said, "Vince Young was the last QB that had the type of talent Lamar Jackson has. The problem was, Tennessee tried to make Vince Young more of a pocket QB than he was." Have things changed in that regard? He says that today, "Coaches just want to win. That part is color-blind. But we [football] still think of QBs a certain way and are now just getting to the point we think of Black quarterbacks the same way we do other quarterbacks." The bottom line is winning. That's the most valid reason to change anything, always—that it works. But Harris adds a note of caution, likely based on experience. "I'm not sure we don't still have a certain way we look at Black quarterbacks." Even if winning ultimately rules, the residual views linger.

Personally, I played probably more quarterbacks of color than any other NFL coach—Warren Moon, Randall Cunningham, Tony Banks, Anthony Wright, Steve McNair, Troy Smith, Jeff Blake. I didn't play them because I was crusading. I played them because we wanted to win, and each guy, at the time, gave my team the best chance to win. You can say, "Gee, coach, some of them were a lot better than others." That's the way it should be. Search for winning talent, not color of talent.

Football IQ—whatever that means...

With the undeniable multiple talents of the Vicks, Newtons, Wilsons, Watsons, Mahomeses, and Jacksons, the game is changing and in a good way. It forces us to reevaluate the way we evaluate, to look for the unknown unknowns—all the attributes we want in a quarterback, not just the physical skills and performance data, but how smart he is, how good a decision-maker he'll be, how fast his mind processes information. SATs don't tell us much. The infamous Wonderlic test at the Combine has proven to be a non-wonder. A lot of coaches have a rule: Don't draft anyone who gets less than 20 out of 50 on the Wonderlic. But Dan Marino, one of the winningest quarterbacks in history, got a 16. On the other hand, Ryan Leaf had a 27 and Johnny Manziel got a 32. So, that tells us... nothing. And IQ? Well, what's that? In fact, the experts even came up with a term to make up for what we didn't know—"football IQ." It's another code phrase or euphemism, not only with racial overtones but with jock overtones too. Football IQ is a catchall, almost defined by what it *isn't*—it isn't standardized test IQ, or academics like math, science, and language. It sort of means, these guys are smart in ways that don't seem smart by the usual measurements. A kind of fast reaction, rapid information processing, combat mentality. They just know where the football is going or should go. Or they can see how defenders are lined up to come at them. Or they can pick up a blitzing linebacker out of the corner of their eye. But maybe they can't divide fractions or conjugate verbs. *Or...*they grew up in circumstances that rewarded skills and abilities developed in backyards and gyms, on courts, on rinks, and on fields: not in classrooms, not from conventional education, but learned in other ways that show they may be smarter than all the rest of us. Finally, after years of bad tests, educational and psychological experts are developing better evaluators of what makes someone "smart." AIQ, or Athletic Intelligence Quotient, is an attempt to explore and quantify the difference between knowledge—the accumulation of facts—and intelligence, the ability to process and act. (More on that in the last chapter.)

But the old perspectives are hard to shake. Even Warren Moon, who had to constantly prove and re-prove himself as a quarterback, complimented Patrick Mahomes on his MVP with these words: "He's special, but does it allow more opportunity for more African American quarterbacks? Yes, because that's kind of our game." Moon clearly expects the battle for legitimacy of the mobile-style quarterback to go on. The reality is, it's here. And it works. Sports is inching toward being what it should be: the ultimate meritocracy. If you're good, you're good.

The most important metric of all: moving the football, no matter how

Run. Pass. Hand off. Just move the ball. If there is one clear lesson we're learning from the "change" in the game, it's an old lesson: All that matters is moving the ball down the field, whether you run, or pass, or hand off, or your defense intercepts and runs the ball back for a TD. Arm strength, passes attempted, completion percentage, yards gained per play, even interceptions…none of them matter if you can't move the ball into the red zone and then score. If you can, then it really doesn't matter how you do it. Sure, there are lots of indicators, but if the quarterback does it in the conventional ways and it works, it works. If the quarterback does it unconventionally and it works, it works. If there's a lesson to extrapolate, it's to look at how many yards the quarterback manages to gain, one way or another. And how consistently he does it.

Even when it looks like something can't be done, some guys can do it, somehow. Pete Carroll on Russell Wilson: "There's so many plays where I'm thinking, 'Russ, get down!' And all of a sudden he pops out and he's still going, and…he finds somebody and makes a twenty-yard play." Somehow he does it. Mahomes's arsenal includes long throws (he's an ex-baseball pitcher), side-arm passes, no-look passes, even left-handed passes, and plenty of scrambles. Somehow he just does it. Lamar Jackson on his own play: "I just had to take what the defense gave me, and sometimes I had to run…I just had to move the sticks." *I just had to move the sticks.* That says it all. That's the game of football.

That's true today and it has been true for a long time. Look at the stats for 2019:

Jimmy Garoppolo threw for 3,978, ran for 62. Total: 4040 yards
Aaron Rodgers threw for 4,002, ran for 46. Total: 4,048 yards
Tom Brady threw for 4,057, ran for 34. Total: 4,091 yards

Patrick Mahomes threw for 4,031, ran for 218. Total: 4,249 yards

Lamar Jackson threw for 3,127, ran for 1,206. Total: 4,333 yards

Russell Wilson threw for 4,110 yards, ran for 342. Total: 4,452 yards

As mobile QBs, Wilson, Mahomes, and Jackson got there by relying on different tools, but their totals, all well over 4,000, are within a few yards of each other. Brady, Rodgers, and Garoppolo—pocket passers—got there by throwing a lot more than running but were all over 4,000 too. They all just moved the sticks.

For historical comparison, Brady had very similar 4,000-plus numbers in his last Super Bowl year of 2018. Peyton Manning relied on his arm in his last great year of 2014, throwing for 4,727 and racking up a negative 24 on the ground. Drew Brees won the Super Bowl after the 2009 season with 4,388 passing yards, 33 on the ground, for a total of 4,421. Dan Marino, in the 1985 season leading to his only Super Bowl appearance, threw for 4,137 and ran for a minus 24, a total of 4,113. At the lower end, John Elway in 1997, a Super Bowl year, had 3,635 in the air and 218 on the ground, for a total of 3,853. And Ben Roethlisberger in 2008, a Super Bowl year, threw for 3,301 and ran for 101: total 3,402.

It's clear that the total yards gained have increased over time. In the twenty-first century, 4,000-plus yards is the benchmark for a quarterback (250 yards per game over 16 games). So when we look at the new style of quarterback, we see guys who manage to make plays with their arms, their feet, and sometimes both on the same play. The point is, they just get it done somehow, someway, and that's the sign of a leader. It always has been. Just like it is in business or politics or the arts. Make it happen. Move the sticks.

So yes, the game is changing. The biggest change is that finally the evaluation of quarterbacks may not be tilted by *how* they gain yards but simply whether they do or not. When we're looking at the draft board, we ought to take a hard look at what the prospects did to just advance the ball, no matter how. Whatever works, works. Wide-open play, scrambling, pocket passes, bombs, designed runs, and high-scoring games. And by the way, fans love it.

The bottom-line factor—eyeballs mean dollars

The changing game has been good for the NFL in every way, especially the bottom line, which is, not to coin a pun, not to be discounted.

We can now watch games in a multitude of ways: in a stadium, at home on the couch, in a man or woman cave, in a sports bar, on the computer, on the phone, streaming or recorded, whole games or RedZone highlights. But we only watch if it's fun, if the game is exciting, with big plays, big surprises, and big, big scores.

How big? Well, in every year since 2010, the total points scored in the NFL season has been over 11,000. That jumped up from hovering in the 9,000 range in the 1990s. Analysts and experts say they like close, low-scoring games. Fans like TDs, high scores, and if possible, blowouts by their team. Higher scores mean they watch more. A lot more.

After a down year in television and cable ratings, maybe exacerbated by the national-anthem kneel-down issue, viewership on every kind of device continues to rise year after year, and sky-rocketed in 2018, up 65 percent on digital devices, 147 percent on phones alone, due in no small measure to the exciting, unpredictable, miraculous play of the new quarterbacks. In 2019, the year kicking off the NFL's centennial celebrations, TV viewership averaged 16.5 million per game, up 5 percent from the year before, which was up from the down year of 2017. A total of 180 million individual viewers watched at least one game in 2019. That's more than half the country! Of the top fifty events or shows aired on TV, NFL games owned forty-seven of those slots. What is staggering here is that the total mind-boggling numbers are people not in the stands—at home, in a car, in a bar, walking, talking, working, not at the game. Virtual fans vastly dwarf in-person numbers. But the NFL revenue is very real.

As of 2019, the NFL overall, as well as the individual teams, have seen record television and alternate-platform viewing revenue. And after the dip of a couple of years ago, in 2018 and 2019, in-person attendance rebounded. PSLs that were being relinquished were snapped up or held on to. Stadium sponsorships are back up. Suites are sold out. Ticket resales on Ticketmaster and StubHub soared. Stadium concessions—food, beer, merchandise—are selling like crazy. Parking lots around stadiums are full. Sports bars are coining money. Apps for viewing are being downloaded in record numbers. Premium cable packages are hot. And apparel—football jerseys—is through the roof. It's worth looking at whose jerseys sold best this past year. In November 2019, just before the end of the season, the number one selling jersey in America was not Tom Brady. It was not Aaron Rodgers. It was not Drew Brees. It was…Lamar Jackson. What is most significant about that is that we can expect a player's jersey to sell best in his team's home market, and it does. But Baltimore is one of the smaller markets in the NFL, so that means Lamar's jersey was being bought everywhere, which means fans were watching him everywhere, which drives viewership, which drives revenue. By the way, Tom Brady hardly suffered. In November he was number two and Patrick Mahomes was number three (from Kansas City, another smaller market), and Russell Wilson wasn't far back at number nine. And by the end of the season, Brady was back on top and Mahomes, after winning the Super Bowl, was a close second.

With or without packed stands, with or without TV ratings, as long as fans can get games on one device/screen/app or another, the NFL is minting money. So…is the game changing? Yes. Higher scoring. More big plays. Happy, big-spending fans. It's moneyball—not the statistics of sports but the bottom line of sports business.

How do we deal with the change? What, if anything, can we learn? Will we learn?

A short course in embracing change—or falling on your butt

Back to school—the Harvard study and the Billick School of Hard Knocks. There are some skills that successful coaches and managers adopt. Or, as I've seen over and over from the sidelines and from the booth, skills they refuse to adopt and then they find themselves out of work.

Adaptability—The NFL has evolved rapidly and substantially in recent years—resulting in higher scores—with rule changes, the use of sophisticated analytics, new offensive schemes, and more and more passing. The study's authors point to Patriots coach Bill Belichick as one who has embraced change instead of fighting it and achieved a long, long run of success. There's a lot of debate in the game about whether Bill Belichick is a coaching genius or a guy who got lucky enough to connect with Tom Brady. I've been in plenty of sports talk show debates—is he lucky or good or both? I'm not here to make the case for Belichick's Nobel Prize, but I will say he recognizes reality and adjusts and wins a lot. Belichick took a team that emphasized strong defense and a run-oriented offense, with a classic careful pocket passer at quarterback, and won three Super Bowls. And then, as the game morphed, he transformed them into a pass-happy offense, jumping from number twenty in the league in passing attempts to number five, and winning two more Super Bowls. Same quarterback, different strategy.

On the flip side, the coaches who refused to budge—who stuck with what worked long after it stopped working—are too numerous to list. But they include three-time Super Bowl winner Redskins coach Joe Gibbs (who was even brought back to Washington a second time but stalled again), Packers Super Bowl winner Mike McCarthy (whose stubbornness and clashes with Aaron Rodgers were fatal), and several more. Meanwhile, Sean Payton won a Super Bowl in 2009 using a fairly traditional offense but began to change with the addition of players with specific styles and skills, notably running back Alvin Kamara, whose speed and moves gained him almost 2,000 yards in a single season. Payton has benefited from the superior play of quarterback Drew Brees but is said to be studying and thinking ahead to a new approach post-Brees. He is unlikely to try to force-fit a new quarterback into a Brees mold, but rather to create an offense around the new guy, whatever that might entail.

The lesson is: Effective managers/coaches "adjust strategy based on team personnel," not the reverse, forcing new players into an old system.

Is the Game Changing?

Small advantages—Given the NFL's stated goal of parity (the worst teams get the highest draft picks and team salary caps) and the business world's playing-field levelers (stock market prices, quarterly reports, investor pressures, internet access to information), leveraging even the smallest edge can make a big difference in both endeavors. For instance, it could mean finding good players that have been discarded by other teams, often in order to stay under the salary cap. Bill Belichick is a master at getting mileage out of retreads. And the Patriots have been leaders in adopting analytics, hiring a Wall Street trader to study numbers (following the lead of their hometown baseball team, which did likewise during the *Moneyball* revolution). Even finding rule loopholes or opportunities can lead to one play that can win one game that can make or break a season—eligibility for a pass, taking a penalty on purpose, and more.

Little by little, NFL teams, and their owners, are investing in more analytical approaches to finding and exploiting those small advantages. Case in point, Paul DePodesta, since 2016 the Cleveland Browns chief strategy officer. (DePodesta is a Harvard econ graduate and an ex–college football player, with a résumé that includes working with Oakland A's manager Billy Beane on sabermetrics, aka moneyball.) How important is the "strategy" role with the team? Look up the front office of the Browns and after you get past the Haslam family owners, there's GM Andrew Berry, and then Paul. Coming out of baseball, where it can take years for players to develop from the minors to the big leagues, DePodesta knows well that the results of analysis take time to show themselves. All sports teams are impatient and NFL teams are no exception. Paul is determined to apply what he knows, the way he knows it: rethink, rebuild, and ultimately realize the benefits. In a press conference after the Browns hired Kevin Stefanski as their head coach, Paul said, "Analytics... [is] having sure frameworks to make decisions under uncertainty... Give you a better chance of being successful, whether that is drafting a player, hiring a coach, or calling a play..." When we asked him to expand on the comment about drafting a player, he said, "Analytics don't work by themselves. They work along with experience. And what you see in games and on film. And over time." Will pro football give Paul DePodesta time to make his "small advantages" add up and pay off? We'll see.

Business managers—that is, successful ones—do the same. They look for and take advantage of small advantages. Some can take the same personnel budget and make it go further than their competitors by hiring unconventionally—maybe by finding a semi-retired sales manager who knows all the customers. Or they may use data in unexpected ways—looking at travel or real estate patterns of a competitor to see who and what they're targeting. Or they may uncover lesser-known government programs and subsidies to gain tax breaks. Small advantages add up.

Collaborate with stakeholders—In football terms, that means making sure the team and the owners are with you, buying into your approach, whether you're winning or not. If they aren't, sooner or later you'll be packing (and more likely sooner). Andy Reid remade the Philadelphia Eagles from losers into winners, made them regulars in the playoffs, and then hit a dry spell. The players were split on Reid; pretty soon so was management. Reid was out. But he was good enough to be back in (and winning) in Kansas City. A similar story played out for Mike McCarthy, who had led the Packers to great success with Aaron Rodgers at quarterback. When the Rodgers-McCarthy marriage hit trouble, so did McCarthy. Like Reid, he is back, but will the lessons be learned? Reid bought in to change with the innovative, decide-on-the-fly style of Patrick Mahomes. Will McCarthy have an epiphany in his next life?

Will most coaches avoid the second-half penalty? In all likelihood, probably not. Remember, in football and in business, the "team" tends to become almost brand-new every few years. You have to have strong relationships and the skills to communicate with a constantly changing pool of talent, personalities, styles, and quirks. Similarly, in both football and business, the coaches/bosses tend to be older (forty to sixty years old), while the teams—young players or young MBAs—tend to be twenty to thirty. Sometimes coaches can adjust and communicate with new players and owners. Pete Carroll had two stints as an NFL head coach—at the Jets and the Patriots—before coming to Seattle, and the third time he has built relationships with young, double-threat quarterback Russell Wilson and the team's GM. Not everyone can do it. You have to swallow your ego a bit and say to yourself, maybe there's another way to do things. Maybe Carroll's eight years as a head coach at USC in between New England and Seattle, in the college culture that turns over even faster than the pros, gave him a crash course in adapting. As Kevin Stefanski told us, based on his experience and looking ahead to his challenges in Cleveland, as a coach—especially a head coach—you have to "just put your arm around a kid," be a combination of big brother, father, and shrink, yelling at some players, patting others on the back, treating all players fairly but not the same. It's no small challenge to try to shepherd fifty-some different guys all at once. Not to mention having to answer to owners who are a lot like demanding stockholders wanting to know why their dividends aren't bigger.

Outsourcing and using experts—Don't try to do it all yourself. You're not good at everything. Do use technology and science. It's there, it's rich, and ignoring it is running from solutions. Most important, find people who know what you don't know. Plenty in the business world learned this the hard way. When digital tech and online commerce emerged, the old guard kept waiting for the fad to fade. Instead it took over. Companies now know what we buy, when, where we are, how much we spend, even why we buy what we buy. Starbucks knows when you walk by and offers you a deal on your favorite drink. Expedia and Orbitz know where you like to vacation, what time of year, how much you spend, and based on your past travel, where you'd like to go next. Facebook knows your friends, family, hobbies, likes, dislikes, and political views. Twitter knows who you like and what you believe. Amazon knows what you read, watch, wear, and eat. And Google knows… well, everything. Any company that doesn't know about customer data, and how to use it, is fast becoming the next Sears.

The same goes for sports teams. Every pro team and plenty of college teams have analytics experts on board, whispering in coaches' ears in practice, during the games, even between plays. The Harvard guys point to Sean McVay and the Rams, who hired a person just to be a "clock management expert." The Raiders put an ex-NFL ref on staff to advise the coaches on whether to throw down the red challenge flag on a penalty. The Ravens have a young kid in the booth next to OC Greg Roman whose "go or don't go" advice on fourth down goes right into John Harbaugh's ear.

More and better data has led to some obvious changes in the game as well as some more subtle ones. First of all, better stats enable us to make better-informed draft picks...defensive player backpedal speed, lateral motion, blind-side quarterback protection, wide receiver separation, even injury history, and many more esoteric/nerdy numbers can all make for improved selections. As far as the game itself, analytics have had a profound impact: First, there's been an explosion of passing—thanks to the college ranks. More passing has meant higher scores, and not only do high scores win games, they make for exciting games, and, as the numbers show, more fans and more revenue, the NFL's true final score. So run-run-pass has given way to run-pass-pass. Or more run-pass options. Or plays that look like passes but turn into runs. Then there's third-down conversions. To a large extent, they've been replaced by going for more yards earlier and making another first down on first down or second down, which of course often comes from more passing or bolder run plays. Going for a first down on fourth down is no longer reserved for late-game desperation; now it's a reasonable option from almost any less-than-four-yard situation past midfield. Today, 60 percent of those plays succeed. That translates to longer time of possession. If you have the ball, that means the other team *doesn't* have the ball, so they can't score.

All driven by data. In fact, stats seem to have improved draft picks' success at every position...*but one.* Completion percentage, accuracy, arm strength all help push the best quarterback prospects to the top of the draft class. But no data seems to be able to help prognosticate which of those picked early, of the good ones, are likely to be the really good ones, the best of the best. *No one piece or set of data can make that prediction for quarterbacks...yet.* Data is not magic, but it gives us an edge, and edges can win ball games. If we use it right, of course. If we look for demonstrable trends and not glory moments. Collectively, used wisely, the data plus experience plus extrapolation can add up to a Q Factor.

Stay curious, keep learning—No matter how much they win, smart coaches keep learning and get coached themselves. They turn to other coaches or experts instead of only having conversations inside their own echo chamber. Belichick got advice from Jimmy Johnson and Urban Meyer—and baseball manager Tony La Russa and Celtics coach Brad Stevens. Maybe the genius of Belichick is tapping the genius of others. Several NFL coaches say they've studied the records and decisions of Andy Reid, Bill Cowher, Don Shula, Bill Parcells, and the legendary Vince Lombardi. I worked for 49ers maestro Bill Walsh and learned more at his side than in all my years of coaching up to and after that. I helped him write his book, and that was a tutorial for me on how to coach an NFL team. Since then, from the booth, I have watched the young coaches, the new schemes, the innovations, the contrarian decisions, and it's a weekly education in staying current. If you don't keep up, you're left behind. Again, go back to the business world: Toys "R" Us, RadioShack, Blockbuster, Kodak—all casualties of not keeping up. Smart bosses hire younger minds...and listen to them.

Be a tough grader—Look at the outcomes, the wins and losses, the profits and losses; don't make excuses, don't wait for miracles.

Results don't lie. So, how did our 2018 draft class QBs do in an era of change?

Obviously, Jackson did well. He's practically the poster boy for the new quarterback.

Mayfield is a pocket passer and he had good moments and not-so-good ones. Unfortunately he's dealing with another kind of change, his third head coach in as many seasons. We'll see.

Sam Darnold is a pocket guy who has been surrounded by a weak supporting cast. He has a solid coach so we may yet see his upside. He won't be a mobile quarterback but he could be a better drop-back passer than he's been.

Then there's Josh Allen, who definitely showed some promise as a bit of a hybrid, a pocket passer who can get out of trouble and who also has a daunting defense to keep opposing scores down, a great offensive weapon for any quarterback.

And there's Josh Rosen, the outlier, a promising pocket passer who has been saddled with a lousy team, a change of coach, a trade, another weak team, and now a very uncertain future.

Though the odds are the longest with Rosen, they can all succeed in the era of change. To state the obvious, they just have to move the sticks. No matter how. If the quarterback does it, he's on the plus side of 50-50. If he doesn't, he isn't. If the jury is still out, it won't be for long.

One more method for embracing change: what not to do

Imitation is the highest form of…suicide—The last method for adapting to change: Avoid the herd mentality. Invoke brutal objectivity. A lot of teams went into the 2020 draft looking for another Mahomes or Jackson or Wilson. And a lot of teams will come out with a guy who kinda runs well and kinda throws well but doesn't do either really well. And the teams will not be prepared to go all in on the changes required. As Greg Roman puts it, "People will move the athletic QB up the draft board because of the success of Lamar, but will make the mistake of not committing to the style of play that they need to." Roman even went out on a limb and offered a specific caution on the upcoming draft. "I don't know that Jalen Hurts [Alabama and Oklahoma] can be a starter and do what Lamar does, but he would be the perfect backup for a Lamar Jackson. Jalen could run a lot of what we do well." For Hurts's sake, let's hope Greg is wrong. Most teams will reach, or sell themselves on a hope and a wish. For the most part, they will get poor copies, not the real deal, as they always have. The NFL is littered with the next–Joe Montanas, or Tom Brady–esque quarterbacks, or Drew Brees–ish quarterbacks. And whoever else. And none of those supposed copies are still playing. Or if they are, not as the stars we hoped they'd be.

If the game is changing, what is it teaching us? What can we learn from what we've done wrong and occasionally right? How can we get above 50-50?

VII

Can We Do Better?

The 2018 draft class has proven to be an ideal laboratory for studying quarterbacks: who rises to the top of the draft, who has performed on the field, who is falling short, where the experts appeared to be right—and wrong. Most important, it has given us some insights to understand why. Everything is happening the way it always does. That is to say, we're being surprised. The top pick of the first round is a question mark. The last pick of the first round is the MVP. The guys in the middle are...in the middle. Except for one who may be heading for the door.

So, what, if anything, can we learn about who, when, and why to make our picks in the future? How do we get better at evaluating young quarterbacks *before* they get to the NFL, so that once they get there, they deliver? How do we spend our money and our opportunities more wisely? One thing we know is how much we don't know. Despite the reams of data available, despite all the analytics we can analyze, despite the years of experience/eyeballing/

instinct of pro scouts, despite their collective gut feel, radar, and clairvoyance, despite the best breakdowns by outside pundits and gurus, despite the Todd McShays and Mel Kipers, despite the ex-players and ex-coaches (like me), despite fantasy football and Vegas odds, we're still not as good at predicting success as we could be. And we should be. How do we use the tools we have more effectively? How do we see past our blind spots? How do we separate the good information from the bad? What can we learn from our misses and our occasional hits? How do we project instead of just hope? *How do we get better?*

The tools/information/clues are there…if we use them better. Even a little better, even 2 or 3 or 5 percent, can translate to a little more success, and a little more success may mean one more touchdown or one more win, which could put a team in the wild card round, and that could lead to the divisional playoffs, and that could mean the Super Bowl. That's how important a little better is. If, instead of picking quarterbacks at 50-50, it was 51-49 or 55-45, it would have profound impact on the game, lots of games, maybe even the biggest game. Think of it off the football field. (There's a whole world out there that isn't playing football.) If the board of directors of a public company is able to find and pick a slightly better CEO, one who has even a fraction more foresight, a tiny bit better grasp of the opposition, faster reaction time when under pressure, the ability to scramble when the competition closes in, that can make all the difference in the fate of the company. It can be the difference between a dividend or a loss at year end. It can mean more investors investing. It can mean knocking off a market leader. That's what a little better can mean.

If the game is changing, we better change with it

Throw away any single piece of data. Completion percentage? Interesting but not by itself. Average yards per pass? Not by itself. Even interceptions don't tell enough without context. Context is actual play, actual games, actual footage. Miles of it.

Throw away the "tried and true" methods of picking. They're tried but not true. The draft won't make picks for you, with the cream rising to the top. Draft order doesn't prove anything except that the order is often wrong.

Throw away the school level or style of play. Small-school quarterbacks don't make it in the NFL...except when they do. West Coast offenses don't translate to the pros...except when they do. Mobile quarterbacks don't succeed as much as pocket passers... except when they do.

Throw away the old quarterback guides. Height, school, IQ, "look." They're not wrong. They're not right. They're largely irrelevant or out of date.

Throw away the height thing. *Quarterbacks have to be six foot three or more.* Bull. But that's a sure way to draft a tall bust. And pass up a shorter Hall of Famer.

Throw away the old intelligence measurements—GPAs, SATs, and, by all means, the Wonderlic test used by NFL teams at the Combine. Most tests have been designed to see how much information—facts, figures, language—we can provide on demand. They have not been designed to measure ability to process information and make decisions; that is, to think. That doesn't mean we shouldn't try to figure out if a quarterback is "smart," but we should first figure out what "smart" is.

And please throw away "he looks like a quarterback." In baseball, they used to say that about pitchers. "They," of course, were old, tobacco-chewing AAA road warriors who could just tell when a major league pitcher came along. Except they were wrong a lot. Quarterbacks don't look a certain way. Okay, they all smile and fist-pump after a touchdown.

If we keep reusing the old bromides, the quarterback clichés, we're sure to keep picking at a 50-50 rate, at best. This is one case where recycling isn't the answer.

The Insteads

In place of the throwaways, we have to use more objective, more open-minded, fresher thinking. Some of it is common sense that maybe we ignored. Some of it is new thinking. All of it is based on what we actually see and know, not what we wish for.

Instead of single metrics, only metrics in context

The 2018 draft class and the cumulative wisdom of past classes have taught us that data is valuable, but not in isolation. We have to look at and use the information we have more objectively, more dispassionately, more in combination than in a vacuum. Look at the numbers—completion percentage, yards gained, TDs to INTs—but view them in the context of each other. And the word "view" is key. Really view/review/study them. That means the tape, film, video, digital files—the record, in motion, of what really happened. Data doesn't play football. A guy does. Data doesn't complete a pass. A guy does. Watch how he does it. Over and over. There is no such thing as watching too much tape. The tape alone will show you a great play. Or a lousy one. But the tape plus the numbers will tell you more. The numbers will tell you how often he does something. The tape will tell you *how* he does it.

As explained earlier, the only good data is data we can project from; that is, trends/patterns/directions, not instances. And the best data is data in combination with other data. Completion percentage is more telling when measured under pressure, like when the QB is being blitzed. And still better when it becomes a pattern, year after year. How did he do from his first to his second season to his third? But that data is best when compared to the tapes showing the reality of a game. Lots and lots of game tapes. How is his footwork when he's being chased? What does his release look like? Does he see the open man when the first read falls apart? Tape, tape, and more tape. Film, film, and more film. Video truth. Don't stop watching until you see a trend. If it's a good trend, keep this guy in the running. If it's not, scratch him. In spite of any single number that may look good.

Really? Do the old vets believe in that too? We asked Gary Kubiak, whose quarterback credentials are a mile long, "Gary, how do you evaluate prospective quarterbacks?" He gave us a two-word answer: "Watching film." That's it? Yup. Not just watching, but watching to compare to the data. He says, "I was old school until fifteen years ago," but he's become "a big believer in analytics" and says now you have to "grow with it, lean on it, listen to it." His litmus test is "watching film" to see if the analytics show up on it.

Instead of the tried and true, find the real truth

Instead of hoping the draft will find talent for us, we have to find it ourselves. A lot of old pros believe the draft process itself pushes the best talent to the top, and the job of a team is just to maneuver and trade draft picks to climb up the ladder and increase your chances of getting that best guy. The draft process is the cumulative information of each prospect's college career—where he played, his stats—plus the evaluation at the Combine, plus the views of scouts, plus the draft wizards in the media, plus the relative needs of each team. All that information and momentum and popular wisdom ought to push the best talent to the top. Does it happen that way? Does reality follow "ought to"? We took a hard look at the results.

Two decades, over 200 quarterbacks. In the last twenty years, over 268 quarterbacks have been taken in the NFL draft. How did we do? No shock: no better than 50-50. The real questions will be why, when, and what can we do to improve that? I looked at the picks as (1) successful, (2) moderately successful—backups, (3) still too early to tell, and (4) busts. I only put the "bust" label on first-rounders, since later picks carry lower expectations. Admittedly my evaluation is subjective, but so is most of the selection process, at least until recently.

1998: This was the Peyton Manning draft, but also the Ryan Leaf draft, the definition of 50-50. The next group fell into the moderately successful bucket—Charlie Batch (number 60), Brian Griese (number 91), and Matt Hasselbeck (number 187)—backups and sometimes starters, largely "system" QBs or game managers, hardly a compliment.

*　　*　　*

1999: This was a colossal bust year, with the first and third picks—Tim Couch and Akili Smith—sandwiching Donovan McNabb at number two, the only one who had a solid career. Then came the eleven and twelve picks of Daunte Culpepper to the Vikings and Cade McNown to the Bears. Culpepper had a moderately successful career surrounded by Hall of Famers in Randy Moss and Chris Carter. McNown didn't.

2000: The busts of 1999 led to a QB-fear year. The only first-rounder was Chad Pennington at eighteen, the ultimate system QB who had an average arm and athletic ability but good field intelligence. Let's not forget that this was also the year Tom Brady was missed by almost everyone and not taken until number 199.

2001: Like the previous year, there was only one QB taken in the first round: Michael Vick, number one overall. Drew Brees was technically a second-round pick, but it was with the number thirty-two overall pick since a team had forfeited a first-round draft choice. Two out of two is a good year for quarterback picks.

2002: Quarterback caution should have continued, but due to team "need," the dangerous motivator, it did not. Three QBs were taken in the first round. David Carr was the first overall pick, and Joey Harrington was the third. Neither lived up to their draft position. Patrick Ramsey was the last pick of the first round, taken by Steve Spurrier and the Redskins. Probably the best quarterback in this draft was the eighty-first pick: Josh McCown, the classic system QB, lasted sixteen years in the NFL with nine different teams.

2003: If need was a factor the year before, it was a demand in '03. Carson Palmer was the first overall pick and had a solid career with the Bengals and Cardinals. Byron Leftwich was number seven and went to Jacksonville, while Kyle Boller went at nineteen to the Ravens (yes, me), and Rex Grossman was taken at twenty-two by the Bears, all less-than-average careers. At best, a 25-75 year.

2004: Maybe it was the law of averages: After a bad year, this one was pretty good. Eli Manning was the number one overall pick to the Chargers, and Philip Rivers went at number four to the Giants (then they swapped when Manning said he wouldn't go to San Diego). Both have gone on to potential Hall of Fame careers. Ben Roethlisberger was picked at eleven by the Steelers and also has had a Hall of Fame career. J. P. Losman went at twenty-two to Buffalo but had only one year as a starter. That flipped the outcome to 75-25.

2005: This was a solid follow-up year with Alex Smith number one overall to San Francisco and future Hall of Famer Aaron Rodgers at number twenty-four. Next was number twenty-five, Jason Campbell, with a nine-year, five-team backup career. Ryan Fitzpatrick of Harvard was the last QB taken in the draft, in the seventh round at number 250, and "Fitzmagic" has had a fifteen-year career with eight different teams.

2006: Big bust year, period. Vince Young went at number three and Matt Leinart at number ten, both disappointments. Jay Cutler was probably the most successful pick, at number eleven, but he had a checkered career at best.

*   *   *

2007: An even bigger bust. JaMarcus Russell was the number one overall (and maybe the number one overall bust in the NFL ever), and Brady Quinn at twenty-two went to the Browns to continue their bad luck at drafting QBs.

2008: After two bad years, this one was solid, maybe solid-plus. Matt Ryan went at number three to the Falcons, while Joe Flacco was taken at eighteen by the Ravens. Ryan has been a very good starter his entire career, and Flacco was a solid player with flashes of brilliance and a Super Bowl ring and MVP.

2009: Another less-than-sterling year, with a one-out-of-three hit ratio. Matthew Stafford, number one overall, has had a good career with the Lions (but not a great supporting cast). Mark Sanchez, the number five pick, took the Jets to the AFC Championship game, but from then on has been a letdown. And Josh Freeman disappointed big time at number seventeen with Tampa Bay.

2010: The bust streak goes on. Sam Bradford was number one overall, showed signs of potential, but couldn't stay healthy. Tim Tebow was the twenty-fifth pick, but was a case study in the importance of skill emphasis in the NFL. A good-throwing quarterback who also has some athletic abilities brings an added asset, but an athlete-first who has some ability to throw has a limited future in the pro game.

2011: This was one of the more interesting QB draft classes. Cam Newton went at number one, despite some worry he was a risk, having only started one year at Auburn. But his one year was an incredible year: He won the Heisman Trophy over Andrew Luck by throwing for 30 TDs to 7 INTs and having a 66 percent completion rate. After Newton, there was a stampede for QBs, from Jake Locker at number eight to Blaine Gabbert at ten to Christian Ponder at twelve. All were thought to be second-rounders, but need took over and they got scooped up early, way too early. All ultimately failed in the NFL. But two players taken early in the second round, Andy Dalton and Colin Kaepernick, had okay-to-good careers, Dalton as longtime starter with the Bengals, and Kaepernick leading the 49ers to a Super Bowl (before having a rough aftermath and endless controversy).

2012: This year looked like a gold mine, with four quarterbacks taken in the first round. At number one, Andrew Luck was as close to being a sure thing as we'd seen. Right behind him was Robert Griffin III (RG3). Luck lived up to his promise and his name, while RG3 had a spectacular rookie year followed by a near career-ending injury. Ryan Tannehill went at number eight to the Dolphins and had an up-and-down career, probably bust-worthy, until 2019, when he was traded to the Titans, came in at game six, and racked up a spectacular 70 percent completion, 22 TD to 6 INT performance, and took them to the playoffs. By the way, he replaced first-round bust Marcus Mariota. And if '12 was supposed to be a gold mine, let's not forget the nugget that most teams missed—Russell Wilson, taken in the third round at number seventy-five. He outperformed all five taken ahead of him. The clues were there but were ignored. Failure to extrapolate.

2013: This was a long-overdue gun-shy year, but not gun-shy enough. After years of first-round overreaches, this year saw only one quarterback taken. E. J. Manuel went to Buffalo at number sixteen, and his career never materialized as a starter.

2014: An oops year. Oops, three QBs were drafted in the first round but none should have been. Blake Bortles went at number three to Jacksonville; the Browns wasted their number twenty-two on Johnny Manziel ("Johnny Football"—really?); Teddy Bridgewater went as the last pick of the round to the Vikings. Teddy's career had a late upturn when he filled in for the injured Drew Brees at the Saints, winning seven games in 2019. Two of the better picks this year came in the second round with Derek Carr (great stats, not enough wins in Oakland) and Jimmy Garoppolo (Brady understudy who took San Francisco to the Super Bowl in 2019).

2015: A cautious but unsuccessful year. Only two quarterbacks were taken but they were number one and number two, Jameis Winston and Marcus Mariota, and both range from so-so to near busts.

2016: Some could argue that 2016 fates are still "too early to tell," but they're sure inching toward "we better know soon." Jared Goff, the number one overall pick, led the Rams to the Super Bowl in 2018 and landed a mega-contract, but he and/or his team fell flat in 2019. Carson Wentz at number two has had solid starts, but injuries are haunting him, causing questions on his durability and overall production. Paxton Lynch went at number twenty-six to Denver, and it's probably not too early to tell he's been a bust. One of the late-draft surprises has been Dak Prescott, a fourth-rounder, who went to the Cowboys, replaced Tony Romo as the starter, took the team to the playoffs, became a Pro Bowler, and has gotten a franchise tag from Dallas.

*   *   *

2017: This draft is worthy of scrutiny, not because of *who* was drafted but because of *when* they were drafted, the order and the outcomes. The number two overall pick was Mitchell Trubisky to the Bears, and he is still trying to prove he was worthy of the high selection. But further back in the pack, Patrick Mahomes at number ten and Deshaun Watson at number twelve are both at the forefront of the style of quarterback play that may be revolutionizing the game. It seems that even when we get it right—picking the right guys—we still get it a little bit wrong, picking them in the wrong order.

2018: This year, the year we are examining under the micro-scope, has been one of the largest-ever first-round quarterback draft classes—five guys. To say the least, these quarterbacks and the order in which they were drafted are worthy of study, analysis, second-guessing, and will provide some understanding for the future.

2019: After the boom of '18, we had three very strong candidates this year. Kyler Murray was number one to the Cardinals (after they discarded last year's number ten, Josh Rosen), Daniel Jones was number six to the Giants, and Dwayne Haskins was number fifteen to the Redskins. All are unknowns so far, but all are starters for their teams.

Observations

Some teams pick badly. In the last twenty years, the two teams that have taken the most first- and second-round quarterbacks are the Browns and the Jets, six each. While the jury is out on their picks from 2018, the jury has been unanimous in finding both teams guilty of poor picks in the past. And keep in mind, that's with changing coaches, changing GMs, even changing ownership. Is there such a thing as a curse? Logic says no. Data says maybe.

Players who drop to number five to ten have an explanation for not doing so well. They fell below the very top. But...Patrick Mahomes and Daniel Jones may prove to be exceptions.

Picks from number ten to twenty seem to have a better shot at success. Maybe we miss them. Maybe some smart GMs see what we missed. Culpepper, Roethlisberger, Cutler, Pennington, and Flacco all did well. (By the way, they also all went to smaller schools. More on that below.)

Selections from twenty to thirty-two have been lethal...usually. They seem to belong in the second round but rise because teams reach out of desperation. And sometimes there are hidden gems there, guys who might have been snagged in the second round that you can steal late in the first. Maybe there's a Lamar Jackson being overlooked. Eric DeCosta, Ravens GM, told me about how they went to great lengths to keep their interest in Lamar secret to avoid competition from New Orleans or New England. That's why Ozzie Newsome traded up to the last spot in the first round, to stay ahead of the other suitors. That's finding the right guy at the right time and getting the right value, or bonus value.

Order of talent doesn't follow order of pick. The number one draft pick of the 2018 class, Baker Mayfield, has shown promise but is struggling. In contrast, the last pick of the first round, Lamar Jackson, set the league on fire. The three QBs in the middle are (a) Sam Darnold—fate unknown, (b) Josh Allen—some good signs, and (c) Josh Rosen—almost out of the game. Mathematically, the upshot is about a 50 percent rate of picking success—think Ryan Leaf vs. Peyton Manning—which is consistent with what we've seen through the years. But the order of those results is hardly what we would have expected. While top QB picks like Deshaun Watson, Andrew Luck, and Cam Newton largely lived up to their hype, plenty haven't. David Carr (poster boy for draft busts), Sam Bradford, Jameis Winston, Blake Bortles, Tim Couch, Joey Harrington, and Akili Smith were all high picks and highly disappointing. At the other end of the spectrum, in addition to the perennial example of Tom Brady as "the guy we missed," there's Drew Brees at number thirty-two (same spot as Lamar Jackson), Russell Wilson at seventy-five, Joe Montana at eighty-two, and Kurt Warner, undrafted free agent and Hall of Famer. We've had plenty of upside-down results. And that will continue until we get better at this.

Instead of *where* a kid played, look at *how* he played

Aren't there some college programs that turn out more pro quarterbacks than others? For sure. Purdue has had sixteen, but the stars have been few and far between—Len Dawson (1957), then Bob Griese ('67) and Drew Brees (2001). USC counts eight, but only one who has made it big, Carson Palmer. LSU gave the NFL seven, but exactly none who have been stars (unless you count Y. A. Tittle, drafted in 1948, playing in the '50s). Oregon, six—other than Dan Fouts, no standouts. Michigan, six—one superstar, Tom Brady. What about Alabama, no doubt the best college football team in modern times? They've won seventeen national championships, five in just the last few years. And when they haven't won, they've been close. The joke is that Nick Saban, the Crimson Tide coach, can't afford to take a pay cut to become an NFL coach. So they must turn out great quarterbacks, right? Not really. Other than Bart Starr from the fifties and Joe Namath from the early sixties, and maybe Ken Stabler, not too many have been successful in the NFL. Alabama has sent lots of future stars to the pros, but in positions other than quarterback. However, 2020 may be a turning point with two 'Bama QBs on the board, Tua Tagovailoa and Jalen Hurts, who transferred to Oklahoma. And at least an NFL team or two are going to bet their futures on a "Roll Tide" quarterback, so we'll see.

So schools and levels of competition haven't been exactly a treasure map to quarterbacks. Even the size of the program hasn't been particularly indicative. Little Boston College has churned out three NFL QBs—Doug Flutie, Matt Hasselback, and Matt Ryan. Carson Wentz came out of North Dakota State. Eastern Illinois gave us Tony Romo and Jimmy Garoppolo. And three-time Super Bowler Ben Roethlisberger came out of Miami of Ohio, playing against opponents like Buffalo, Akron, Ball State, Bowling Green, and Kent State.

Instead of style of offense, conference, height, weight, or hometown, look for performance. Period.

If the obvious clues were reliable, like conference or level—SEC, Big Ten, Big 12, Pac-12, ACC, Mountain West, big school, small school—or style of play—wide open, run and gun, pocket, shotgun, pistol, pro style, West Coast—or where he grew up—small town, big city, Sunbelt, rust belt—or what he looked like—stocky, lanky, angular, boxy, tall, taller—or his grades or his economics or his ethnicity—if any of those, or all of them combined, could tell us who's going to make it and who isn't, we wouldn't be scratching our heads every year asking, "What the hell just happened?" The clues aren't clues. They're a collection of legends, easy answers to hard questions. And easy answers are most often wrong. Here's a guy who is six foot five, rugged good looks, raised by hardworking middle-class parents, grew up in Montana, multisport jock, played football every Friday night in high school, swamped with full-ride offers, went to Washington State, Pac-10 Offensive Player of the Year, took his team to the Rose Bowl, has an arm like a rocket launcher, and is impossible to knock down in the pocket. No wonder that guy was taken number two in the first round. If he isn't a model for an NFL quarterback, who is? Okay, now how about a guy who's barely six feet tall; didn't play tackle football until he was in high school; son of an affluent trial lawyer; got injured in high school; received only two college offers and took the one with the best academics, not the best sports program; had a good college career but didn't get drafted until the second round. Not exactly the prototype NFL quarterback, right? Well, the first guy, the surefire guy, is Ryan Leaf. The second guy is Drew Brees. Not to pick on Ryan Leaf, because he had plenty of personal challenges, but only to say that the obvious clues may be obvious but they're hardly a guarantee of anything. Same goes for Drew Brees in reverse.

Instead of GPAs, SATs, and Wonderlics, look for AIQ

If a quarterback is the leader on the football field, how do we determine who has the intelligence, judgment, reason, vision, and guts to lead? It's the same problem businesses face when they look for executives and ultimately CEOs. Do they recruit only from Ivy League schools, the hardest colleges to get into? Or do they hunt for hungry, driven young people trying to prove their worth? Is it discipline or imagination? Or both? And how do you measure the "it"?

The scuttlebutt in football is that some coaches don't want a player who is "too smart" because he'll be hard to coach. Of course, that's a bunch of bull. I've coached plenty of high-IQ guys who were extremely coachable, smart enough to know what they don't know. And plenty of not-so-bright lights who couldn't be taught to turn a light on. And everything in between. There are even coaches who don't want a kid with too high a Wonderlic test score. Personally, I prefer a guy without a Wonderlic score, since it doesn't tell us much of anything. Nor does an SAT or, in most cases, even a GPA. SATs depend on accumulating facts and knowledge and being able to spit them out on demand—no minor skill but not indicative of whether a guy can process information in 2.5 seconds. GPAs are dependent on even more variables, from level of classes to level of school, to class size, to whether the teachers gave easy grades to jocks or the reverse. A 4.0 is not a 4.0 everywhere or all the time. The Wonderlic test was created in 1936 to gauge cognitive ability, specifically in mathematics, language or vocabulary, and reasoning. It has been used by the NFL since the 1960s. With only fifty multiple-choice questions, so it could be given and scored quickly, right at the Combine, it seemed like a good idea at the time. We didn't have anything else. And now they give out the test to all NFL teams for free. It's good PR for them. But as far as I can tell, there is only one number that comes out of the Wonderlic that is reliable. Zero. There is zero correlation between Wonderlic scores and NFL success. So, what's better?

Interview the kid and ask better questions. Ask hypotheticals—some about football, some about life. "If you see a dime defense and the play is supposed to drop the ball into their coverage, do you dump it off to a running back, roll out and look for a breaking receiver, keep it and run, move around until the coverage changes, or throw the ball away?" And ask him to answer very fast. "When you're being blitzed from the left, do you look right? *Answer fast.*" "On a quarterback keep, what if the hole left of center closes? *Answer fast.*" "When you meet a girl you want to go out with, do you ask her right away in a crowd or wait until no one else is around?... If it's raining, do you wear a hat?...Do you ever run yellow lights?" It's not just what his answer is, it's how fast he gives it and whether it makes sense. It doesn't have to be what you would do. Let's say you never run yellow lights. Maybe you want your quarterback to be gutsy enough to do it. But not red lights. Also look for dumb answers. Cocky, full-of-himself answers. Confident yes, cocky no.

Ask other people. Teammates, roommates, friends, parents, coaches, teachers, next-door neighbors. Look for people who know him away from football. Sure, most will tell you the good stuff, but if you listen closely, people tend to tell the truth. *He's a smart kid but not as smart as he thinks he is... He's quiet but don't let that fool you.*

It's much harder work for you to do the detective work than to look at a test score, but it may tell you more. You have to know if he's smart enough to lead. You're not looking for all the facts he can regurgitate. He'll learn the facts of plays, formations, packages, schemes on your team, from your coaches. Not the date the Magna Carta was signed (with all due respect to the year 1215 and the beginnings of constitutional democracy). You're looking to see if he can process and think with the information on the chalkboard, in his playbook, on the practice field, and on the football field. Is there a way to measure that ability? It looks like maybe yes.

Can We Do Better?

There's an emerging field of intelligence evaluation that shows a lot of promise—athletic intelligence. (Although it's called "athletic," it's equally applicable to first responders, firefighters, EMTs, military officers, pilots, even entrepreneurs, any endeavor that requires evaluations of "smart" by pragmatic and situational gauges.) There are several variations, but essentially, evaluation is based on something called the Cattell-Horn-Carroll test, one of the dominant assessments of intelligence. A basic tenet of the Cattell-Horn-Carroll theory is that "intelligence is a stable genetic trait." That means, if you have intelligence, you have it. It *doesn't* mean the usual tests always find it. If we get better at finding it, we will find better minds to perform better, to think and act more effectively. So say Scott Goldman, PhD, and Jim Bowman, PsyD, co-founders of Athletic Intelligence Measures, which administers the AIQ (Athletic Intelligence Quotient). Here's how Scott explains the need for a better test. "People use 'intelligence' and 'knowledge' interchangeably when they're not. Intelligence is the ability to acquire, process, and apply information. If you have a puzzle and you don't already know the answer, then you use intelligence to problem-solve it. When you already possess the answer, that is knowledge, or experience." So the AIQ doesn't test what you know. Rather, it measures how you solve for what you don't know as well as how you acquire new information. For example, the AIQ measures visual-spatial processing and decision-making; that is, what someone sees, how he/she processes it to come to a solution, as well as learning efficiency, which indicates how many "reps" are needed to absorb the information, and how well a person can recall it later when needed. It's like playing against a shot clock in basketball, or a play clock on the football field, or what happens in the next seconds after the snap.

One of the keys to Goldman and his team's success is that their test is not delivered on paper or in a written form. The tests are done on an iPad, with instructions given visually and verbally, in the native language of the test-taker (baseball teams are taking the tests to Latin American countries, using the Spanish versions developed to align with local dialects), and instructions are repeated as necessary without penalty. The questions are in the form of gamelike exercises, not unlike Tetris. They are not language- or culture-dependent. But they are timed because, like a sports activity, there is temporal pressure to find a solution. You must process fast and correctly, not one or the other. Goldman says one of the most common responses from athletes after taking the test is, "Damn, that was hard...and fun."

Is it credible and predictive? Clients seem to think so. The company has a database of six thousand elite athletes across all five major leagues (NFL, NBA, MLB, NHL, and MLS) as well as Olympians, Power Five conference schools, special forces in the military, and e-sport gamers. In the NFL, they have been collecting data since 2012 and have over two thousand players in their database. For 2020, they are under contract with eight teams, and tested over four hundred players at the East-West, Senior Bowls, and the Combine. And remember, unlike the Wonderlic, this test is not free, so they have to believe in it to pay for it.

Does it work in football? Goldman says, "Yes, it accurately measures what it is intended to measure." But, does it predict? He adds, "Well, nothing really predicts in sports. If you could predict game outcomes, you should go to Vegas." Goldman is too much of a scientist to promise outcomes, but as a scientist, he offers data. They have found "statistically significant" correlations between the AIQ and outcomes such as rushing yards, sacks, interceptions, and "weighted career approximate value" (Pro Football Reference's Approximate Value stat—seasonal value, per player).

Does it work specifically for quarterbacks? So far, they've tested over a hundred quarterbacks or quarterback prospects. Goldman offers one example that he can share (carefully worded out of respect for his non-disclosure agreements with his clients). The AIQ found eleven quarterbacks with superior scores on a "narrow ability." Examples of narrow abilities are: spatial awareness—knowing where the end zone is when you're in motion or turned around, and being able to recalibrate; reaction time after distraction—a blitz or change in coverage; adjustment to stimulus—defensive shifts; learning efficiency—how quickly the athlete absorbs and comprehends new input. Six of the eleven QBs demonstrated scores on reaction time after distraction, a narrow ability which, when coupled with other key factors, is believed to be indicative of QB mobility: Patrick Mahomes, Lamar Jackson, Kyler Murray, Daniel Jones, Teddy Bridgewater, and Ryan Tannehill. The other five who showed superior scores on this ability (perhaps lacking other needed factors) are no longer in the game. That, by the way, is a 54 percent success rate, well above our 50-50. And the more he tests, the more he learns.

By way of anecdotal examples, someone leaked Baker Mayfield's AIQ to *Sports Illustrated* as one of the top-scoring quarterbacks of his class or of any class. And Lamar Jackson showed clearly superior scores in several elements of the AIQ, displaying, in Goldman's words, "the cognitive abilities to be a good QB."

None of that guarantees anything, but it seems to reveal much more than we've known before. As Goldman says, "The test is not a predictor; it's a descriptor. In other words, it is meant to help teams understand *how* the player is successful as well as *how* the team can maximize their abilities."

My conclusion is, it's early and more tests will tell us more, but the AIQ is already a better "descriptor" than most we've seen. The real lesson is, it's not the same; it's change.

A subset of "smart"—character and leadership

There is no test for character other than life itself. But one company that also utilizes the AIQ, Premier Sport Psychology, does give a behavioral profile test called DISC (they got it from Athletes Assessment out of Australia) that seems to show correlations between real-life behavior and performance. Premier currently consults with teams in the NFL, NBA, MLB, NHL, USA National Teams, and a university athletic department within the Big Ten Conference.

DISC is a behavioral assessment that looks at/for four traits: dominance, influence, steadiness, and compliance. Just by the names of the traits, you can see that if the DISC test works, it could really give us a preview of how a kid may perform. Dominance can be a clue to natural leadership...or power madness. Influence can tell us if that young person's words and actions sway others...or turn them off. Steadiness can reveal cool under fire... or panic. Compliance may be the key to getting along or causing revolt when it comes to crunch time. Justin Anderson, PsyD and founder of Premier, himself a quarterback at the University of Minnesota Duluth and three-sport high school athlete, explains it this way: "DISC looks for a behavioral profile. Like being right- or left-handed, there's no right or wrong way." But he says it helps to know which way a person is wired. Can you really alter or modify someone? Yes, like when you break an arm and learn to use the other arm. But when under stress, people often return to the baseline, their original arm. DISC looks for these traits, but underlying the traits are motivators, what drives people. Some people want to be the best, period. Others are after money or security. Some are looking for a good relationship. If you know the motivator, you can connect with the athlete better and maybe elicit better performance. If you don't, you rely on what would motivate you, not him.

Has DISC worked in looking at quarterbacks? Anderson says yes, cautiously. He has given the test formally at Pro Days in the NBA and on top-30 visits in the NFL (when teams ask certain players to come to their facilities). But he has also employed it informally, not giving the full test but relying on his own experience to sit in the interview room at the Combine while GMs or coaches talk to a prospect. During the interviews, Anderson observes the clues to see if a kid would show a strong trait, which may tell us how the person will deal with problems. For instance, a high D (dominance) might be indicated by a strong handshake, looking right in your eyes, or sitting assertively. A high I (influence) would be seen in a more extroverted, emotive type, maybe quick-witted. Low I would show as more reserved, less personable, even speaking in lower tones of voice. S (steadiness) gives a picture of how a person deals with pace—particularly changes in pace, stress, or attack—and whether the person has patience and persistence and prefers not to shift gears. And C (compliance) indicates how a person deals with rules, detail, accuracy, and data. Does he rely on facts? Does he aim for high standards?

Prior to the last two drafts, Anderson sat in on several quarterback interviews, even asking his own questions on occasion. The interview lasts fifteen to eighteen minutes, so it's a reasonable conversation length, long enough to reveal, short enough to maintain interest. Overall, he sees a high-D kid as likely to have command, be strong in the huddle, and have a clear drive toward goals.

Influence is important too, but he notes it can be expressed differently by different people: strong, quiet types or strong, expressive types. Anderson says it's good to see a level of S, or steadiness, but not have it be the ruling trait for most quarterbacks. Impatience can be good too. Similarly, compliance is good up to a point. Know the rules. But then you may have to break rules to overcome adversity.

The test claims to have another benefit: what you can do with the results. The company maintains they can identify areas for improvement and even provide tools to improve or modify behavior. That last element is a big promise, but if it's true, we could find ways to lessen or eliminate insecurity or knock down and recalibrate arrogance. Their results to date are modest.

But these are the kinds of tools we need. Especially if we put them together with "going to the film"—that is, looking at the evidence from the past, meticulously, repeatedly. In the case of personality or character, that means digging into the anecdotal past of these star players. Digging deep. College, high school, middle school, summers. Coaches—not just of football but other sports too—teachers, parents, next-door neighbors, ex-girlfriends, summer bosses, anybody who had good, bad, or neutral contact. That means, if possible, not just the people who want to give a good reference, but also those that can offer insights. *He played on our middle school baseball team and he had a terrible temper... He took piano lessons, and if it hadn't been for football, I thought he could be a musician... We broke up in the tenth grade but he was nice about it... He got in trouble but always got out of it because he was a hotshot.* Of course, look for patterns, not just isolated stories. There's always someone who wants to say something glowing. And someone who wants to be a naysayer. And we must allow for mistakes. Kids do dumb things. (So do adults.) We're not looking for flawless kids. We're looking for kids who learn from their mistakes, who show patterns of improve-ment. Kids who really do mature. And there are signs, if we look hard enough. It's your job to go to the film—the film of life—over and over and over. Every kid we see in the NFL has a past that gives away his present. Sometimes it's good, sometimes not so good. Lots of times we don't want to face it because he has an arm like a rocket launcher and can pinpoint a moving target. Personality and character matter. They seem to be opaque; that is, hard to view and assess. But maybe not. Maybe new tools can enable us to get a window into personality and character in advance of the draft and see what they look like and even how to shape them.

Dr. Anderson's approach, while maybe raw in its development and database, takes a fresh look at personality as a determining fac-tor for a player, particularly for a quarterback. While the AIQ (Gold-man and Anderson know and share each other's work) may "tease out aspects of intelligence," we need to know how a player uses that intelligence, what his go-to tendencies are. Anderson uses the expression, "Knowledge suffocates the ability to process," meaning you need to stay present, weed out distractions, not get bogged down in information overload. Personality may well tell us if a player has the tendency or trait to let too much input overwhelm decisions. Anderson points to the contrasting cases of Christian Ponder, a first-rounder who seemed to overprocess and let anxiety rule, and Brett Favre, who could filter and process at lightning speed.

Most critical in the personality equation, says Dr. Anderson, are tendencies and compatibility. He and his test can tell us a lot about a player's personality and character traits. But are those traits compatible with what the coach or scheme demands? DISC can identify a beauti-ful, perfect, well-honed round peg. But a coach may have a perfectly formed, sharp-edged square hole. Not a fit. On the other hand, when the fit works, it is powerful. Joe Montana and Bill Walsh. Andy Reid and Patrick Mahomes. When you put a quarterback in situations where he has a high chance of success or cannot fail, he gains confidence. When you do the opposite, he bleeds confidence. Anxiety and confidence have an inverse relationship. Confidence is the most fragile body part on the football field. Yet NFL teams do little or nothing to train coaches to adjust to the player—instead of the reverse—especially the quarterback, to welcome and utilize change to build confidence.

Which brings us to the issue of fit...

Instead of drafting a quarterback, look for a marriage

A quarterback is only as good as the match with his coach or coaches. There is an age-old debate about who's the most important person in a football organization: the quarterback, head coach, GM, or owner. We could look around the league and draw our conclusions. Instead, we went back to our Harvard Business School experts/weekend football fans for their take. They actually studied the question. Logic and outcomes tell us that the "who's most important" controversy quickly comes down to the quarterback and the head coach, though the other two figures, GM and owner, can play important parts. We asked Dr. Groysberg the question directly, "Okay, who is it?" (By the way, on the subject of relative importance, Groysberg declined to acknowledge himself as the lead author of the study, but rather as one on a team of equals.) For the answer on the football field, Groysberg turned to the favorite sports bar argument—Brady or Belichick? The consensus seems to be Brady in that case, but it's close. The question of who is more important in general is answered by the draft.

Can We Do Better?

The 2020 draft as evidence

As always, the draft was the symbolic kickoff of another season of NFL excitement. But this one was different. It came in the midst of the global COVID-19 pandemic. That meant no stadium hoopla, no fans in attendance, no players walking onstage and shaking hands with the commissioner. All remote. All distant. All virtual. So was it a downer? Hardly. Broadcast from Roger Goodell's basement, from team "war rooms," from players' homes, surrounded by anxious families, fans starved for sports flocked to their screens—15.6 million watchers, up 37 percent from the previous year! Viewership literally "Zoomed"! As for the outcomes, they reinforced what we knew. In the past twenty-one NFL drafts, the number one, top-of-the-board pick has been a QB fifteen times. With the 2020 draft, that makes sixteen times. The consensus "best player in the draft" was Chase Young, defensive end from Ohio State, but he was picked second, not first. The number one overall pick, and no surprise to anyone, was QB Joe Burrow out of LSU, who went to the Bengals. As predicted, the Dolphins essentially gave up on Josh Rosen by taking Alabama QB Tua Tagovailoa at number five. The Chargers followed at number six with Justin Herbert, QB from Oregon. Green Bay, with Aaron Rodgers at QB, hardly had an immediate need but couldn't resist Jordan Love from Utah State. (Remember past Packers GM Ron Wolf drafting a quarterback in seven of eight drafts while he still had Hall of Famer Brett Favre.) Four quarterbacks in the first round. And QB Jalen Hurts went to the Philadelphia Eagles in the second round, despite the Eagles' healthy Carson Wentz. The results are flashing in neon: *Quarterback—Quarterback—Quarterback.*

But on the other hand...

The head coach in football, more than any other sport, actually determines the play on the field, whether it's offense, defense, or even special teams. He's the play caller. Or at least he's getting the plays from his coaches and then deciding what play to call, what the quarterback or linebacker hears in his earphones. Nobody has more influence over strategy and tactics, with the possible exception of a military general. As Boris and his team remind us, the trophy for the biggest win in sports, the Super Bowl, is named for a coach, Vince Lombardi, not an owner or GM or even a great player. But hey, what about that GM? He's on the hot seat to size up players and put the personnel together, trading, signing free agents, and of course, drafting. My longtime GM Ozzie Newsome turned our franchise from a loser to a winner, with two Super Bowls. He found Ray Lewis, Ed Reed, Jonathan Ogden, Jamal Lewis, and plenty more. I give him the lion's share of the credit. Well, maybe I should give the credit to the owner, Art Modell, who put Ozzie in charge, but we'll look at owners in a minute. Ozzie and his successor, Eric DeCosta, get the credit for drafting Lamar Jackson. That's a pretty good case for the importance of the role. The same might apply to Ron Wolf at the Packers or John Dorsey in Kansas City and Cleveland, and now Howie Roseman of the Eagles.

But can't the owners get some love here? After all, they pay for all of this. And they make the initial picks of GM and head coach... and if they're smart, they don't try to pick the quarterback. Some teams turn over the reins to the GM, some to the coach, and some try to do it literally as a family. Sometimes that works—like in New Orleans and Kansas City—and sometimes it doesn't—like in places that have family feuds instead of family harmony. Some have just one guy who calls almost all the shots, like Jerry Jones in Dallas. When it works, he's brilliant, and when it doesn't, he's a dictator.

All that is conjecture. What did the researchers find? First, overall "combined leadership"—all four roles working in sync—accounts for most success. But within that, there are some key revelations. Statistically, over a thirty-plus year study of results, of what the authors call the "explained variance" in wins and losses, owners get credit for 11 percent of success, GMs about double that, coaches almost 30 percent, and quarterbacks 37 percent. The quarterback is three times as important to winning as the owner...if you don't count the fact that the owner signs the QB's paycheck. Together, the GM and coach add up to over half of the successes. But quarterbacks and coaches together get credit for two-thirds of the success.

And here's a key finding: Of the explained variance (as opposed to the unexplained variance, which are those factors that cannot be specifically attributed), owners and GMs were more important in the past than today. QBs and head coaches are now the pivotal figures. The quarterback's contribution has risen; the head coach has stayed about even, dropping slightly; but the GM, already lower than the other two, dropped a fraction, and the owner's influence dropped a good deal. Why? A more wide-open, offense-driven game—more passing, more run-pass options, and more innovative, on-the-fly plays. A game that demands a great quarterback. The league MVP award now almost automatically goes to a quarterback: 2015—Cam Newton; 2016—Matt Ryan; 2017—Tom Brady; 2018—Patrick Mahomes; 2019—Lamar Jackson; and Peyton Manning five times. So it's the quarterback. But we still haven't figured out how to find the right guy. FiveThirtyEight.com, the statistics, polling, and metrics website, wrote: "NFL scouts, coaches and general managers—the world's foremost experts on football player evaluation—have been notoriously terrible at separating good QB prospects from the bad through the years."

The marriage—arranged or true love?

It takes more than just identifying the guys who appear to be good or potentially great. It takes something else. It takes a match. It takes a coach who wants that guy who's about to be picked, who wants and will adjust to that style of play that taps the player's strength, and will not try to jam him into a scheme that ties him in knots. It takes a coach who knows how to talk to and work with a kid, literally a kid, who has enormous talent but needs to hone it and direct it. Some coaches I've seen over the years work far better with veterans just because they don't have to explain as much. With young QBs, we should remember what Kevin Stefanski says, "put your arm around the kid" and be his "father, brother, shrink, and confessor."

It's easy to see the matches that have worked and the ones that haven't. Belichick and Brady, though they may not be best pals off the field, together are at the top of the success ladder, leading to the who's-most-important debates. But well before the two of them came Joe Montana and Bill Walsh. I was there; I saw it; and it was as remarkable a display of how to nurture a youngster into a leader as I've ever seen. Would Montana have done as well for someone else? I doubt it. Would Walsh have done as well with another quarterback? Based on what he did in developing Steve Young, I'd say yes. In recent times, we've seen the Hue Jackson–Baker Mayfield mismatch, and Aaron Rodgers and Mike McCarthy's divorce over irreconcilable differences. On the other hand, Sean Payton and Drew Brees have been in sync from day one. The same can be said of Pete Carroll and Russell

Wilson. Andy Reid showed he "gets" quarterbacks, especially mobile QBs—Donovan McNabb in Philly, then a late-career Michael Vick, and then in KC, bonding with the most innovative quarterback in football, Patrick Mahomes. Put Mahomes into a Green Bay offense and I venture to say it wouldn't be nearly as game-changing. As we've said, one of the best pivots in football in recent years was John Harbaugh, moving from the very conventional, and largely successful, pocket-passer offense with Joe Flacco to the wide-open—very, very wide-open—you-don't-know-what-to-expect offense of young Lamar Jackson. And I emphasize young because John, in his late fifties, has been remarkable about bonding with a raw but immensely talented kid. John has done most of the adapting. And that's why they're winning. It's not the quarterback. It's not the coach. It's the match. It's the marriage. And like a marriage, sure, one person earns more money. One person manages the family. But they are not often the same person. So they better be a good match.

We know that college and pro quarterbacks who go through a lot of change in coaches often struggle to find themselves, or their game, or the best schemes. But it's more than just consistency; it's the fit between the quarterback—in style of play, in communication, in personality, sometimes even in sense of humor—and the coach. At the risk of repetition because it warrants emphasis, a coach who has tunnel vision for the old pocket-passer offense and tries to jam a mobile QB into that model is likely going to see a guy uncomfortable with his role and a team struggling to make it work. A coach who is not open to another style of play better make sure he and the GM agree to draft a quarterback who fits his style, not just the next guy up who is ranked high. When the GM and coach don't agree, they get the wrong quarterback for the coach or the wrong coach for the quarterback. And as we well know, if/when the team has taken a first-round QB and things go wrong, the coach will be the casualty, not the kid. But in spite of how much sense it makes to have a good match, we—NFL coaches and teams—keep trying to force-fit bad matches.

One interesting observation, or hypothesis, is that maybe, from the been-there-done-that experience, former QBs make good mentors for QBs. And going further, maybe former backup QBs are even better mentors because they faced longer odds. They understand the game from the perspective of the kid carrying the weight of the world, the need to rally and improvise and rise to the occasion to keep the game, your team, and often your career alive. Nobody has to scramble, literally and figuratively, like a backup quarterback. You come into the game as a second choice, and then you're asked to save the day. Joe Montana had to do it. So did Tom Brady, replacing starter Drew Bledsoe. Brett Favre did it. Steve Young did it after Montana. Aaron Rodgers did it after Favre. Ben Roethlisberger did it. Kurt Warner did it. Jim Plunkett did it back in the 1970s. They all became starters and stars. But it seems it's the guys who didn't become stars who may have more empathy, more affinity and comradery with which to connect to young quarterbacks—big brothers, tough love, coaches in every sense.

The backup-as-coach brotherhood may be just a theory, but history gives it some validity. Take Tom Flores, a starter and backup with the Raiders, later head coach of the Raiders and Seahawks, working with quarterbacks Ken Stabler and then Jim Plunkett, who led the Raiders to two Super Bowls.

Frank Reich originally backed up Boomer Esiason at Maryland, then among others, Hall of Famer Jim Kelly in Buffalo and Kerry Collins at the Panthers. Hall of Fame executive Bill Polian, former GM in Buffalo, said Reich was "the greatest backup quarterback in

NFL history"... sort of a compliment, I think. But Frank has been something of an offensive whiz as a coach with the Colts, Cardinals, Chargers, and Eagles, and head coach of the Colts in 2018, taking them to the postseason.

Sean Payton was a backup to a variety of unknowns in the Arena Football League and the CFL, and was even a strikebreaker in the NFL with the Bears, hardly a distinguished playing career. But he's considered one of the best offensive and coaching minds in the game as head coach of the Saints since 2006, in perfect harmony with Drew Brees through all of those years.

Jason Garrett was with the Cowboys, behind Troy Aikman on two Super Bowl–winning teams. But after his playing career, he went on to become offensive coordinator and then head coach of the Cowboys from 2011 to 2019, achieving success with quarterbacks Tony Romo and Dak Prescott. In 2020 he became offensive coordinator of the Giants.

Jim Harbaugh played as a starter and backup with several teams, then after a hot run as head coach of Stanford, became head coach of the 49ers and worked with Colin Kaepernick to take the team to the postseason three times and ultimately, the Super Bowl.

Doug Pederson was a classic backup QB who later became an offensive coordinator and then head coach of the Eagles, working with Sam Bradford, drafting and developing Carson Wentz, and creating a near-miracle season when Wentz went down and Nick Foles took over, upsetting the Patriots in the Super Bowl.

Gary Kubiak was an unsung backup to John Elway at the Broncos, but went on to become an offensive coordinator loved by QBs, head coach of the Texans and later the Broncos, taking them to the Super Bowl. He is the ultimate mentor, returning to the game after a break to become assistant head coach in Minnesota, and taking Kevin Stefanski under his coaching wing as they both resurrected the career of Kirk Cousins to guide the Vikings to the playoffs, and Kevin to a head coaching job.

That's a pretty good record for backup quarterbacks as coaches. Especially if you compare it to Hall of Fame quarterbacks turned coaches. Only one, Bart Starr, even got his team to the playoffs, and it was in a season shortened by the strike in 1982. Maybe there is something to this empathy thing. There is definitely something to the idea of the coach and quarterback being on the same page. When it works, the coach and the quarterback essentially form another entity, a third party, a unit stronger than the two components. True synergy. And clearly, when they are not in sync, they are less than the two parties, a negative not only for themselves but for the team.

Alignment—a word for marriage in business and football

"Alignment" is a business term that is very applicable here. Alignment means that a company must have its goals, personnel, and resources all aimed in the same direction. Without alignment, the company cannot achieve its objectives. We see it on the plus and minus side all the time. Southwest Airlines on the plus side; Northwest on the minus. Target and Costco on the plus; JCPenney and Sears on the minus. UPS and Amazon on the plus. Blockbuster was a big plus that became a bigger minus. But in football, to a large extent, we've not seen much purposeful alignment. I would conjecture that if we did, we'd get better at picking quarterbacks, and several other positions.

How do you do it? The same way business does. Set out your objectives, your strengths and weaknesses. Of course, objective number one is to win, but what is your timeline? One season or within four? What are your strengths? Good defense, running game, receivers? What are your weaknesses? Offensive line, special teams? What is your coach good at? Working with players with years under their belts? Or kids? Or both? Adapting to change, or discipline in a given system? Mentoring or strategizing? Accept reality. If you have a two-year horizon to win, a good defense, and a coach who works well with a traditional scheme and veterans, draft a quarterback who shows he can work in that situation, not one who doesn't. If you have a coach who can embrace the skills and abilities of a more mobile, maybe less rigid kind of QB, who is willing to rewrite the team playbook, and a GM who can make the personnel changes needed, then go for the other kid. But don't try to force-fit one into the other. If you do, then expect to fire your coach, and expect an extra year at least of adjustment of quarterback to coach and vice versa.

Any NFL team that is about to draft a quarterback should ask and answer these questions...honestly:

A. What quarterback do you rank highest on your wish list, and what is his style of play? What are his strengths?
B. What style of play does your team use now?
C. Are you willing to embrace major change, including schemes and roster, to maximize the strengths of the new QB?

If A doesn't match B and you cannot commit to C, don't draft that guy. If they do match—go for it. Without alignment, in business, football, or marriage, you're headed for trouble—angry stockholders, another losing season, or alimony.

We can do better

The 50-50 rule can be improved, at least a little. And a little can mean a lot. Enough to shake up outcomes. It is not a single metric or practice. It is a composite. That is the Q Factor—the collection of practices that can provide an edge:

Extrapolate. Don't look at any one incident on the football field (or anywhere in life, for that matter). Look for a pattern. Look for a trend. One of anything tells you nothing.

Look at data, but never one metric in a vacuum. Don't be seduced by one big number. Make sure metrics are borne out on film—not highlights, but game after game.

Look for decision-making and leadership. They're not just God-given gifts; they can be demonstrated with evidence... or absence.

Look for intelligence but look to measure it differently. Don't rely on the old tools that measure accumulation of knowledge or facts. Look for evaluations of thinking and processing.

Look at character. It matters and it will show later.

Throw out old guidelines—size, economics, ethnicity, school, scheme. Look for performance, no matter how, no matter where. Did this guy advance the ball?

Don't draft out of need. It's the worst evaluator of talent there has ever been. The corollary is, don't talk yourself into a guy. Need tends to make you do that.

Make sure your QB and coach match. If they don't, one will leave soon, probably the coach.

Can We Do Better?

Accept and embrace change. If you don't adapt, you become extinct. It's true of dinosaurs and coaches.

Most important: Extrapolate. Don't imitate.

The mobile quarterback came on big-time in the past few years. So now everybody will be looking at the draft board, saying, "Find me a Patrick Mahomes. Find me a Lamar Jackson." They might as well say, "Find me a unicorn." These guys are great quarterbacks. One can run or throw, run a little and then throw, and even throw side-arm. The other guy can run and run and run, and then surprise you with a great throw. But what they do is advance the ball. Somehow. Some way. More times than not. They're smart. They lead. They find a way.

The next great quarterback is on the board. He may be a mobile QB. Or he may be a pocket passer. Or both. He may be big. Or not so big. He may be from Clemson or Florida, but he may also be from Harvard or Duke. But one thing is sure. The evidence is there, *if* we'll look for it. Once we see evidence, real hard evidence, then we have to make sure it recurs, that we can see it over and over, play it and replay it. If we can see more than an incident—a real trend—then we can project or extrapolate. Then we know something. Then maybe we've found someone. Only then. But the question is: Will we look at a hint of evidence and be sucked in too fast, as usual? Will we draft out of need and hope and talk ourselves into what isn't there? We can do better than 50-50, maybe a good deal better, but it will take brutal honesty and a willingness to dump the old thinking and embrace change—a change of thinking.

Acknowledgments

No business is more collaborative than sports. Any coach will tell you he is an amalgam of every coach, player, scout, trainer, owner, or administrator he has ever worked with. I have been extraordinarily lucky to have been associated with many of the great coaching talents in the game, including LaVelle Edwards, Tom Landry, Bill Walsh, Denny Green, and Tony Dungy. The number of assistant coaches that have formed and enhanced my abilities are too numerous to list but include people like Marvin Lewis, Jack Del Rio, Rex Ryan, David Shaw, Mike Smith, Mike Singletary, Mike Pettine, and Mike Nolan, all of whom have gone on to become head coaches. In addition, the likes of Ozzie Newsome, Phil Savage, and Eric DeCosta, among the best ever personnel people, have had a huge impact on my perspective of the game. Of course, the gift of being allowed to work with the countless number of players, which includes twelve Hall of Famers, is what coaching is truly about.

Now, thanks to my friend and colleague Kevin Byrne, I was able to collaborate with co-author Jim Dale, who in turn brought the counsel of agent David Black, who led us to the wisdom of editor Sean Desmond. Together with Jim, in *The Q Factor*, hope-fully I have been able to convey a lifetime of learning in the game I love.

Brian Billick

To borrow an overused sports cliché (is that redundant?) *The Q Factor* was a team effort, of course, led by a quarterback. Despite years as a coach, Brian Billick was the book's quarterback, in NFL parlance, an "elite quarterback," who understands the game, is disarmingly honest about what he knows and doesn't know, is candid, funny, and openminded, a combination of pretty rare traits in Super Bowl–winning coaches. The rest of the team was comprised of, first Kevin Byrne, communications impresario of the Baltimore Ravens and great people connector who led me to Brian; then David Black, my long-term literary agent (and diehard Jets fan), who not only represented me, Brian, and the property, but also helped shape the concept from its earliest stages; Sean Desmond, our editor at Twelve, who was an incredible partner, encourager, reader/improver (and true football addict); Rachel Kambury from Twelve who was my conscience, reminder, and fixer; contributing experts including Gary Kubiak, Paul DePodesta, Kevin Stefanski, Eric Mangini, Scott Goldman, Justin Anderson, John Verros, Boris Groysberg, Alex Olbrecht, Jeremy Rosen, and Ron Shapiro; my son Andy who went with me to three Super Bowls and schooled me on the game from age eight on; and of course, my life teammate and wife (who knows the difference between a pocket passer and a mobile QB), my MVP on all books and all things, Ellen. Other than those people, I pretty much did it myself.

James Dale

About the Authors

Brian Billick has spent his entire professional career in football, spanning high school to small college to major college, and finally the NFL. He is a Super Bowl–winning head coach who has overseen the highest scoring offense in NFL history and the lowest scoring defense in NFL history. He has spent the last twelve years broadcasting games and doing shows for Fox and the NFL Network. In addition, he has written or co-authored four books: *Developing an Offensive Game Plan*, *The Winning Edge* with Bill Walsh, *Competitive Communication* with Jim Peterson, and *More Than a Game* with Michael MacCambridge.

James Dale has collaborated as co-author on books ranging from sports to negotiation to medicine to politics, including *We're Better Than This* with Congressman Elijah Cummings, *Together We Were Eleven Foot Nine* with Hall of Fame pitcher Jim Palmer, *The Power of Nice* with agent/negotiator Ron Shapiro, *Alpha Docs* with cardiologist Dan Munoz, and the *New York Times* bestseller, *Just Show Up* with Cal Ripken Jr.